# TINY SETBACKS, MAJOR COMEBACKS

*From Brooklyn to Europe*

## CORIN "TINY" ADAMS

**MASCOT**® **BOOKS**

*"Tiny had the capabilities to score 30 points a game, but her personality off the court matched her personality on the court. She was always too unselfish. Whether it was the ball or a good deed, Tiny just always wanted to give!"*

*-Donald Beasley, Morgan State University Women's*
*Head Basketball Coach 2005 – present*

# TINY SETBACKS, MAJOR COMEBACKS

## From Brooklyn to Europe

CORIN "TINY" ADAMS

# Table of Contents

# Thank You

I want to first thank every single person who has purchased my autobiography. I really appreciate it, as cliché as that may sound. For someone to take the time out and purchase a book about my life is an honor and truly humbling. I thank you all from the bottom of my heart!

Secondly, I want to thank the people dear to me; the ones that have helped me in any way during the many struggles I've faced during my short time of existence on this earth. Without you in my corner, I could have easily gone another route and not been able to accomplish the things I did. Your support was a difference maker to me.

I would also like to thank everyone that has believed in me, pushed me, wished me good luck and congratulations, enlightened me, or just gave me a compliment about the person I am or my game. You keep me going and motivated to do the unimaginable.

Last, but not least, I would like to thank the strongest woman I know, my mother, Gwendolyn Youngblood. I would like to thank her for instilling her wisdom in me, teaching me the things she has, always being there, shaping me into the person I am today, and for just riding out with me on this journey, no matter what was put in our path. We've been through it all, and no matter what she has always been supportive and been down for me.

Please email me at ta9apparel@gmail.com with thoughts, critiques, and concerns or just to say hey. I'd love to physically thank every one of you that purchases my auto biography.

# Foreword

I have always believed that the main reason people decide to join the sport business is not the money, but the emotions that come from working in this field. Money, the little or lot that there is, is only the means that allow us to live our dreams. Athletes play for adrenaline that only a game can give: for a win, for a basket at the buzzer, and for the crowd. The emotions of an agent are different. We don't play, nor do we score; the joy of our work is when we meet people like Tiny and are able to help share and contribute to their success.

I was very impressed with Tiny from the first conversation we held via Skype. We had been introduced by another client of mine, and I cannot thank her enough for helping me meet Tiny. Since our first conversation, I speak to Tiny practically on a daily basis. I have gotten to know who she is as a person, and it has lead me to truly appreciate and admire her. She is incredibly perseverant, determined, and above all, has an extraordinarily intelligence that will surely bring her much success in life, even when basketball is long over.

Tiny is a volcano of ideas, and each day she has a new, innovative one. The #TA9 brand, her website, video documentaries and photo services, and the creation and promotion of this book are just a few examples. Women's basketball in Europe is a niche sport, and while Tiny has never been (up until now) a WNBA star, she has already sat at tables with major companies in the industry, and been interviewed by major radio and television stations. Her will to succeed helped her grow and rise from a small college basketball program to a globe trotter, with a better than average physique, good hands, and basketball smarts that often keep her a step ahead of competitors. She has seen her share of career struggles, which included dealing with charlatans and dishonest and naïve profiteers. Regardless, she has handled everything with pride. Like many of us who have had to make the most of a bad situation, she always finds a way to rise above her circumstances.

Aside from her intelligence, what you cannot not love about Tiny is her big heart. The heart that she throws on the court every game allows her to always come out like a winner, regardless of the final score. I remember, for example, when she made me feel small and selfish on Christmas in 2013. That day, we spoke about Christmas while she was playing in Sarajevo, and, despite not having a first level salary, she decided to spend a portion of what she had to provide a less fortunate family with Christmas dinner and toys for their children. In addition to doing things like this, she has helped other players without contracts countless times to obtain their dreams or get one step closer. This is Tiny—a smile to the world, filled with so much generosity! She deserves every little or big goal she plans on reaching.

In the end, you shouldn't be surprised if one day soon you hear about her, her future success stories, or her and her faithful dog, Buckets. This woman will go far! Those of us who know her are more than lucky, because the world needs more people like Corin 'Tiny' Adams.


Lorenzo Gallotti
Two Points Agency
FIBA & FIP Agent

# Introduction
# For My Hoop-Dreamers and
# Dream Chasers Everywhere

*"To accomplish great things, we must not only act, but also dream; not only plan, but also believe." -Anatole France*

It's crazy to me, the number of people that have encouraged me to share my story. "Tiny, you should do a blog." "Make sure you keep us updated through social networks and emails." "The world needs to hear your story, Tiny." "You should write a book." Words of encouragement like this were heard more often than I could imagine. At first, I'd just brush it off or respond with half-hearted acknowledgements like, "true," or "I got you," never really giving it much thought. Who am I to write a book? I haven't even made it.

It just didn't seem like I was interesting enough to consume readers' time with my words and my thoughts. I'm just plain old Tiny. After sitting down and thinking about my journey and struggles, how I've managed to overcome them and carry on, I started hearing the opinions of those close to me. I came to the conclusion that it was not just a good idea, but a great idea!

A lot of you may know me—my past, personal stories,

accolades I've earned, and many other chapters from my life—but very few know the entire journey, from the struggle to the success, from the beginning of my life and career to where I am today.

Not only will I tell you about my journey from start to finish, I also would like to enlighten you about the things I've had to learn through the mistakes I've made. I want to provide insight and advice to anyone looking to pursue many of the same dreams I have, or how to persevere to accomplish your own goals.

On a daily basis, I find myself educating and enlightening my fellow hoopers, the dreamers, and my peers through my words, my attitude, and my actions. One of my mottos is aspire to inspire. Helping people is something I love to do. It's something I do whenever I can. One of the primary reasons I believe writing this book is a great idea is because I know it can and will help somebody—perhaps somebody I know or somebody I don't know, it doesn't matter. There's no telling who will pick this book up or get access to it. Just knowing this brings a smile to my face, and gets me excited about writing my autobiography.

This book isn't just for the African-American female basketball player audience. I want this book to touch and inspire people of all ages, professions, races, sexes, sports—basically anyone out there with a dream. I'm living proof that things don't always go as planned, and things may even knock you down and take you back a couple steps, but every tiny setback is a set up for a major comeback! As long as you keep your faith, work hard, and execute your plans to the best of your ability, good things will happen!

# Chapter 1
# The Early Days

*If you're passionate about something or someone,*
*you should go for it, no matter what!*
*#Tinyism*

The year was 1995. Jordan was averaging thirty a game, the Bulls won the NBA championship, Penny Hardaway was still hooping, and there was a little girl in Far Rockaway Queens, NY falling in love with a sport. This sport would forever change her life.

Those familiar with my story may already know that I was born and raised in Brooklyn. Every family get-together took us to Far Rockaway, Queens to my grandmother Ruth Youngblood's house. These consisted of food, drinks, laughs, sports, and, simply put, good times. The adults would be in the basement and my brother, my cousins, the younger friends of the family, and I would be in the backyard until it got too dark to play. Most of the brood were boys, so it was only a matter of time until I transformed into a tomboy.

My family produced some pretty good athletes, and if you didn't play a sport, you were a die-hard fan. During the year that I was seven years old, my grandma had put a hoop in the backyard. I'm not sure what holiday it was, but it was there when we arrived at her house, and that was the first time I ever picked up a basketball. That day, most of my family came into the backyard. My grandfather, Alonzo Youngblood, was on the grill, and it was almost time to eat. The backyard was large, so while the grownups were getting the food together my brother, cousins, and I played until lunch was served and the grownups made us stop.

Since I was just a beginner, I bounced the ball with two hands, shot under-handed, and traveled every time I touched the ball. Everything you weren't supposed to do in the game, I did. I was terrible, but I was having fun and, at that point, that was all that mattered. Between bonding and getting some cheap shots in (because I was a hack), I was loving every minute.

Before they made us stop to wash up and eat, some of the grownups took shots and played with us. My uncle, Anthony Youngblood, was good at basketball, my grandmother had played in high school, and, though my mother and aunts played handball, they even took a couple shots.

My uncle shot first, made a couple shots, and stopped shooting because he wasn't missing. He said sarcastically that we'd be there all day waiting for him to miss. After that, my grandma, who was well-known in the family for her hook shot, took a layup, a couple bank shots (which she bricked), and then did her renowned hook shot. The hook was all net! Once she made that, everyone in the backyard cheered; from that moment on, I knew basketball was something I wanted to play.

The fact that my Grandma was so well-rounded in so many aspects of her life blew my mind. From that day forward, I lived in that backyard, until we broke a couple of the rims and began going to the parks. My grandma's house became my first and last stop of the day. I wasn't big on video games or TV (though I played a little NBA Jam here and there); for the most part, I just wanted to play basketball and try to beat my more athletic cousins and brother.

Over time, my family saw that I was becoming serious about basketball and I was improving steadily. That next year, my third grade year, I played on my elementary school team. I also attended clinics and tournaments at the St. John's Recreation Center in Brooklyn. Any chance I got to be associated with basketball, I begged my mom to make it happen.

That year, I became an official tomboy. I was still the smart, cute, sweet little girl everyone knew, but at any given moment you'd catch me rough housing and playing with a bunch of boys. I did it all—basketball, football, suicide, and all the other games the boys played. I wasn't interested in single and double-dutch rope games with the girls, even though it would have been much safer. It was only a matter of time before my favorite subject in school became gym (my fellow physical educators are probably going to let me have it for using that term).

We got the opportunity to play all period, and I got to hang out with my favorite teacher. Prior to falling in love with gym class, math was my thing! I loved it and still do, but math just didn't give me that same thrill. They were both the highest grades on my report card. Like all students, once I really enjoy and love something, I apply myself even more.

I attended Public School 92 on Parkside Avenue in Brooklyn, NY. PS92 was an elementary school that went from kindergarten to fifth grade. It was about two blocks from the apartment building I lived in on Lenox Road. While attending, I met one of my most influential teachers. Her name was Ms. A. She was my gym teacher and I was her teacher's pet. I loved helping teachers, but with Ms. A. it was more than that. She constantly pushed me and cheered me on. She encouraged me to be better than the boys and told me that nothing was a boys-only activity. She was the one that suggested I join the elementary school's after-school program and other extracurricular activities. I immediately got the applications and became more involved with what was going on at school. I also noticed that all the boys I had secret crushes on were in the program, and I was sold.

The elementary after-school program was called the Jackie Robinson Center for Physical Culture (JRC). All participants would do one activity (arts and crafts, sports, dance, etc.) and one educational subject, twice a week. We had to learn a pledge, wear a uniform, and be on time. They taught us discipline and helped us with our studies. It was the perfect way to keep us out of trouble.

I resided in the Flatbush Avenue area, which was one of the most dangerous neighborhoods in Brooklyn. There was a lot of gang violence, drugs, and crime going on, so it was definitely good to have somewhere to go after school. The after-school program took place on Tuesdays and Thursdays. If you didn't register quickly enough, some of the more interesting activities filled up; as luck would have it, the first rotation of basketball was already full. I ended up having to take tennis as my activity and math as my educational subject.

Playing tennis was cool, but it was nothing like basketball. Sometimes I think my mother wanted me to continue to pursue a career in tennis. Throughout my childhood, she always styled my hair with beads. I had every color bead in my hair, sometimes all at the same time. If you didn't see me, you could definitely hear me coming. Everywhere I went, people compared me to Serena and

Venus Williams. Eventually, my aggressive style on the basketball court led to losing a lot of the beads, so she put them in less often.

Once the first session was over, I got accepted into basketball. My first jersey number was five and my very first coaches were Coach John Lalane and Coach Heather Domacase. My very first serious basketball crush was on Richard Campbell. My friends will tell you that, to this day, my greatest fantasy in life is to find my Quincy McCall from the movie Love & Basketball and to have an Asian baby. Call me a dreamer, but one day I will find my Quincy, and, if I'm lucky, he'll also be Asian.

Richie was a year younger than me and he played like a mini Allen Iverson. He was fearless and very talented, and he was so cute and little. He was probably about four feet tall, but watching him play was amazing. I don't think he knew, but I always watched him closely. Between gawking in amazement and gawking because I adored him, I was studying his every move. He was way better than me at the time, but he definitely inspired me to get my game up.

I made friends at the JRC with the boys from school who lived close to me. Soon I began to play with them outside of the after-school program, as going twice a week to JRC wasn't enough for us. We began playing before, during, and after school, in the park out back of PS92. Soon we had our own little basketball clique. Everyone lived between two and five blocks from the school, so unless someone got in trouble, we were in 92 Park faithfully. Before school, we'd get our snacks and then go play on the half court against each other. After school, we'd go get freshly baked chocolate chip cookies, a quart of juice, or the Chinese food restaurant special of the day.

My mother held me to above-average standards in school. She took education very seriously, especially once she got on the school board. There was no way she was going to be in that light and have me not doing well in school. She made sure I was doing what I had to do, and if I didn't meet her standards, she'd punish me. Punishments like taking the phone or TV away didn't really have an effect on me. She made sure she hit me where it hurt. She recognized my love for the game, so it wasn't long before she began using basketball as both motivation and punishment. I wasn't the perfect kid; I slipped up once in a blue, and when I did, she'd use basketball against me.

Basketball was all I wanted to do. It was something I enjoyed and had so much fun doing. I was now playing all year round, all day, every day. Playing that much basketball led to me running through more and more pairs of sneakers. I was a pretty simple kid. I didn't ask for much. I just wanted sneakers and permission to go to the park and hoop whenever I wanted to. This was when my sneaker addiction started, an addiction I'm still struggling to overcome. Up until eighth grade, I didn't realize that, once it got cold, I'd need clothes to go with the twenty to thirty pairs of sneakers I had.

I had to wear a uniform. After fifth grade, I had a lot of sneakers and basketball shorts, but my regular clothes consisted of about five pair of jeans and maybe twelve shirts. I didn't go anywhere but to the park and school, so I didn't care about clothes. The result is that I know nothing about fashion to this day. I just knew my sneakers were fresh and that I should make sure I matched. These are the very things I believe in today, and are probably why my friends make fun of me.

Thanks to PS92 and Ms. A., I decided that I wanted to make a living out of playing basketball and teaching physical education. Fortunately for me, with hard work, dedication, and perseverance,

I'm doing just that. I'm a professional basketball player, as well as a certified physical educator. Whenever I return from overseas I work as a substitute teacher, primarily teaching physical education. Basketball and children are my passions, so I plan to be around both for as long as I live.

I attended JRC until I graduated from PS92 and met a couple other girls that played ball. Girls began showing up at 92 Park. In fourth grade, there was another girl that joined the JRC team. Her name was Charmonique Watt. I honestly felt like she was always on my heels, and that made me a better player. It was exciting to have another good female hooper from the same neighborhood to relate to, and occasionally gang up on the boys with.

At that time, I was still ignorant to the girls' basketball world; if you asked me, there weren't too many good girl basketball players around. Within the twelve block radius, I knew of only Charm, an older girl that lived next to 92 Park named Tameka, and myself. Tameka hung with an older crowd of boys from the neighborhood, and she could hoop! She was a good player, but it was evident that basketball was more of a hobby to her. She just wanted to chill with her boys and have fun. She wasn't taking basketball seriously or trying to make a career out of it, but she could have. Charm has followed in my footsteps, as we both traveled from JRC, to 92 Park, to the same middle school and team, same division in high school, same AAU team, and even the same state in college, with her attending Towson and me going to Morgan State. Her mom and my mom were even involved with the school board together.

Charm is also pursuing her pro career, and it's honestly been an honor to watch her grow. She was like the little sister I never had, on and off the court. One thing about her game—her jump shot was always money. We were two of the few girls in the area that hooped and made it out of the hood. Basketball took us many places, introduced us to many people, and, most importantly, got us free college educations. Not many people get the opportunity to experience the things we have.

Looking back, not more than three or four of the boys we played with made it out. Unfortunately, today, when I go back around 92 Park, I see some of the same dudes in the same places. They always wish me well and show love. No matter what I achieve or where I've been, I'll never be one of those people that make it and get all Hollywood. With success, I believe you should remain humble, no matter what.

# Chapter 2
# A T-spoon of Progress

*The more you play the game, the higher your IQ will get!*
*#Tinyism*

After elementary school, I started venturing out of the neighborhood. We wanted to play against different people and different competition. We started going to MS2 Park, Wingate Park, and MS61 Park; I also started going to St. John's Recreation Center with my mother and grandmother a couple times a week. They had memberships to the recreation center, so they went on Tuesdays, which was Ladies' Night, and sometimes on the weekends to work out or attend boot camp. I would attend the clinics for the kids my age, and just run around and play with the boys.

I joined one of the "biddie" teams (ten to twelve year old division), and that's where I met one of my lifelong friends, Kenya Kirkland, and one of my favorite coaches, Coach Lloyd. Today, Kenya is an assistant coach at Jacksonville University, after a star-studded college career playing at Georgetown for the Lady Hoyas.

Coach Lloyd was in charge of anything that had to do with the gymnasium. He coached us, reffed us, organized the leagues, and did whatever he could to take care of us. Once I started coming to the Rec on the regular, Coach Lloyd began helping me with my game and looking out for me.

I was getting comfortable with traveling around Brooklyn by myself. At that point, I was starting middle school, and for my sixth grade year, I begged my mother to let me go to MS2, which was right across the street from PS92. She agreed, but assured me that if she didn't like how the school year turned out, I'd be transferring the next year. I wanted to go to MS2 because all of my friends were going there. I tried out for the middle school team and, though I made it, so did everyone who tried out, so it wasn't much of an accomplishment. The team was decent, but we didn't win much. After losing a few games, people stopped showing up, and our season went down the drain quickly. I even stopped attending myself. The reason I had been excited to go to MS2 was because I thought I'd be on the team with the boys that I played with all summer. I didn't know they were going to separate the teams by gender.

MS2 was beefing with MS61 that year, so, in addition to fighting a lot, the school developed a bad reputation. My mother was still on the school board, and there was no way she was going to let me stay there for another two years.

My last two years of middle school were spent in a well-known school for the gifted called North Star Academy (MS340). It is located in Brooklyn, near the Grand Army Plaza area. I was going into a much stricter environment, totally different from MS2. We had to wear full uniform, head to toe: ties, stockings, skirts, shoes, the whole nine yards. In MS2, and even in elementary school, I had gotten away with just wearing the shirt or pants, but that wasn't going to fly at North Star.

I got there the first day and realized there was no park! There was a hoop attached to the gate in one of the parking lots, but it didn't have a rim. On top of that, the school and parking lot was so small that there wasn't any room to play. Once I got inside, I looked for the gym. To my utter dismay, there was no gym! Oh my God! What am I going to do without basketball all day? There actually had been a gym at one point, but it was turned into two classrooms and a storage room. If it hadn't been pointed out to me that there were painted backboards near the ceiling, I would have never known.

I finally learned that gym class took place in the lunchroom and the hallway next to it. MS2 had two gyms, and here I was at a school with none! I was heartbroken. No friends, no gym, no team, no fun at recess, no nothing! I wanted to get out of there, but my mother wasn't having that. She had pulled some strings to get me into the school, and there was no way she was reneging. This was one of the best schools around, and education was always number one to her. Later down the line, I made some friends, and between lunch time and the train rides to and from school, I found some of the cool kids. I even found some boys to crush on.

It was getting cold, so I couldn't go to the park and play like I wanted to. I was going through basketball withdrawal bad. I even tried to go and play in my gloves, but that didn't work out (you're not a real hooper if you haven't played in gloves or in the rain!). My mother began asking around about basketball teams, and a friend of hers told her about a basketball program in our neighborhood. The next weekend, I went to see if I could tryout and be a part of the team. The name of the program was Fundamental Youth

Association, or FYA. This organization had different age groups, and was coached by the well-known Coach Screen.

The first time I went to work out, I was a little intimidated. The boys were way more talented and bigger than the ones I was accustomed to playing with. I was still young in the game and sort of a rookie, so I didn't have the same confidence that I have now. The first day was cool. I got invited back for the next week, and I was told that in two weeks, we'd have a game. I knew I had to work out more to ensure I could stay on the team. I asked my mother to get me a membership to the Rec, because I wanted to start going more frequently. My school may not have had a gym, but there was no way I was going on without basketball.

I ultimately made friends at North Star, and basketball was now back in my life (they also put a rim on that hoop in the parking lot). In the mornings and at lunch time, we played three on three, horse, king of the court, Utah, or just shot around. Once people found out that I played ball and that I was good, I became more popular. Playing and competing against some of the best players at school led them to invite me to tryouts for the team. When they told me about it, I wondered how we could have a basketball team when we did not even have a gym. Little did I know that tryouts and practice took place at a school about five blocks away. Once I made the team, I had FYA and my North Star teams to look forward to.

I consider myself to be an unselfish person, and I was even more unselfish on the court. I would always look for my teammates instead of trying to create for myself. Often times, my mother, coach, and even my teammates would scream at me to shoot, but if it wasn't a wide-open layup, I wasn't interested in taking it. I was more interested in trying to cross someone and then pass it to a teammate, so they could score.

On both teams, I had several teammates who were very talented, and often took over as the leaders of the teams. I admired and looked up to them. On my North Star team, there was Joseph Dixon (Lil Joe), and on my FYA team, there was Quasim Pugh (Q or Qua). Qua went on to play college ball at Norfolk State, after transferring from the College of Charleston. Joe was a year older than me, and Qua was a year or two younger. They both averaged double figures, and were getting lots of attention by being the best players on the teams.

The only time I took over games or put up numbers was in the park with my friends. I didn't have a scoring mentality. It seemed like a totally different game when there was a referee on court. It took me some time to play the same way on the hardwood as I did on concrete. I adjusted and began playing the same game everywhere when I started participating in summer tournaments. Almost all summer tournaments took place outside on concrete in someone's park, so it felt the same whether there were referees or not.

FYA and North Star gave me a little taste of the organized basketball life: consistent practices, games every week, traveling to games, and just the camaraderie that came with being on a team. I was the only girl on both teams, but being on those teams was very important to me. While playing for FYA we were competitive, but I don't remember winning any of the tournaments we played in. In contrast, the North Star Academy team went undefeated in the PAL (Police Athletic League) tournament and won the championship.

Playing in that PAL tournament was really an eye opener. For one, everyone on that team could hoop. We had a good fan base every game, which included the families of all of my teammates, minus mine. On top of that, we had customized our uniforms. PAL leagues just give out t-shirts with their logo on the front and a number on the back. However, our Coach Davis got us matching shorts, and customized the shirts with the nickname of our choice. Between how we looked, played, and were supported, we definitely had some swagger to us.

Before the nickname Tiny stuck with me, there were a couple other nicknames I went by. In middle school, I was introduced to the WNBA; the fact that there was now somewhere for female basketball players to play professionally in the United States increased my desire to play ball. I'm the type of person who has favorite players instead of favorite teams. When you're invested in teams and they lose, it hurts more—just ask any long-term Knicks fan, they'll tell you. If I root for a team, it's either the team that has my favorite player on it, or any team from New York.

New York's women's professional basketball team is the New York Liberty. When I began supporting them, the players included Vickie Johnson, Becky Hammon, and my first favorite, Teresa Weatherspoon (aka T-Spoon). I was able to meet her a couple times, because she was often in the community. She would come to St. John's Recreation Center to play open gym with the older girls, speak to the younger kids like me, and to get her hair done at a nearby shop. Being able to interact with her made her, by far, my favorite player at the time. I didn't really consider her a celebrity, but more of a mentor, someone to look up to. I loved the person she was and the way she ran the team.

Prior to my coach asking us to come up with nicknames for our jerseys, I just went by Corin, but once he asked and I gave it some thought, I began calling myself T-Spoon, Jr. It fit, and my teammates liked it, so we went with it. I was always short, so T-spoon also related to my height (as compared to a tablespoon), so it seemed like the perfect nickname.

I tried to play in every tournament possible. The PAL tournament gave me one of my very first nice sized trophies. That feeling of accomplishment that came with bringing that trophy home was a feeling like no other. At that point, I had already received five to ten pocket rockers, but they didn't compare to the size of the PAL trophy. Pocket rockers were those trophies that were small enough to fit in your pocket. My goal became to get as many trophies as I possibly could. I used to watch the NBA players and other professional athletes show off their trophy rooms on TV and in magazines. I knew that someday I wanted to have my own trophy room—not necessarily to brag, but to have an opportunity to relive some of my accomplishments, and recognize how far I'd come.

*Honoring my childhood idol and Women's Basketball Hall of Famer Teresa Weatherspoon with a TA9 shirt*

# Chapter 3
# The Birth of Tiny

*You should focus more on proving yourself right than proving them wrong!*
*#Tinyism*

One of a child's deepest fears is losing their parents. Living in Brooklyn, I've had quite a few scares over the course of my lifetime. Flatbush was a place where gun violence and crime took place on a regular basis. Between the shoot-outs, drive-bys, and robberies taking place on or near my block, I was scared for my mom's safety whenever she went out at night. I can remember a time she called during a shoot-out, explaining to my brother and me that she was hiding and would try to get home as soon as it was safe. She wanted to tell us she loved us, and to do her best to assure us that everything was okay, even though it was quite the contrary. Hearing the fear in her voice, as well as the gun shots in the background, made me wait by the door until she arrived home safely. Fortunately, no one in my family was ever harmed by the frequent shootings in the neighborhood, but there was one particular scare and blessing that I'm reminded of every year since.

Many New Yorkers had their personal fears turn into realities on September 11, 2001, when the World Trade Center was attacked. My mother works for the Board of Elections on Broadway, and her office is just a couple blocks away. The train station she used to get to and from work was minutes away from the Twin Towers. She frequently went for lunch a block or two from the site of the disaster, so imagine the fear in my heart when, in class, I was receiving only partial details of the situation on that infamous morning.

I was in eighth grade, in my first period class, during the first week of school. Some parents came to pick up their children, as news of the attack began to spread. The teachers were meeting and talking in the hallways. Some of my classmates were getting calls and texts from their parents. It was pretty chaotic in my middle school. When I finally got word of what had been going on, my heart dropped and my eyes began to water. I called my mother's cell, job, and our house, and received no answer. I was terrified. I began to think the worst, and contemplated life without my mom.

Luckily, she had decided not to go to work that day. I eventually got in touch with her, and I was as happy as can be. As my fear turned to joy, I thought about all of those families who lost someone that day. It could have easily been any of us in their situation, and after all this time, I get the same feeling every year on the anniversary of the tragedy. I can't even imagine what they went through and continue to go through. I want to forever send my condolences to the victims of 9/11 and their families.

Once things calmed down around the city, my final year of middle school continued like any other. I was still playing on the school's team, with FYA, and I was going to the rec more often.

Towards the middle of the year, the time came to apply for

high schools. I picked my high schools quite randomly, without much more thought than eenie-meenie-miney-mo. My mother suggested one school, and didn't necessarily care about my choices. I didn't particularly care either, which led me to haphazardly narrow down my selections to two boroughs: Brooklyn and Manhattan. I flipped through the listing of schools and randomly picked two or three from each.

When I say randomly, I mean it. I flipped through the pages, counted to three and stopped—whatever page I stopped on, that's what I put down. I can't remember my choices, but my mother's choice was Brooklyn Tech, the best academic school in Brooklyn. To get into Brooklyn Tech, I had to take a test and complete a tedious application. We agreed that if I didn't get in, we'd pick the best academic high school out of my careless list of choices. I was accepted to each of my choices before I went to take the test for admission to Brooklyn Tech. My brother, Raling Herrera, Jr., was already attending the school. He loved computers, science, video games, and every gadget you can think of. If I got in for the upcoming school year, he'd have been a senior, while I would have been an incoming freshman.

When I went to take the test, I killed the math section, but then I began thinking about how I felt when I first attended North Star. I looked around the classroom, and it was a very diverse culture. At that age, I wasn't very open-minded, and I quickly decided I really didn't want to be here for the next four years. My brother often complained about how much work he had to do, and how big his books were. I wasn't looking forward to that, so I sabotaged my results, answering only half of the remaining questions, and deliberately flunked the test. I completed half of the other sections, as I didn't want to make it too obvious, but after I felt like enough time had passed, I just shaded the letter B for every remaining answer. Not many people knew that I did that. I don't even think my mother knew until now. After it was announced that I didn't get in, James Madison High School was my best academic option. It was located on Bedford Avenue in Brooklyn. It was about forty-five minutes away from my house by bus, and about twenty minutes in the car.

Before I attended Madison, I was playing in my last games with FYA. That summer, I started taking my talent to a high level. I was getting a good amount of playing time, despite being the only girl on the team. With more time on the court, I got more confident. I was doing things now that I may have practiced before, but hadn't necessarily thought I could pull off in a game. One of the first tournaments we played in to kick the summer off was the Clarence Norman, Jr. Classic, in Brower Park. This became one of my favorite tournaments. My mother was very cool with Assemblyman Norman, Jr. He lived up the block, and actually gave me one of my first jobs. My mother worked to help him get re-elected. To make things easier for her, my friends from the neighborhood and I helped out. We hung posters on the corner light poles, handed out flyers on election days, and slid pamphlets under doors all around Brooklyn. It wasn't a legit job, but it was easy money and a nice little hustle.

That was the third year the assemblyman held the tournament in Brower Park. I played every year on an all-girls team. This year, I was playing with the boys, and he was excited to see if I could hold my own. That I did, and even though we fell short in the tournament, I turned some heads in the park that day; one in particular was the head of my future coach. After the game, Coach Edwin Llopiz (aka Munch), came up to me. He was a big, heavy-set man, who represented the teams from the Parks Department. He was coaching both boys' and girls' teams, and he had decided he was going to be entering a team in several girls' tournaments that summer. He asked me if I wanted to play, and I decided that I would. He said, "Great, we have a game tomorrow." From that point on, ninety percent of the time that I was playing in a tournament in NYC, I was playing with Munch. I still play with him to this day.

That summer, we played in seven tournaments, including well-known leagues like Nike Swoosh, C & C in Wingate Park, Kingston Park Tournament, and Rod Strickland. After winning the Nike and Rod Strickland tournaments, we were invited to more and more tournaments. We made it to nearly every championship game. We were turning heads and making a little noise.

We had a core group of girls, basically the same age, and we were all relatively the same height. As long as you play hard, your size doesn't matter. Heart over height is one of my many mottos. We did not play with a legit center, but we played defense and we played together. In the championship games that we occasionally lost, it was usually because the other team was much bigger than we were. We played against some of the best AAU (Amateur Athletic Union) teams in the city and the nation. We played against the mighty Exodus, who had legendary city players like Epiphanny Prince (who would score one hundred thirteen points in a high school game in 2006), Kia Vaughn (the eighth overall pick in the 2009 WNBA draft), Anjale Barrett (who played point guard for Maryland), and many other big names in the city. We faced the Douglass Panthers and the Gazelles, who featured Melanie Murphy (Stanford University's standout point guard), Tina Charles (WNBA All-Star), and Marissa Flagg (current Seton Hall Director of

Operations).

Our arch-nemesis was Team Mika. We often played them, and we lost to them only twice in four years. We earned many trophies and jerseys, as well as something far more important—respect. The little scrappy team from Brooklyn was getting it done citywide, and we couldn't wait until the next summer. Most of my teammates were the same age as me, and were also entering their first year of high school. I was the only one to attend James Madison, while the rest of my teammates went to Benjamin Banneker, Lincoln High School, Grand Street, Martin Luther King and others; schools that, I would later learn, were basketball schools. Those schools had the best girls' teams in the city. I was ignorant to the basketball world and how things worked. I learned from my mistakes, or just simply found out the hard way.

As this amazing summer ended, it was time to become the new girl again, for my freshman year at Madison. Madison was far from a basketball school, but both the boys' and girls' varsity teams competed and hung with the best. The girls' team always made it to the playoffs, and had some well-known players. Coming from a small school like North Star, I had to adjust to such a big school, and to going to classes by myself. By about the second week, I was beginning to get the hang of things. From the metal detectors to changing for gym, I was getting accustomed to it all. I made some friends from class, hooping in gym, and the commute to and from school. I bumped into a lot of familiar faces from my neighborhood, FYA, Flatbush, and even people I'd met the past summer. One of those familiar faces was Frances Lyons. She was one of the stars of the girls' basketball team at the time. She was a year older than me, and we had met while I was playing against her with Munch. She was surprised to see me, and wondered why I didn't tell her I was coming here. Fran went on to play college ball at Brooklyn College, and was ranked thirty-second out of five-hundred in field goal percentage in the nation in 2009-2010. We were both excited that we'd be playing together, and she said she'd let me know when tryouts were. Fran was a very physical post player, a little undersized for college, but perfect for high school. She was a straight bully on the block who finished well. We felt we could be the perfect one-two punch, I just had to make the team. Tryouts weren't until the end of October, so the only time I played ball at Madison was in gym class or after school, at nearby parks with my friends.

October rolled around and it was time for tryouts. The school had a junior varsity team, which was for freshman and sophomores only, and a varsity team. Varsity was for the best players, but mainly the upperclassmen. If you were talented enough to play varsity, though, it didn't matter what grade you were in. For a freshman to make varsity was a big deal. When I got to tryouts, I was so amped. I watched the girls that were trying out (along with the returners) shoot around a little, and thought that this would be easy. I usually played with boys, and after this summer with Munch, most of these girls were below my level. The tryout was run by the new coach, Coach Bill Dumont. Coach Dumont also coached the softball team, which was his pride and joy. Last year's basketball coach retired, and he decided to take on the position, since he had knowledge of the game and had coached Madison's team years ago. Dumont, a fiery coach, was also my chemistry teacher. Up until that point, I was struggling a little bit in his class. I had a grade average of about seventy-five at that point. Prior to high school, I was used to getting good grades without studying. Subjects like chemistry and other sciences require studying to get above-average grades, and I wasn't doing much. I wasn't into class participation either.

Dumont started the tryout by introducing himself and the returners, and by letting everyone know we'd do a couple drills and play full court after that. Once he finished talking, Fran looked at me and asked "You ready, youngin'?" I shook my head to assure her I was.

I did well in the layup and ball-handling drills. I felt there wasn't anyone in that tryout that was better than me, so my hopes were high. Once the drills were over, they split us into teams and started playing games. For some strange reason, I wasn't put on a team. Coach Dumont told me to sit on the side for a little, and he'd let me know when to get in. Little did I know, the strange reason I was left riding the pine was because I was only about five feet tall, and he already decided to put me on junior varsity, regardless of my game.

We didn't have a relationship; I wasn't even sure he knew my name, even though I was in his class. I sat on the side for about an hour and a half, and I was furious! I wanted to go home, but I decided to stay. With about fifteen minutes remaining, he finally told me to get on court. Most of the returners were on the side talking with him and the assistant coach, and he was hardly paying any attention. Once I got on court, Fran sensed I was upset, and knew what was up. I went crazy as soon as I got the ball! I was all over the place! Stealing the ball, scoring, diming her after I crossed over some girls. I had that gym going crazy. Once Coach Dumont started paying attention and saw what I could do, he blew the whistle and ended tryouts. He told the upperclassmen that he'd be in touch, and the rest of the underclassmen that they would be on JV. He pulled me into the other gym with Fran, the assistant coach, and the returners, and started going crazy. He asked, "Adams, how did you do all of that?" Fran had told him I could play, but he hadn't expect anything like that. He just shook his head and said, "But I don't understand it, you're just so tiny." He asked everyone if they saw this move I made, or this shot I took, and kept spilling on himself at how small I was. He told the returners that it was official. He didn't know which girls he was going to pick to complete the team, but one thing was for sure; Tiny was on the team. Everyone looked around, like, "Who is Tiny?" He said to the assistant coach, "Yeah John, we're calling her Tiny from this day on." From that day on, I was no longer Corin or T-spoon, Jr.—I was Tiny. I also didn't have to worry about chemistry anymore.

# Chapter 4
# From A Lady Knight to
# a No Limit Soldier

*When dealing with new experiences, you should
always be open-minded!*
*#Tinyism*

Becoming a James Madison Lady Knight made my transition into high school pretty easy. When you're a part of a school team, you get a lot of attention—sometimes it is positive, and other times it can be negative. No matter what though, after a certain amount of time, everyone knows who you are. Being well-known can add a lot of unwanted pressure that some athletes just aren't ready for. You experience the pressures of special treatment (both good and discriminative), representing your school everywhere you go, having to be on your best behavior all the time, and even having to choose your friends wisely. Your allowance for mistakes instantly shrinks to a minimum, regardless of age, maturity, or knowledge.

Being a student-athlete is a full-time job. You have to manage your studies, as well as handle your business on the court or the field. Fortunately for me, I have never struggled with being a student-athlete. The best way to deal with balancing school and your sport is to always be prepared, manage your time, be organized, and show your teachers you care about your education. No matter what level you're at, there is always an academic standard you have to uphold to remain on the team. Teachers are the ones who put the grades in, so it's important to develop a relationship with them. There are two types of teachers you experience while being a student-athlete: the cooperative teacher and the hell-raising teacher.

The cooperative teacher is more lenient than the hell-raising teacher. That teacher will try to help you as much as they possibly can. They'll often give you later due dates, special assignments, excuse your tardiness and absences, and provide other accommodations that you may need to pass their classes. The hell-raising teacher will not cut you any slack, at all! Their number one goal seems to be making life a living hell for you. They hate most athletes and don't believe they deserve special treatment. None of this has been proven, and it is entirely my opinion, but I think the hell-raising types are jealous of student athletes. They likely envied the athletes growing up, and now take it out on the athletes in their classes. They finally wield the power, and they are paying us back for all those years of their childhood that they despised the athletes.

The cooperative teachers may have been student-athletes in the past, participated in extracurricular activities, or just are flat out cooler. They know what you're going through, and don't mind helping you along the way. Regardless, it's entirely on you whether you pass or fail. My number one rule when it comes to being successful is holding yourself accountable. Depending on your sport, you're going to miss a lot of class, so excused absences on top of unexcused absences would be setting yourself up for failure.

Once I made the team, the students, teachers, other faculty, and even the school safety agents all knew and loved Tiny, and it was all thanks to Dumont. He not only gave me an everlasting nickname, he provided me with the support I needed to make it through high school. Dumont did everything, from helping me understand chemistry to giving me extra bus passes to get home. To this day, we keep in contact, and I thank him for all he's done for me. Dumont is one of the smartest men I have ever met, let alone been coached by. He could break down things to me in ways that I could understand, and also teach to anyone else in the same situation. Being from Flatbush, I never really interacted or communicated much with people of different races. Growing up, I witnessed a lot of stereotyping, prejudice, and hatred towards other races and people who simply were different from what we saw in the hood. Building a relationship with Dumont, a Caucasian, contradicted those beliefs, and allowed me to become a well-rounded, non-judgmental person. Often your surroundings can influence your beliefs, especially the negative ones, if you aren't an open-minded individual. I have him to thank for the way I turned out and developed, both on and off the court.

My freshman year, we had best team of my four years there. We had a strong starting five and some good role players coming off the bench. Our starting five included Fran, who played the 4-5 (Power Forward/Center); Jackie Cavalcante, a great shooter who played in the backcourt with me at the 2 (Shooting Guard); Monique Murphy, who was the older sister of Brooklyn standout, Melanie Murphy, and basically our Paul Pierce at the 3 (Small Forward). Filling out the starting five, we had Jessie, a hard-nosed softball player who was like our Dennis Rodman. Coming off the bench, our sixth man was Kristine Dillon (PF/C), the only other freshman to make varsity with me. Dillon was the tallest person on our team, and even though she wasn't as talented as Fran, she played her role well. Dillon was a rebounding machine, and at the time that was all we needed from her. We weren't a basketball school, but we had talent and competed with the best.

Though we were talented, we never were able to get out of the second round of playoffs. I often think back and wish I knew some of the things I know now. I promise the results would have been different. Like most athletes, I often wish I could go back and do things a little differently. That's a part of evolving as a player.

During my freshman year, our boys' team was equally talented, but they struggled with a problem we didn't—ineligibility. I always felt there was someone on the boys' team that mirrored my talent, and could have been my potential Quincy McCall. At Madison, that person was Tyrone Cooke. Unfortunately, he could've been my little boo thing, but I didn't tell him about my crush until about five years after. Little did I know, the feelings had been mutual. When I found that out, I just shook my head in disbelief, because he was very handsome.

Ty and I were outstanding guards, with great ball-handling ability and great court vision. There were many talented ineligible male players at Madison. I would see some of them in gym class or in the summer, doing their thing, and would just shake my head. They just didn't want to go to class or do their work. I would talk to a few of them that I was close with, including Tyrone, but it was no use. If those guys were eligible throughout their four years at Madison, we probably could have been considered a basketball school. With the talent that both programs had, we would have been winning and putting Madison on the map.

After my freshman year, Dumont upped the ante and made our schedule a little more challenging. He even added some holiday tournaments for us to participate in. I am a firm believer that the more you play, the better you'll get. That's why, to this day, I try to live in the gym. I'm what you would call a gym rat. I'll go anywhere, anytime, anyplace, just to hoop.

By sophomore year, I took my talent to another level, and opponents, coaches, referees, and spectators began taking notice. I was being mentioned among the best in NYC and the tri-state area. Between Dumont's choice to have us play against some of the best public and private schools in NYC, and the fact that I was playing all over NYC in the summer with Munch, Tiny became well-known and well-respected. To be successful and prosper in the basketball world, you have to work hard, know how to use your talent, and get the proper exposure. Your exposure comes from playing at basketball schools in the winter, and playing on Amateur Athletic Union (AAU) teams throughout the spring and summer.

AAU is one of the largest non-profit volunteer sports organizations in the United States. A multi-sport organization, the AAU is dedicated exclusively to the promotion and development of amateur sports and physical fitness programs. AAU tournaments are where college scouts get to watch you play and decide whether to recruit you for their schools and universities. A free education to college should be the ultimate goal for all basketball players, especially for players from the city who likely wouldn't be able to go to college if not for the scholarship system. My focus, however, was scoring trophies and newspaper clippings. I didn't see the bigger picture.

Ms. Rochelle Murphy, the mother of Monique and Mel Murphy, saw me play quite a few times. I was on the same team as her older daughter Mo, while Mel and I played for rival high schools. Towards the end of my sophomore season, after we played

Midwood (Mel's school), Ms. Murphy asked if I'd be interested in being a part of an AAU team she was affiliated with called the Gazelles. I told her to give me the info, and I'd consider it and talk about it with my mom. Usually, I'd be quick to say yes to anything basketball related, but at that time my mother was beginning to complain that I was never home. Her worries about me being in the street with a bunch of people she didn't know were beginning to get to her. I had just gotten her to start being comfortable with me going all around NYC with Munch, so I knew I couldn't just give Ms. Murphy a straight answer without consulting my mom.

Once my mother and I saw the price for playing on the team, we both said no, immediately. If your AAU team isn't sponsored, it can be very expensive, as you have to think about the costs of travel, hotels, uniforms, and food when traveling to other cities. All we knew was that playing with Munch was cheaper, almost free, and I didn't see a difference between playing with Munch and playing AAU with the Gazelles. I passed that opportunity up, which was a bad decision. At that time, the Gazelles had a good program, and the next summer, we played against them a couple times. They had players like Melanie Murphy (Stanford), Tina Charles (UConn, WNBA), Marissa Flagg (Iona), Diatema Hill (UMass), and a couple other notable players from the city.

That next summer, Munch started to turn it up a notch for us. We kept our team intact until we all left for college. Since we were now serious contenders around NYC, Munch wanted to look and act like a team. He came up with a team name, No Limit, and team colors—white, navy blue, and baby blue. Munch's wife, Valerie Llopiz, would always come to our games and act as our team mom. So it was her, Munch, and their ten to twelve daughters, known as No Limit.

They also welcomed us into their immediate, real life family. Munch and Val are very family-oriented people, so on weekends, holidays, or birthdays, they were always celebrating and we were always invited. We even used to have sleepovers at Munch's house. We really bonded as a unit, and it brought us closer together, which resulted in us playing even better. Occasionally, we'd pick up a few new players, but our core team was Kenya Kirkland (Grand Street, Georgetown); Juanita Chapel, aka Shea Shea (Grand Street, Globe); Kimberly Blakney, aka Kimbo (Benjamin Banneker, Farmingdale State); Danielle Smith, aka Baby D/Big Momma Buckets (Benjamin Banneker, Temple); Quasha Llopiz, aka Qua (Benjamin Banneker, Farmingdale State); Krystal Parnell, aka Grandma (Bishop Loughlin, Bergtraum, Towson University); Amanda Burnett (Grand Street, South Carolina State); and Keona Jones, aka Africa (Grand Street, Monroe). After receiving my favorite nickname, Tiny, the year before, I was now being called my least favorite nickname ever—Keyfood.

When I first started playing with Munch, I used to pack bags at grocery stores. That was my hustle to get a couple dollars in my pocket. I mainly worked at Keyfood grocery stores, and sometimes, if I was being lazy, I'd go across the street from my house to C-town. When I'd come to the games, I'd come right after work, with plastic bags tied to my book bag with my sneakers in them. My teammates would see my plastic bags and make jokes and clown me. One day I was late, and my phone was dead. I never changed my answering machine recordings, so I was still using my old nickname, T-spoon Jr., on there: "Yo, what's up, you've reached T-spoon Jr. I can't answer the phone right now, so leave a message." Munch and Quasha were taking turns calling me, and Qua said, "Daddy, you know she prolly packing bags at Keyfood again." At the same time she finished her sentence, the phone broke up during my recording right when I said T-spoon Jr., and it sounded a bit like Keyfood. As soon as she heard it, Quasha started laughing. From that day forward, they have tortured me with that name. It's grown on me, and I kind of like it now since they shortened it to just Key. To ninety percent of the people I know I'm Tiny, but to the other ten percent that make up my No Limit family, I'm Keyfood.

The memories of my No Limit family are limitless. I'm the only one that made it to the professional level, but everyone either played in college or has a degree. Most are coaching and still playing in the summer. Kimbo and Baby D were the tallest people on our team at about 5'9, but we always played as if we were the biggest people on the court. Everything about No Limit was unique. We practiced once a week, didn't have any set plays, didn't have any big post players or centers, didn't have sponsors, and certainly didn't have much money. All we had were big hearts and a will to win. Everything we got, whether trophies, uniforms, or just a spot in a big tournament, we earned. Some of the championships we won were Nike Swoosh, Rod Strickland, C&C Showcase, Conrad McRae, 35 Park, and Kingston Park. We were runners up in tournaments like Slam Jam, Rose Classic, and Fordham University.

I have countless memories of playing with No Limit, but my most memorable moment was shared with Kenya Kirkland. Kenya and I were the captains of the team. I was always the lead by example, quiet kind of leader. I didn't really like to be that player that's constantly talking and telling people what to do, because, in the back of my mind, I knew I was capable of making the same mistakes.

Kenya, on the other hand, was the outspoken, put you in your place, no BS type of captain. We were like good cop, bad cop.

Everyone knows I like to laugh and joke around, so, while I was making jokes, Kenya was trying to get us focused. As close as we were off the court, we were even closer on court. We'd go to St. John's Rec and play against the boys outside and inside, get on our bikes or the train and hit up different parks and hoop all day. It was very rare that we could both be on court at the same time and not know what the other one was thinking. We had amazing chemistry; the type of chemistry needed to pull of this unbelievable play we did back when we were around fourteen years old.

When you're a young player, you have the luxury of just going on the court and playing. You don't necessarily think about things you should do until the situation occurs. When I was playing with No Limit, I rarely stretched or even tied my shoes all the way to the top. I just showed up, warmed up a little bit, and played. It wasn't until college that I started taking stretching and tying my shoes tighter. I started doing it because I began getting sore and twisted my ankle one day. This particular weekend, we were playing in the fourteen and under Nike Swoosh girls' division. On one play, I got the ball on a fast break off a steal, and as I pushed the ball on the break, my sneaker fell off—but I kept going. Usually when I'm on a fast break, I'm either with Kenya or Shea Shea. Shea Shea wasn't down the court yet, but Kenya was on her way. Kenya ran behind me and picked up my shoe before she caught up to me on the break. I've always been a pass first guard, so no matter who or where you are, if you're open, I'm going to pass it to you. Once Kenya caught up to me on the break, she was open, so, not realizing she had my shoe in her hand, I still passed her the ball. She saw the ball coming to her, threw me my shoe at the same time, caught the ball, scored, and got an 'And-1' (when you score, are fouled, and get to shoot a free throw). It was the funniest, most incredible play I think I have ever been a part of. We left the park with a win and one of the best highlights to ever happen for No Limit and the Nike Swoosh League.

# Chapter 5
# For Better or Worse: Tiny Setback #1

*The more painful a mistake,*
*the more pleasant the lesson will be.*

*#Tinyism*

As my high school career continued, I started to understand the game and dominate at a high level. As a junior, I averaged nineteen points and nine assists. During my senior season, I averaged twenty-one points and five assists. My senior year numbers were strong, considering I was up against a lot of double teams and box one defenses. It was time for me to start thinking about college. Without a score for the SAT and ACT, no college will consider accepting you. I was also a great test taker. I rarely studied, but once I understood a topic, it was embedded in my brain.

I've passed every important test I've taken on the first try, with a couple exceptions—like my first chemistry Regents in high school. I didn't pass that one, because I forgot to go. In NYC, each student has to take a Regents exam, which is a big final for every subject they have studied. I wasn't used to going to school on a separate day just to take a test, so it slipped my mind. I had a game that day, so that was all I was focusing on. A friend of mine asked me how I did, and that's what triggered my memory. It wasn't a huge deal since I could reschedule it, but my friends made fun of me for being such an air ball.

As a junior, my mother and I decided that I should take the PSAT, to see how I would do. I did well enough to give me confidence, so I took the SAT soon after. At this point, I was just taking the test to attend college academically, as I wasn't hip to the college basketball scene. I knew nothing about the NCAA Clearinghouse, or the qualifications needed to be eligible for an athletic scholarship. Surprisingly, neither did my guidance counselors.

Before I took the SAT, I asked my guidance counselor what would be considered a good score. She told me to just try to get 500s or better, all the way across the board. My goal was to score 500 in reading, math, and on the essay. I ended with a 1550, well above the average score of students in my school, and a little above my goal. My guidance counselor expressed how happy she was for me, because with that score and my GPA, I was definitely eligible for a grant or scholarship. At the time, I didn't know how expensive college was, but once she told my cheap a** we were getting a discount—that was okay with me.

By the end of my junior year, I had my SATs out the way, basketball was going great, and I couldn't ask for a better life. Little did I know, things would start to change. Things getting worse before they get better is the ongoing story of my life. I always experience a slight set back, and then, once the pressure is on, I grind my way up to making a nice little comeback. Before my junior season ended, basketball at Madison began to look like a nightmare for me. Fran was graduating and, worst of all, Dumont decided to resign from his coaching position.

Dumont's passion was softball, so he stayed around as long as he could, but he stepped down after my junior year. He knew we weren't going to be very good, and, with so much on his plate, he didn't need the stress. I understood, but at the same time I was a little hurt, because I loved him so much. Every coach I have ever played for, I've had a special relationship with and truly loved, except for his replacement. Richard Tighe became the coach my senior year, and I didn't really care for him as a coach. Between his need to fill some mighty big shoes and the lack of talent we possessed as a team, my senior year felt like the worst year ever. I put up the best numbers I had in high school, but I didn't have much help around me. After a while, the game plan became to stop Tiny, and you'll beat Madison. Although it was frustrating, it helped me as a player and got me prepared for college basketball.

Before Dumont resigned, he would really look out for me. He did things like put my name in the local newspapers and websites. He even promised me that, if I continued to play the way I did, he'd retire my jersey on my senior night. When I was in eighth grade, they retired the school's first basketball jersey at Madison, that of Justine Paxhia. She was one of the best players to ever play at Madison, and also the previous coach's favorite player. She went on to playing Division 1 basketball at St. Francis College in Brooklyn. During my junior year, Dumont retired Fran's jersey. No one had ever grabbed more rebounds or had more double-doubles than her, so it was definitely justified. Seeing those two jerseys on the wall motivated me to get mine up there as well. Dumont was always a man of his word, and he shared that promise with Coach Tighe.

Before I entered my senior season, I vowed to enjoy my

summer as much as possible. I sensed that my senior season at Madison was going to be a catastrophe on the court, so I wanted to have as much fun as I could prior. That summer turned out to be the most important one for my future basketball career.

No Limit was associated with some of the best people in the girls' basketball world. One person in particular was the late, great Coach Apache (RIP). Apache Paschall was a well-known coach of the AAU Program Exodus, St. Michael's Academy, and Nazareth High School. Apache was known for impacting girls' lives all over NYC. His primary goal was to help girls get college educations by way of basketball. After playing and competing against Exodus, Munch and Apache became cool. He taught Munch about the girls' basketball world, and was much like a mentor to him. Apache told Munch that we were talented, and that he had to try and get us into college. We quickly learned that basketball was bigger than trophies and uniforms. Basketball was something that could change our lives for the better. Apache helped us register for our first AAU tournament in Atlanta. No Limit was known through NYC, but on the national level, no one knew who we were or what we were capable of.

Apache spoke to Mike White, who ran the tourney. He asked him and the other coaches to watch out for us. Unlike the other well-known AAU teams, we weren't sponsored, and we were less fortunate than the girls we played. One thing about the No Limit family though, we grind for whatever need. We fundraised for months, asked our families for money, sold candy, begged on bridges, trains, asked for donations, and just tried to get money any way we could. We had to get to Atlanta, one way or another. Between hustling the money, and still competing in the tourneys around NYC, it was a long summer. Eventually, it was time to head to Atlanta. I'm not sure how much we raised, but it wasn't a lot of money. It was enough for some cheap uniforms, two hotel rooms, a couple buffet dinners a day, and gas for Munch's Expedition. We weren't stylin', but we were there.

Going down was a long trip, but we were family, so it was a fun road trip full of laughs and music. It was Munch, Val, and eight of the No Limit soldiers. Our mantra was Any Means Necessary. You'd be surprised at how big that Expedition truck actually was. Munch and Val sat in the front, of course, and four of us sat in the second row, while the other four actually laid out in the back with our bags. Good thing Munch's windows were tinted, because I doubt we were legal.

The way we grinded to make that trip happen gave us a chip on our shoulders. We didn't win the event, but we did well enough and shocked everybody at that tourney. We didn't have a center or any plays, but we always played hard, scrappy, and together—no matter what. That trip opened a lot of doors for all of the No Limit hoopers after us. People were emailing Munch, and the phone was ringing off the hook.

Before you play the games in most AAU tournaments, they make you sit through an educational presentation that tells you about college basketball, the NCAA, the NCAA Clearinghouse, SAT scores, and everything you need to know to get to the next level. Those were all things we needed to be aware of, so that trip was really the start of this journey I call my career.

The summer was almost over, and that meant a lot of family birthdays were on the way. During mid-August, we celebrate two of my aunts' birthdays, in addition to my cousin's birthday, with most celebrations taking place at my grandmother's house. Usually, if I'm not with the fam in the basement, or in the backyard hooping,

I'm upstairs in my grandmother's room, watching NBATV or any game that's on at the time.

On this particular day, I got upstairs and found what I was going to watch. I left my phone on the bed and went back downstairs. I wanted to get some food and a drink before I got comfortable, even though I wasn't supposed to eat in Grandma's room. When I returned, I had a couple of missed calls from Munch. I called him back but got no answer. A few seconds later he called me back and said, "Yo, I got someone that wants to talk to you. You gonna bug out, yo!"

I asked who, not really knowing who to expect. He told me I was on three-way call with someone well known in the basketball world who was close to Mike White, the man who ran the tournament we just left in Atlanta. I honestly can't remember the gentleman's name, but he introduced himself and told me his experience and involvement with girls' basketball. At that point, I was still trying to figure out exactly what this call was about.

He had watched the No Limit girls play last week, and was blown away. He told me about one person in particular, the reason why he was contacting me. That person was Coach Quentin Hillsman, the current head coach at Syracuse University, who at the time was the assistant coach. He said Coach Q was interested in me, and had asked him to find out if I would be interested in attending the university. At that time, I didn't know much about college basketball and didn't even really follow it. I watched a couple times, and knew the big schools. The only thing I knew was that I had a crush on Dee Brown, who played at Illinois. That was really the only team I followed closely. I knew of Duke, North Carolina, and Syracuse, so when he mentioned Coach Q, I was hyped and so was Munch. I told him that of course I was interested!

Once I hung up that phone, I was in shock. I sat on the bed for a while before I went downstairs to tell my family what had just transpired. I just sat there and thought, 'Wow, maybe you are a little better than you give yourself credit for. This might actually become a reality for you.'

After that phone call, I spoke to Coach Q once or twice on the phone, and then, every few days, he'd send me postcards from Syracuse. Those postcards were to assure me that they were interested and couldn't wait until I was able to attend the school for a visit. Once he started sending postcards, the word got out, and I started to get more and more letters from other programs. My stock must have risen a little more than he had expected, because soon he asked me to verbally commit to Syracuse. Once you verbally commit to a school, it sort of lets everyone know you're likely to attend. It's like a sign to other programs to back off.

After I verbally committed to Syracuse, the college letters slowed down a bit, but, at the time, I didn't think it mattered. All I thought was, oh well, I'm going to the 'Cuse! It didn't really seem like a big deal to me, but once my friends found out and the girls' high school basketball blogs in NYC posted it, I began to realize that maybe it was. Everything was fine until it was time to sign my letter of intent. I didn't know much about the process, but I knew that after you verbally committed to a school, it wasn't long before you had to sign the letter of intent for your scholarship. I inquired to Coach Q, but I suddenly wasn't getting any responses, and those Syracuse postcards I was getting slowed down to maybe once a week and then to none at all.

People were continuously asking me for answers I didn't have, and no other schools were contacting me, because they thought it was a done deal between me and Syracuse. Everything seemed to come to a halt, and I didn't quite know what to do. My senior season was about to start, so things were about to get even tougher. It would have been less stressful, going into a rough season, knowing my future was already squared away. Instead, I was going into my senior season unsure of what I was going do after graduation.

Eventually, I spoke with Coach Q, and he said that, even though he was still interested in me, it wasn't his call. The head coach had his eye on a player with a better resume than mine, who they were going to sign. Coach Q said he was still advocating for me, but it wasn't looking good, and he was sorry.

I'm not very good at handling failure or rejection, and I realized that my dream had been stripped away in a blink of an eye. I was experiencing my first real set back, and I had no plan on how I was going to come back. They say you shouldn't put all your eggs in one basket, and this was a prime example as to what can happen if you do!

# Chapter 6
## "11"

*You never really know who's watching, so make sure you're portraying the right image!*
*#Tinyism*

After that experience, I wanted to make sure that I worked on my game as much as possible. I wanted to work on my weaknesses, and make sure that if or when people doubted me, I'd be able to prove them wrong and prove myself right.

Surprisingly, Munch and I got another phone call. It was Coach Q, who wanted to apologize again and see if he could help me in anyway. Coach Q knew the situation I was in, and even though I still hoped things would work out with Syracuse, they were not going to. He told us that he had a lot of friends in the college basketball world, and would see if he could spark some interest in me.

Days later, Munch was contacted by Coach Donchez Graham from Morgan State University in Baltimore, Maryland. Coach Graham and Coach Q were very good friends, and, interestingly enough, Coach Graham had actually been at the tournament in

Atlanta, and saw us play. Coach Graham was entering his second season as Morgan State's assistant coach, and Morgan was his alma mater. Graham played football at Morgan, and was a Baltimore native. He coached various AAU teams in the Baltimore area, so he was well known.

The first thing Coach Graham did was give us our props for the way we held it down in Atlanta. He wanted to invite the No Limit family on an unofficial visit to Morgan State. At that time, I was the only one to actually have some sort of commitment to a college, so the trip very big for us. This was a great opportunity for No Limit as a whole, so of course Munch agreed. After a few phone calls back and forth to set things up, we were on our way to Baltimore.

Morgan was about three hours away from Brooklyn, so it wasn't a bad trip. We were able to visit and come back in the same day. Just like our trip to Atlanta, we piled up in Munch's Expedition. It was my mom, Munch, and all the upcoming seniors of No Limit: Kenya, Kimbo, Baby D, Shea Shea, and me. We were actually our starting five for most games.

Driving around the neighborhood of Morgan before we arrived, I realized it wasn't really any different from Brooklyn. We joked about how it was The Wire, a hit show at the time that took place in the urban areas of Baltimore. Once we got out the car, I felt right at home.

We thought very highly of all colleges we had seen, because of the way they were portrayed on TV shows and movies. Coming to Morgan's campus brought us back to reality, however. That was 2006, right before Morgan made many upgrades and became one of the best looking Historically Black Colleges and Universities (HBCU) in the country. The fact that they were renovating was actually one of Coach Graham's biggest selling points. After giving us a tour of the campus, which was actually already pretty big, he informed us that they were building a new library and a state of the art student center with a movie theatre and bowling alley.

After the tour of the school, we sat and met with the coaching staff. We spoke about our senior years and what to expect from college. The head coach, Donald Beasley, was also a former football player at Morgan and he was in his second season head coaching. Beas had come to Morgan during the previous season. He replaced the previous coach, so he wasn't able to bring in his own players. He had to simply work with what he had. He expressed his need to bring talent to the program, because of the team's history. The Morgan women's team won about ten games in the past three seasons. They weren't used to winning, and that was a culture he wanted to change.

Beas also coached in the AAU circuit in Baltimore, but he was most successful coaching boys at the junior college level. He had won a championship, and was looking to eventually do the same at Morgan. Towards the end of the visit, we got a chance to scrimmage against some of the current players at Morgan. Beas said he had heard a lot about us, but he wanted to see it before he believed it. We stretched and played for a little while, but you could tell we were kind of nervous. Even though this wasn't a regular game, Munch called a timeout. He called us over to see what was wrong, but, before he could even talk, my mother, being the aggressive, crazy lady that she is, stepped in. She screamed at us like she was the coach, let us know the opportunity at hand, and told us to get it together and do what we do. She reminded us that our parents couldn't afford to pay for college, and this was our opportunity. Everybody did their thing like we usually did, and Beas was impressed. It was not only fun, but eye-opening that this was something we all could be doing next year.

Beas was so excited, he jokingly said, "Sign these girls right now, Graham." He was truly interested in signing me, Kenya, and Kimbo right on the spot. As for Shea Shea and Baby D, he liked them, but he wanted to check exactly how many other scholarships the school had available.

We all spoke about the visit in the car. Kimbo and I loved it, so we were in. Kenya, on the other hand, thought Morgan was a little too hood. She wanted to attend a school opposite of Brooklyn, to get a different experience. Shea Shea and Baby D didn't really say much, because they were waiting to see if the scholarship money was available. My mother and Munch liked the idea of me getting a scholarship, and figured I'd be in good hands with Beas and would be able to get an opportunity to play as an incoming freshman. My mother especially liked that I had family in Bowie, Maryland, which was only forty-five minutes away from Morgan.

With my senior year of high school right around the corner, as long as I handled my business, it was going to go by pretty smoothly. I only had four classes my senior year, so the only thing I really had to worry about was staying out of trouble until practice started. After the first month of school, Kimbo and I signed our letters of intent to attend Morgan. All we had to worry about now was performing well on the court, and graduating off the court—at least, that's what I thought.

Unfortunately, Kimbo was having trouble with her SAT scores. She had to take the test a couple times to get the proper score to be eligible for her scholarship at Morgan. Kimbo ultimately never got a high enough score, and decided to go to a junior college. Junior college is the route some athletes end up taking, when they don't have good grades or high enough scores on the SAT/ACT. They attend for a year or two to get some college credits under their belt, with hopes that they can eventually transfer to a four year school. I remained positive for both her and me. I was positive she was still going to come to Morgan after junior college, and I was positive I was going to hold it down until she got there.

Mid-November rolled around, and it was the first game of the season for the Lady Knights. Between adjusting to a new coach and a team with less talent, the evening was very frustrating! Even worse, I fouled out and felt like the refs were against me. I stormed out of the gym like a spoiled brat. I've never done anything like that, but being a senior, the best player in the school, and having friends in the crowd shouting things to boost my ego may have made me a bit big-headed that day.

Coach Tighe came right after me, and taught me a lesson I definitely needed to learn. He put me in my place, and even threatened not to retire my jersey, because my actions showed I didn't deserve it. He was right, and from that day on, I respected him and we did our best to work together to help our Lady Knights win. He taught me about being more of a leader. I didn't realize how much my teammates looked up to me and watched everything I did. If I illustrated that I didn't believe in or support them, what kind of leader could I really be? Although I didn't agree with Coach Tighe's coaching philosophies, one of my biggest attributes is the ability to be coachable. This is something I take pride in, because of the stereotypes of superstars and specifically players from NY.

We had a rough season, but we got better as it went on. Coach Tighe kept his promise and retired my jersey on Senior Night. I was the third and final jersey to be retired at Madison to this day. The last home game was an emotional night for me, but I was thankful for every minute. To have my friends and family cheer me on was an amazing feeling I will always remember.

When I think back on it, I did some pretty amazing things during my years at Madison. My jersey was retired, I held numerous assist records, scored forty points in a game (that we lost by more than twenty), was a McDonald's All-American nominee, and I even scored a shot from the free throw line on my knees. I try to visit whenever I can and keep up with the girls' team, and I still keep in contact with my number one guy, Dumont. I'm hoping one day I can possibly return to teach PE and coach the girls' or boys' team there! Shout out to the MAD HOUSE!

# Chapter 7
# A Time of Mixed Emotions

*Regardless of your feelings, remain humble and grateful!*
*#Tinyism*

Once my jersey was retired and the season ended, the end of my senior year flew by. The only thing left to do now was pass my classes and regents exams. After the senior trip and prom, it wasn't really necessary to attend school until graduation. I still attended most days, but I spent most of my time at the gym. I began to lift weights in the school's weight room because everyone suggested getting stronger in preparation for college. St. Johns Rec had a weight room so between Madison and St. John's, I made sure I got at least one workout a day. When I worked out at Madison I would usually be by myself. I loved going to St. Johns Rec more because there would be other people there to challenge and push me. After six o'clock it's adult hours, and although I was still only seventeen, Munch and Coach Lloyd used to let me in the building.

I'd spend my time playing with the adult men and with the adult women on Tuesdays. Playing with men that are older and stronger than you always elevates your game. It's much more competitive and more physical playing with men. When I played with the women I felt as though it helped improve my basketball IQ. Being the youngin' on the court, they'll always tell you what to do or what you are doing wrong. Sometimes they did it nicely, and sometimes not so nicely.

St. John's Rec definitely made me tough and helped prepare me for college basketball. If I could consistently perform well against the old heads, there was no doubt that I would dominate those my age in college. Growing up, when I came to St. John's all I ever wanted to do was play on the "big girl side". The "big girl side" consisted of former and current college, professional (both overseas and WNBA) or recreational female players from NYC and the tri-state area. All ages and sizes came to hoop when it came to ladies' night. It was always good competition. During ladies' night if you wanted to get a good run in, you had to make sure the five you played with were decent. Once you lost a game there was going to be a wait to get back on the court. When I was younger I used to just sit on the bleachers and watch them go at it. Sometimes I'd watch in awe but I'd say to myself "They're good, but I know I can hold my own."

The summer before college, they let me play with them because they needed one player to make ten. I did well and held it down. They didn't really want the younger girls to play because this was the only competitive open gym in NYC and they didn't want us young girls taking their spots. They looked forward to Tuesdays at the Rec, so there was no way they were going to let me and the younger girls take their shine. After a couple years went by though, and some of them got older, my fellow youngins and I eventually took over the "big girl" side! With so many of us getting better, and playing at a higher level, we began giving them a run for their money!

Once I got a chance to officially play there, I was there bright and early every Tuesday after. Munch used to let me in around 4:30 or 5 and I would lift weights then shoot around until there were enough girls to run a full. I held my own, so the big homies didn't mind me playing. I always took their constructive criticism well and made whatever adjustment they suggested. After playing with them for months I formed relationships with most of them. They became my big sisters, aunts, and grandmothers. I even began playing in the unlimited summer leagues with some of them. They helped me mature as a player and made me feel accomplished.

It's like what Drake said, "My idols were now my rivals." The two players I looked up to the most were my current big sisters, Renee Taylor and Nastassia Boucicault. If anyone ever compiled a list of the best guards to come out of NYC, they'd be at the top of that list. After killing the high school/AAU circuit around the city they both attended junior college a couple years apart at Monroe. Renee went on to attend the University of Miami and Stass attended Shaw University. Renee ended up playing professionally overseas in Spain, Israel, Switzerland, Ukraine, and a couple other countries. Stass won numerous championships at Shaw and played professionally in Puerto Rico. These two were who I tried to play like and model my game after. They possessed the ability to play the combo guard position, meaning they could play the point guard spot and also shoot or score like a 2 guard. They both had a crazy handle, court vision, and the ability to create plays for themselves and others. Every time I played well against them, I'd secretly be hyped. Over the years I've formed great relationships with them. They really are the big sisters I never had.

I recruited them to No Limit to play with Munch. Having the three of us on court at the same time was fun to watch. Our peers would jokingly say we were cheating by having the best guards in the city on court at the same time, on the same team. We played in all the unlimited leagues in New York, as well as money tournaments in New Jersey, Vegas, and Maryland. I now knew how some of the young up and coming NBA players felt playing with and against their idols.

After training constantly, June finally rolled around and it was time for graduation. To me it symbolized achievement and new beginnings; the achievement being getting my diploma and the new beginning being college. It actually turned out to be somewhat of an emotional roller coaster for me. Before graduating from school there are certain dues that you have to pay. My mother asked my "father" Ronald Adams to split the dues with her. It wasn't necessarily that she needed him to, it was just the principle. For whatever reason, he never gave her the money. That made my mother so upset that she sat me down one day and told me the truth. The truth of the matter was that Ronald Adams, the person I'd believed to be my father for the last seventeen years, actually wasn't. Imagine my sense of shock. I felt hurt because they had been lying to me all this time. I also wanted to know and meet my real father. I felt like my mother had betrayed me.

My mother and I have the type of relationship where we can tell each other anything. I know she thought it was in my best interest, but this really hurt me. I expressed how the situation made me feel and she explained that at the time she and my real father were going through some issues. She wasn't sure if she was going to have me or not as a result. Once she made the decision to have me, she was dating Ronald and he said not to worry, and that he would be my father. I now realize how great a man Ronald was for taking in a child that wasn't even his, as he already had four children of his own. Ronald was a very handy guy. He could cook, clean, fix, and basically do anything with his hands. In addition to working security and maintenance at his father's church, he always did side jobs for friends. He was always busy and doing something throughout the day. I regret it now, but once I learned he wasn't my father, I became rather rude towards him.

I was still playing in tournaments here and there to stay in shape so I'd ask him to come to my games, and he would always say he was coming. He'd come to one or two, be late for another, or just not show up at all. He started missing more and more games. It was most likely because of the side jobs he was working, but I didn't care. Telling me you were coming to my game and not showing up is the equivalent of breaking a promise to me, so I was upset. After a while I stopped inviting him and eventually cut him off all together. I was still hurt about being lied to, so I justified my actions because he wasn't really my father. After graduation I even decided that I wanted to change my last name. Throughout my life I have actually had three last names: Adams, Herrera, and Youngblood. Adams was the first name given to me when I was born. Youngblood is my mother's family's last name and Herrera comes from when my mother was married to my brother's father. I almost made an irrational decision to change my last name officially to Youngblood because I no longer wanted anything to do with Ronald or his name. Fortunately, I changed my mind and kept my name. Everybody knew who Corin Adams was and no one knew who Youngblood was. Plus, I liked being first for things like attendance, and other things that went in alphabetical order.

Instead of changing my name, I just didn't speak to Ronald

again until April 2013. At that time I was playing in Portugal and began thinking about him and my actions. I realized that I had been an absolute brat about the situation, so I began reaching out to get contact info for him. My Adams siblings had no idea what had happened and I still kept in touch with them as if they were my real brothers and sisters, so I got the contact info from them. When I returned from Portugal, I called Ronald to wish him a happy birthday, to thank him for what he did when I was younger, and see if we could get back in touch. As soon as he answered the phone I began to get emotional. With tears in my eyes and that lump in my throat, I said "Happy Birthday, Daddy. Do you know who this is?" He answered and said "Thank you darling, I have an idea. I hope it's who I think it is." I said, "It's me. Corin." He expressed how happy he was to hear from me. We chatted briefly and he even invited me to his birthday party. At that point in time I wasn't really ready for that, so I told him we should do lunch instead. Before hanging up he said to me "I'm so happy you called. I remember that day in my father's church when you said one day, you were going to make it, and when you did you wouldn't forget me. You said you'd call me, and you did! I've been waiting for this call for a long time and I'm so happy to get it…on my birthday too. Everybody always asks about you and I just say you're fine, without really knowing. But now that I know for sure, I can get to bragging. My baby graduated college and is living her basketball dream!"

The whole time he was saying this I was on the other end of the phone crying my eyes out. I felt so many emotions, but I was happy there were no hard feelings between us. The fact that he remembered a moment we had shared made me both extremely happy and sad because of how I had acted.

Rekindling the relationship between me and Ronald made me

want to find my birth father even more. Unfortunately though, during the holiday season of 2014, my mother informed me that my birth father, Jimmy Johnson, had passed away the previous April. She added some even more shocking news. Apparently, I had had an older sister, who also played professional basketball overseas. The only information my mother could gather from her source was that her name was Monique, she was about three years older than me, and her mother's name was Robin. After missing out on the opportunity to find my father, I plan to do everything I can to find my sister. I don't know how I am going to do it, but I hope I get a chance to meet her before it's too late. For those blessed enough to have their parents and siblings in their lives, please cherish it. I'd give anything for it.

Although I sometimes perceive his absence as a curse, it's also been a gift. I believe everything happens for a reason. So there may very well be a reason why he wasn't in my life. The fact that he hasn't been around has made me who I am and is also the number one reason my mother and I have the relationship we do. In reality my mom is my mother and father. I even give her gifts on Father's Day to illustrate that. He may not have been around to shape me into the person I am, but no matter what there's still this void in my heart that meeting him, even just once, would've filled. Sometimes you just need closure.

# Chapter 8
# Brotherly Love?

*One of your top priorities should always be to protect your feelings.*
*If you don't, then who will?*

*#Tinyism*

Prior to graduation I lost another male figure in my life—my brother, Raling Herrera. Around the same time that I decided to be done with Ronald Adams, my brother seemed to be done with my mother and me. I still don't completely understand it, but I'm hoping to reconnect with him very soon.

Growing up we got on each other's nerves, like most brothers and sisters. After I got serious with basketball, we began to get much closer. Raling was my complete opposite. He stood at 6'5" tall and was interested in nerdy things like technology and architecture. We did have two things in common though, basketball and music. Having spent most of our childhood at each other's necks, both literally and figuratively, getting close to him during our teenage years was an amazing feeling. Unlike my father, Raling's father was always around. Raling Sr. was one of those smothering parents. He loved Raling so much and would do anything for him. Those types of parents always mean well, but, from the children's perspective, a smothering parent can be a bit annoying.

I will always remember Raling Sr. trying to give us garlic every time he would come by. He would say, "Here Corin and Raling, eat this garlic. It's good for you and will prevent you from getting sick!" He cared for me as if I were his own. He performed his parental duties to the best of his ability, and he spoiled Raling and always did whatever he could for him. Before I turned fifteen, Raling Sr. thought it would be a good idea if my brother moved in with him. We lived in a small, two bedroom apartment in Flatbush with my mom, and things were getting a little crowded as we got older and Raling kept growing. Everyone agreed it was a good idea and they moved to a house about fifteen minutes from our apartment on Foster Ave.

Things were a little different when my brother moved out, but I would often ride my bike or take the train to his new house to hang out with him. When I didn't have games I'd go over there and we'd go hoop in the park, play video games, listen to the latest rap music, eat Chinese food, or just chill. My brother wasn't the best basketball player, but he was decent. Although he was 6'5, in his mind he was a guard from the AND1 mixtape tour. My brother used to be a dribble head. A dribble head is someone who dribbles the ball way too much. He always wanted to 'cross' people. He used to dribble so fast and so low. Often times his moves would work, but seeing a big 6'5 player dribbling so low to the floor, then throwing a no look pass was just hysterical to me. The faces he would make were quite entertaining.

When we used to hoop in his neighborhood, we'd either play two on two or full court. When we'd play two on two people wouldn't expect us to be as good as we were, so it was fun and a bit of a challenge for us. We would sometimes hustle people off the strength of their doubt. When we'd play full court games we would just try to make highlight after highlight. He would cross someone and then pass it to me for an open shot. I would do the same and try to throw him an alley-oop. My brother never played on teams or in tournaments, but he loved basketball as much as I did. We'd be in the park in the summer for hours. Even some winter days, we'd put on hoodies and play one on one, shoot around, or a game of horse just to hoop.

After living with his father for a year or two my brother wasn't particularly happy. Raling wanted to move back with my mother and I, but my mother told him no. She felt it didn't make sense because he was almost twenty years old and we were still in that small apartment. My brother was not happy with her answer, and became angry at her for quite some time. In the back of his mind he always felt my mother treated me differently and loved me more. He thought that the fact that she didn't let him move back in proved his theory to be true.

She may have treated me differently, but what parent treats all of their kids the same? She loved us both dearly! My mother explained to us that her different actions towards me stemmed from the fact that my father wasn't around and his was. After not being allowed to move back in with us, my brother started hanging out a lot to get away from his father and the house. He began to act differently. Before we knew it he was this new, more "gangster" Raling. When we were around each other he seemed like the same Raling to me, but I don't think his father or my mom liked it. After some time he began to despise both my mother and his father. He didn't communicate with my mom, and I began to get busy with basketball. The more basketball I played the less time I had to see him or speak with him. I would reach out and we'd both seem too busy for each other. After a while it felt like he cut my mom and me out of his life, for reasons I don't understand. I've reach out to him periodically for about ten years now and he's only responded twice. He's never once responded to my mom. She checks up on him by way of his father, but there's never any direct communication.

The first time he responded to me, I had contacted him from my friend's phone acting like a newspaper reporter from my college. Prior to that he had ignored every message directly from me, which was why I came up with the whole newspaper scam. I was desperate! I had contacted him and asked if he'd be interested in doing an interview and surprising me at a home game. He responded, but simply stated he wasn't interested and didn't care to surprise me. I will never forget how bad I felt after his response. Being rejected by someone you love has got to be one of the worst feelings ever. I'm not one to give up on people or things, but I had to leave him be for a while for the sake of my feelings.

The second time I got a response from him had I texted him a heartfelt message asking for closure, forgiveness and an explanation. It was one of those days I thought about him and just couldn't bear to continue to think about it without some answers. He actually responded and said that nothing was my fault. He said he didn't mean for me to feel like he hated me. He said he still loved me, but there were just some problems he needed to fix in his life. The fact that he responded gave me hope that one day we'd be reunited. Those responses let me know that he at least cared a little. Maybe not as much as I would have liked him to, but at the point, it was enough. Every now and then I still reach out and let him know he's being thought of and is definitely still loved. I'm just hoping sooner than later I'll actually get to see, hug, and speak to him again!

I graduated from James Madison High School on June 26, 2006. Although it was rainy, there wasn't much that could ruin that day for me. I had many people present that loved me unconditionally, including my mother, grandparents, and peers. There's just something about people telling me they're proud of me that means so much. It makes me feel humbled and honored. On and off the court one of my priorities are to make sure that whatever I'm doing, there will be someone, somewhere who is proud of me. Knowing that I'd reached a milestone and great things were ahead put a nearly permanent smile on my face. On top of all that, once the ceremony was over I knew my family and I were going to go out to eat one of our favorites, seafood. One thing about my family is that we love seafood. My mother is actually allergic to some seafood, but she still eats and loves it anyway. After saying goodbye to my friends at Madison and enjoying a great meal with my family, it finally hit me. I was a high school graduate and in less than three months I was going to be attending college for free on a basketball scholarship. My dreams were becoming reality!

In regards to my achievements, I've learned to have a delayed reaction when it came to getting excited. Throughout my life I've experienced many let downs that I've wasted my excitement on. I'd get excited a bit too quickly, and be forced to experience a major low following a false high. So now, when good things happen it takes me a little longer to actually get excited and feel good about myself. It's sort of a defense mechanism that has resulted from having the rug pulled out from under me a few too many times.

# Chapter 9
# Summer Love

*When someone is both on your mind and heart, it's damn near*
*impossible to suppress the thought of them.*
*#Tinyism*

After graduation, I planned to work out even more, work at my annual summer camp job, play basketball and have as much fun as possible with my family and friends. I began playing in the unlimited basketball leagues all around NYC with some of my big homies from St. John's Rec. I played in West 4th, Rucker Park, and Uptown Challenge in Harlem. Playing those games in the unlimited leagues helped me gauge exactly what I needed to improve on before my college career began. I played against professionals, other college hoopers, and some of the best veterans in the tri-state area.

My weekdays typically consisted of working at the camp from 8 a.m. to 4 p.m., and after work going to hang out with one of my close friends, Marissa Austin. Marissa lived close to my job so it was easy to stop by most days. She'd either come to hoop or work out with me, or I'd meet up with Kenya or other friends that wanted to work up a sweat. Once my workout was over I'd go home to shower, eat, sleep, and do it all again the next day. On weekends I played two or three games a day in the unlimited tournaments, get-togethers with my friends or family, or just hooping in a park. Unless one of us was busy, you'd always find Marissa, Kenya, and I together. It was like we had recruited her as our third musketeer. We had known Marissa for some time, but never hung out with her until she became part of the No Limit family. Prior to that, she was the enemy. We'd play against her in different tournaments and during the high school season. Marissa played for Abraham Lincoln High School in Brooklyn, NY. Their girls' team didn't get as much recognition as the boys' team, but Lincoln produced many well-known basketball players. Stephon Marbury, Sebastian Telfair, and most recently Lance Stephenson of the Charlotte Hornets all graduated from Lincoln. Marissa was a good athlete. She was a nice size, wasn't too slow, and had a great jump shot. Her game reflected her personality, and she knew and always played her role.

Marissa was a quiet person. Once you got to know her though, and she opened up to you, you'd quickly see that there was more to her personality. I honestly believe just being around Marissa made Kenya and I better people. At the time we all became close friends, we would spend the majority of our time at her house. Marissa and her family were known for helping those in need, taking care of close friends and family, and being always willing to do or give whatever it would take to help. We used to spend about three or more nights out of the week at Marissa's house. Whenever we stayed, we'd for sure get great home cooked meals as well as genuine hospitality.

Being with Marissa and her family reminded me of the importance of family and being willing to give no matter what.

Marissa's family adopted Kenya and I as sisters, and that's something I will always be grateful for. To this day I acknowledge her and her family as my own. Later down the line Marissa and I got closer than ever and it wasn't long before she became not just a close friend, but something like my twin sister. We often knew what the other was thinking, finished each other's jokes or sentences, and people started to say we even looked alike.

One characteristic we both share is our ambition. Marissa always finds a way to inspire me. To be successful, your immediate circle of friends and family should motivate and support you. Marissa has been on her own for the past couple of years, by choice. No matter what odds are against her she's always found numerous ways to come out on top. Whether it's moving to a different state or working three jobs while in school, she got it done. Being on her own was a choice she made and stuck with, and I couldn't be more proud of her. No matter what decisions I make or what obstacles are ahead, she supports and reassures me that it can and will be done. I always do the same for her. I love my twin, and our time and blessings are coming. We just have to continue to work hard and believe!

In addition to gaining a sister in Marissa, I was in for another surprise relationship with Jeffrey Haynes. Jeff was one of my first real relationships, and strangely, my last. I met him at Wingate Park in Brooklyn, NY. To this day, he has a piece of my heart. I'll never forget the first day I saw him. He had the biggest afro, and caught my eye instantly. It had been a couple of weeks since I'd been to Wingate to hoop. Hooping with Marissa and Kenya, I usually ended up going to the parks around their house or to St. John's Rec Park. I walked into Wingate Park one beautiful sunny day, saw Jeff, and he's been the man of my dreams ever since.

Between his fro, looking so adorable, and the fact that I was surprised I had never seen him before, I couldn't stop staring. He was playing full court with all the people I knew and played with regularly in Wingate. I immediately called "next" hoping that he'd either stay on court to play against me or stay so I could put him on my team. Fortunately he won, so he stayed on court.

Whenever I play with the guys there are two things that take place: a little flirting and a little trash talking. If there's someone on court I find attractive, I'm going to "basketball flirt" as much as possible. Basketball flirting works better for me if the person is on the other team. One thing that turns me off instantly, though, is a guy who absolutely sucks at basketball. If you can't hoop, sorry, but there won't be any basketball flirting coming from my end. If you suck and try to flirt with me, I'm going to actually try my hardest to kill you on the court. It's petty and shallow in a way, but I can't help it. Since Jeff was so cute and could play a little bit, I put operation "Quincy McCall" into action.

Jeff had a great smile and the most adorable dimples. He was taller than me, had on nice hooping gear with the swagger to match, and could shoot a little. He was ideal for me! When it comes to basketball flirting, I have a little system. First, I just look at the person for a while. I see what I can pick up on-site first. I call this the scouting stage. I scouted Jeff from the moment I walked into the park. He was athletic and looked like he knew what he was doing on court. He didn't really post up or play down low, so that made it possible for my second step to come into play. The second step is making it known that I was going to guard him. Once I announce I was guarding him, there would usually be a joke right after my statement. As you know, I'm small, so most of the time the guys I basketball flirt with are bigger than me. Once I'd say I was guarding them, someone would usually ask if I was sure because of the size difference. My response would be something smooth like, "Don't worry, he's not going to score," said with a smile, of course. This is the beginning of the actual flirting stage, where I throw a couple signs to see if that person is interested or not. After that is the in-game stage, during which I try to be competitive, physical, and cute, all at the same time. This is either the last or second to last stage of basketball flirting. If it doesn't end there, it leads to what I call the bagging stage. This is when I get some kind of contact info from them. Sometimes the in-game stage leads to them beating me to it and asking me for my number. It all depends on the moment and timing. While we're playing, I'll be touchy-feely, while scoring and making plays at the same time. Guys like girls that can hoop, so I figure that if they see I'm actually good, it's a plus for me. It sucks that sometimes there's someone watching that may say something like "That girl is killing you." Guys like girls that can hoop, just not when they embarrass them.

After playing against Jeff for a few games, we got to play on the same team and were able to flirt and exchange smiles. It was "like" at first sight. I noticed he was friends with some people I grew up and went to North Star Academy with. When it came to social networking at the time, AOL Instant Messenger and Sconex were the main outlets. Facebook only allowed college students to register, Myspace wasn't that popular and anything else wasn't known about yet. I went home and immediately turned into Inspector Gadget in order to find him on Sconex. I had to know more about him, most of all if he had a girlfriend. As you know, if a female really puts her mind to it, she can find out anything, especially on a social network. So of course, I found him.

After stalking his profile, I realized we had a lot of mutual friends. I just couldn't believe I hadn't seen him prior to this. Keeping calm, I didn't send him a friend request. I called it a strategic move. I didn't want him to think I was sweating him. The next day after work, however, I went to Wingate hoping to see him. At first he wasn't there, but after a game or two I heard someone on the side say something like "You wouldn't do that if I was on court." I looked over and it was Jeff, looking even better than before. He had his hair braided and smiled at me with those adorable dimples. I was so happy to see him, and I think he knew it. We played again and he asked for my AOL screen name and phone number. Back then AOL Instant Messenger was the big thing, so asking for someone's screen name was very common!

Once again I rushed home to my computer and he was online. We chatted the whole night and from that point on he was my boo. I'd go to the park to hang out with him. We'd talk on the phone and online, and go on cute little dates. It was puppy love.

I had never really been the relationship type. I was always gone, too busy with basketball or just not that interested. It was different with Jeff. Usually I'd like someone for two or three weeks and then get bored or turned off somehow. Jeff made it past that and I genuinely liked him a lot. Each time I saw him or spoke to him, I liked him more. Hanging out and spending time with him made the last couple months before college well spent.

Before I knew it, the last week of the summer had arrived and I was preparing for my departure to Morgan. It didn't really occur to me that in a week I was going to be away from my family, friends, and everything I was used to. Most of all, I would be away from Jeff. We used to speak about me leaving and joke about him coming to Morgan with me. It wasn't until that last week that I really thought about the fact that I wasn't going to see him for a while. Up until that point I didn't think I'd be so caught up on him.

Cherishing my last few days at home, my mother and I thought it would be a good idea to have some sort of party. I agreed to it and we actually had a going away bowling party. All my family and closest friends attended and it was a great night. Seeing everybody that was important to me one last time before embarking on my journey sort of made me emotional. The people that attended were my mom, grandparents, aunts, uncles, cousins, Kenya, Marissa, Kimbo, a couple people from my high school, Kristine, Jeff and one of his best friends, Najee. After playing a few games of bowling Jeff and I went outside to talk before he and Najee had to leave. We both expressed how sad we were that I was leaving, and how much we were going to miss each other. I never had really been in a relationship, let alone a long distance one, so I wasn't sure what was going to happen. After we hugged and kissed I told Jeff I wouldn't forget about him, and that if he wanted to be with someone else or take a break I wouldn't mind because I knew he'd be lonely. I just figured I didn't know what was going to happen at college and I didn't want him to be here in Brooklyn waiting for me. It just didn't seem fair. Without taking my suggestions into consideration, he said he would be okay and that he just wanted to be with me.

I went off to Morgan and things were okay between us until December. I came home for the holidays and it was like we had lost our connection. Things seemed weird between us. I was excited to come home to see him, but when I got home it seemed like he was avoiding me. We played phone tag for a little bit, but we both seemed too busy to connect. At one point his phone "broke". I didn't know what was going on, but deep down inside my feelings were hurt. All the months talking to him that led up to this point, and for us not to even see or really speak was something I couldn't understand.

We even exchanged Christmas gifts in a weird way. I had to meet his friend Najee to give and receive his gift. After that I said okay, that's it. I'll take the hint. So even though I was upset, disappointed, and hurt, I still reached out to him before I left. I expressed my feelings and said that we were still cool, but it was evident things weren't the same between us. Once I got back to school, it took me a while to get over it. In my mind Jeff was the perfect guy for me, but the timing wasn't right.

To this day we still do the cat and mouse game. I've been gone the past five years chasing this hoop dream. I'm sad to say that every summer I've come back he's either had a girlfriend, or worse, a baby. The chance that we'll be together gets slimmer and slimmer, but there's still a part of me keeping hope alive. Every now and then in the summer time we'd meet and catch up. Whenever I see or speak to him, I always wonder what might have been.

# Chapter 10
# Intro to College Life: Tiny Setback #2

*Holding yourself accountable is a very vital part*
*of achieving any goal.*
*#Tinyism*

The time had finally come, and I was off to Morgan to start the next chapter of my life. My mother and I were joined by a close friend of the family, Kurt (aka Squeeze), who loaded up my mother's Jeep Liberty and traveled with us to Baltimore. That Jeep was filled with nearly everything I owned. We were still living in that small apartment and my mother made it clear that since I would no longer be there, she wanted her space back. The car was packed with all of my sneakers (maybe forty pairs at that time), my clothes, my bootleg movie collection and any other belongings I had. Squeeze was a crazy fast driver, so we got to Morgan in record time. It only took us two and a half hours to get to there, including stops. Squeeze was definitely fast and furious; all he needed were a few CDs and he was good to go.

Once we pulled up to the school, I called Coach Graham, who met us in the parking lot of my new residence, Blount Towers.

Blount Towers was where the female freshman that lived on campus stayed. Right across from Blount Towers was the dining hall and Rawlings, the male residence hall. In Blount Towers everyone had one roommate and shared a quad with two other rooms, except for the RAs. In each quad there was a community bathroom with four showers, sinks, and toilets. That year my coaches recruited six freshmen so, fortunately for us, we were able to have our own little hooping quad. It was perfect because most of the time we all had to be up at the same time or on our way to the same places. The other five freshmen were: Phylicia Jones, Brandi Williams, Aaries Reed, Ciara Banks, and my roommate, Mahala Thomas. Even though everyone had a different kind of swag because of where they were from, we got along well. We were the new faces of Morgan State Women's Basketball and our main goal was to turn the team into a winning program. The season before, the Lady Bears' record was 4-23. In 2004 they were 4-24, and in the 2003 season they were 3-26, with a grand total of 11 wins in three full seasons.

After three consecutive years of losing records the athletic director, Floyd Kerr, felt it was time for a change. He hired Coach Beasley, who recruited us to help make it happen. In addition to the freshmen, we had one other new comer on the team; Shalane Price (Lane). Lane transferred in from a nearby junior college, Baltimore Community College. She was born and raised in Baltimore, so Morgan and their history was nothing new to her. She was just as anxious as we all were to change things at Morgan.

I had assumed my college experience was going to be just like the movie Love and Basketball. I use that movie as the blueprint of my life. As soon as I stepped foot onto the Morgan campus, I thought I was Monica Wright Jr. The very first time I walked into

Hill Field House, Morgan's gym, as a Morgan State student-athlete, all I heard in my head was "point guards lead from the front, not the back, Monica." Not only did I feel that the coaches were going to be hard on me, I was also worried about how the upperclassmen were going to treat me.

We had four seniors and three juniors on our team. The fact that they played for Morgan for at least the past two seasons meant that they experienced losing almost their entire college careers. I was concerned that the culture we were walking into was negative. Knowing that we were here to try and change that, I wasn't sure if they were going to embrace us or hate us. On one hand, they could be excited that we were here to help them finally start winning. On the other hand, they could have looked at it from a somewhat envious point of view, as if we were there to take over the team.

It actually turned out to be a little of both, but we did win games! The four seniors were Latricia "La-La" Jones, Whitney Johnson (Whit), Shana Phillips (Sheezy) and Sarissa Gaskins (Rissa). The juniors were Dominisha Britton (Nisha), Britney "Big Brit" Griffin, and Latonya Grady (L). L transferred to Morgan after she had partied at the school a few times. She was one of our walk-on players. A walk-on player is someone who isn't recruited, but attends the school and is good enough to make the team. They don't receive scholarship money at first, but if they prove themselves they sometimes receive partial or full scholarships the following season. Our only sophomore was another walk-on. She was a baby genius with a crazy jump shot. Her name was Monet Johnson.

After meeting the team for the first time, I wasn't really sure what to expect. All I knew was, this was my squad for my freshman campaign at Morgan. Freshman year turned out to be a real eye opener for me both on and off the court. It is exactly why I recommend going away to college for at least one year. Whether or not you are an athlete, it's very beneficial to experience campus life and to be away from home. I learned so much about myself and what it meant to be independent. Going away for college can be extremely expensive, however; my freshman year tuition was about $20,000, with increases every year after that. If you can afford to go away for college, even just for a semester, do it! I guarantee you won't return to your hometown the same person.

It was a very interesting year for my partner in crime, Phyli, and I. We instantly clicked, having so many things in common, and became inseparable. If I made a list of everything I was happy to gain from Morgan, Phyli's friendship would easily be in the top three. Once we learned that we both had a sneaker addiction, it was pretty much a wrap. Phyli actually may have been more of an addict than me. She worked at Finish Line back in VA for a few years, which made it easier for her to get her sneakers. We also had many of the same ambitions, goals, views, favorite players, and most of all the same infinite love for the game. People often tell me they don't know too many people that love basketball more than I do. I can honestly say Phyli loved basketball just as much as I did. If we had some free time or a break between classes, we'd try our best to get to the gym and if we weren't playing, we wanted to watch basketball as much as possible. We used to watch the boys' team, intramurals in Hurt (the secondary gym at Morgan), or any of the neighboring colleges' games. Morgan St. was surrounded by several other schools, including Towson University, Coppin State, Loyola, UMBC, Goucher College, and BCCC.

Our gym was frequently in use, but open gyms didn't last long. Whenever that happened, Phyli and I would drive over to one of the other schools and hoop with them. Phyli and I damn near hooped at every gym around Morgan. After a while, we were so well known that we used to conduct our own open gyms at Morgan. We put the word "open" in open gym. We invited people from the other schools, as well as the local female hoopers in Baltimore. Before we knew it we had one of the most competitive open runs in Baltimore. The best part was that our coaches didn't mind. It was always competitive so regardless of who was there, and our coaches knew we were challenging ourselves and trying to get better.

Phyli and I spent most of our social life together as well. We attended school events, ate together, and had most of the same friends. Prior to Morgan, I didn't have much of a social life outside of what I did with my "No Limit Family". Parties and things of that nature weren't my cup of tea. I attended a few, hung out, and had a good time, but I wasn't about that life. Phyli's social life was very similar to mine. All she really did in VA was work, play ball, chill with her family, attend church and church events (because her parents were pastors), and attend an occasional party with her friends.

Morgan State University is an HBCU, and most HBCUs have the stereotype of being party schools. Now I won't say that this is true, but I feel that, no matter what kind of college or university you attend, there are going to be parties. House and dorm parties, school parties, club parties, parties to promote something, parties to raise money, pep rally parties for school spirit, and on and on. You can walk around and get a personal invite, flyer invite, or a Facebook invite for a party every day of the week. Early in the semester, the ultimate 1st party of the year was taking place. Some of our teammates were talking about going and the promo team hyped it up so much throughout campus that we wanted to see what was up. There were so many different promo teams at Morgan, including promoters, street teams, hosts and DJs.

In my first few weeks at Morgan, I saw some familiar faces. There were a lot of people from Brooklyn, and the majority of one particular promo team was from NY. We had mutual friends and they had seen me hooping in the gym a couple times, so we showed each other love 'cause it's the Brooklyn way. They knew some of the upperclassmen on my team and said they'd take care of us if we attended their party. Phyli and I didn't really need much more convincing. After seeing who was going to the party from our team as they made arrangements, everything was set. We were on our way to our first college party.

Phyli, Mahala and I were the only ones to go to the party from the new crew. It felt like all of the upperclassmen were our chaperones. Phyli and I threw on our best Jordans, shirts to match our sneakers, and jeans. Mahala wore something a little more casual with flats and we headed over to meet up with the upperclassmen. Most of the student-athlete upper classmen at Morgan State stay in the Argonne apartments. Argonne is to the right of Rawlings and diagonally across from the gym, so it's pretty convenient. When we walked into Argonne ours eyes lit up. The upperclassmen were applying make-up, had their sexy shoes and freak 'em dresses on. We were shocked since we normally only saw them in their basketball clothes. They looked at us the same way we looked at them like, "That's what y'all wearing?" While we were waiting for them, some of their friends came over to see which club they were going to. We were introduced and their friends waited for them while chilling with us. Some of them came in with alcohol, cigarettes, weed, and Black n' Mild's. They called it the "pregame" and even offered us some. Although we quickly denied the offers, we still had no idea what we were in for.

We were completely out of our element. We left around 10:00 and drove in several cars. Once we pulled up to the club, a few busses from Morgan pulled up at the same time. There was already a line down the block, so as the busses dropped loads of people off, I knew we were never getting in. Our teammates drove around a little more and we finally parked. Trying not to act as shocked as I was, I just followed my teammates' lead and kept it cool. Once everybody parked we went to the front of the line. LaLa spoke to one of the promoters and just like that, we skipped everybody!

Phyli and I just looked at each other and laughed. We got to the booth to pay and show our IDs, and the doorman put X's with permanent marker on our hands. I had only been to a club once in NY and I used someone else's ID, so this was all new to me. I asked, "Ummm what's these Xs for, yo?" "Alcohol. You're only 17 so the Xs on your hands let the bartenders know not to serve you any drinks. If you're seen with a drink in the club you'll get kicked out." "Oh, iight thanks."

As soon as I walked away, I saw my homeboy from Brooklyn, Zeke. I met Zeke once in the summer on Kimbo's block. We were telling him that we were coming to Morgan to hoop, and he said, "Kim, you know I got y'all." When I saw Zeke I had one of my famous Brooklyn shirts on, and he looked at me and the shirt and just laughed. We said hello and chopped it up for a little. He asked if I wanted a drink and I told him I was good. He apparently didn't see the X on my hand, but after talking to the person in the booth I had a little fear in my heart. I saw a couple of the bouncers on my way in and I wanted nothing to do with them.

The club was packed! I just chilled with my teammates, danced a little, and people-watched all night. I couldn't believe some of the stuff I was seeing. I think Sheezy or Whit saw how shocked I was and they told me, "Don't worry, Tiny. You'll get used to it." My first college party was a success and they even gave the girls' basketball team a shout out on the mic.

In Maryland, clubs close at 2 AM, so around 1:35 they started to clear the place out. We began heading back, but we didn't leave with the same amount of people we came with. We were missing four girls. Phyli and I just got in whatever car they told us to and went back to Blount Towers. When we got back to Blount, everyone was asleep in our quad except for Phyli's roommate, Brandi. After the night we had, it was only right we told her everything she missed. Once we told her about our night and started putting things we saw together, we realized where some of the girls we came with ended up. They ended up attending their own private after party. That was definitely the icing on the cake! That night opened our eyes to some of the ins and outs of college life, and we realized just how ignorant we were to certain things. In the beginning it was shocking, but after a while we knew so much that we often predicted things before they even happened. As we became upperclassmen ourselves, we tended to educate some of the freshman. We still let them experience things on their own, but we gave them a heads up if and when they needed them.

After the first couple of weeks, I got the hang of almost everything. I knew where my classes were, my schedule, who to go to when I had a problem, and even where to get some of the best food on and off campus. I was adjusting to my new lifestyle just fine. We were now entering the 'preseason' of college basketball. Most preseason regimens consist of two or three workouts a day, plus conditioning, weight training, open gym, individuals and sometimes even core training. That first week or two my body felt terrible. I was sore as HE double hockey sticks. I wasn't too fond of stretching, icing, or ice baths yet, so I just simply had to suffer and work through the pain.

Not in all my previous years of playing had my body felt the way it did those first two weeks of the preseason. Although my body was feeling bad, that wasn't my hardest adjustment. Prior to preseason we played open gym as much as possible. Off the court my teammates and I were pretty much in sync. We knew enough about each other to gel and not step on each other's toes. But on the court, being the flashy player I was, it took us a little longer to synchronize. Coming from a program like No Limit where everyone was able to score, I was more interested in crossing over a girl and making a pretty pass to my teammate. I knew nine times out of ten they'd complete the highlight, and that was really all I cared about. I didn't really care about scoring because it wasn't really necessary. I wanted the "oohs" and "ahs" and to make the crowd go wild.

At Madison during my senior year, I was counted on to put points on the board, so I rarely focused on the highlight plays unless they were automatic buckets or assists. Entering Morgan, I shifted my focus back to being a passing, highlight-creating point guard. Since I was new on the team, I wanted to share the ball and get everyone involved to create some kind of chemistry. There was just one problem, which was that my teammates weren't used to playing with someone like me. They either weren't ready for my no look passes or just didn't have the coordination to catch them. The few passes they did manage to catch rarely ended in a finished play. Between me turning over the ball trying to hook them up, or them not finishing it, the experience was very frustrating. It wasn't long before I began to get lectured about "KYP", Knowing Your Personnel. Coach Clarke, one of the other assistant coaches at Morgan, preached this to me day in and day out. Coach Clarke was my mentor. She held me down on and off the court. Most of the lessons found in this book come from Coach Clarke. To know your personnel basically meant knowing the limitations of your teammates. It meant knowing what they could and couldn't do, so that you could put them in situations where they could succeed. Coach Clarke told me that the passes I was throwing were great, but my teammates weren't ready for them. Since they weren't ready for them, the passes looked good, but on paper it would just amount to another turnover in the box score.

In the beginning I figured if I did it daily, maybe in a week or two, they'd get used to it. If they got used to it we could be more successful and I could continue with my flashy play. Unfortunately the coaching staff didn't view it the same way and actually seemed to get mad at me. I was instructed to stop passing (not entirely, of course), and to make plays for myself.

While trying to adjust to my new role one of the scariest moments of my life occurred. A few weeks after preseason began I learned that I was ineligible. Being ineligible meant that my scholarship was null and void, which meant my tuition wasn't covered and my schedule would be dropped. Being ineligible meant that I wasn't really a student athlete from a technical standpoint. The cause of my ineligibility was that the requirements for my NCAA Clearinghouse Profile weren't complete. If you're on a collegiate team and you become ineligible, NCAA rules actually forbid you from physically being part of that team. You can't work out, play, or take part in any official team activities until you are eligible again. I went from trying to adjust to my new role to technically not having one at all because I was no longer a part of the team.

The NCAA Clearinghouse processes academic qualifications for all prospective Division I and Division II athletes and determines whether they are eligible to compete. The academic qualifications are known as core credits. Every student athlete had to be sure to complete all core credits in high school or junior college prior to becoming eligible to play any collegiate sport. Those core credits include two years of English, two years of math, one year of a science, and so on and so forth. Prior to attending Morgan and registering for the Clearinghouse, I knew for a fact that I had completed all of the core credits necessary. The issue wasn't with me or my actual high school transcript. The issue was with Madison and their collegiate department. Basically, they didn't update things in their system that transferred students' core credits correctly to be made available in Clearinghouse's database.

I didn't even really understand what was going on or know how to get it handled. Whenever my mother or I called to get answers, Madison didn't seem to know either, or simply gave us the run around. After weeks and weeks of trying, I began to get worried. Things didn't seem like they were going to get handled and the season was approaching.

As soon as I stepped foot in Morgan, Beas and I formed a relationship in which we always seemed to be on the same page. I'd go to his office on a daily basis and we would just pick each other's brains for hours. At that point I wasn't practicing with the team at all, I was also sneaking into class because my scholarship money couldn't be used, and after a week I wasn't even able to eat free on campus anymore. I went to the academic coordinator of the athletics department, Ms. Watkins, who brought my ineligibility to our attention. I asked her what my options were and she told me I could "red shirt" this year if my coaches were willing to pay for it. Red shirting is when you sit out a year without participating in any official team activities. Red shirting would allow me to attend classes and earn college credits, which would eliminate the Clearinghouse issue. Another option was to take out a loan and play as a walk on. Without Clearinghouse I wouldn't be able to accept the scholarship money because that was a requirement, but if I paid my own way no one could really tell me that I couldn't play. There was no way I would willingly go into debt for $20,000, though. The last option was to find some way to get Madison to update their system and my core credits as soon as possible. She said I'd need someone to apply pressure on Madison's staff to ensure that would be done.

I called Munch and told him my issue. We called everyone around NY affiliated with girls' basketball and tried to determine who could help us. We got into contact with Rochelle Murphy, who knew me from the Gazelles AAU team and through her daughters. Ms. Murphy was very anxious to help. She knew my story and how hard I've been working to get to this point. She knew a lot about Clearinghouse and AAU. She was also an athletic director at a high school, so she knew exactly what needed to be done.

A few weeks before the season began everything was taken care of and I was eligible for my scholarship. During the time I was ineligible I didn't just sit on my butt and feel sorry for myself. I knew one way or another the situation was going to be handled, and I didn't want to be unprepared or behind in anything. I still snuck into and attended my classes. I let my teachers know what was taking place and they worked with me. I still turned in my work and projects. When I wasn't in class, I worked out on my own.

I did the same things my teammates were doing. I just had the luxury of doing it at my own pace, without a coach on my back or any penalties. I was still able to play open gym with my teammates, even though in preseason, open gym was only a few times a week. Since I didn't want to get out of shape, I also went to Hurt Gym to play recreationally with some of the regular students. I may have had a tiny set back, but there was no way I was going to be unprepared for my major comeback!

The team took another hit when Mahala tore her ACL before the season began. Mahala was an athletic wing player with great explosiveness. If she didn't start, she was still going to get a lot of playing time. I realized just how quickly basketball could be taken away. Once I returned to the team, I was more driven and focused than I was when I first got there. I was willing to make the necessary adjustments and help my team win by any means necessary!

# Chapter 11
# A Historic Freshman Year

*Being a part of history is good, but being*
*legendary is even better!*
*#Tinyism*

I vowed to never put myself or my team in that situation again. I made sure from that day forward I was there for my team. Throughout my career at Morgan, I missed only one game, and that was an exhibition game. The competitor in me just wouldn't allow me to miss competition.

Once I returned to the team it was mid-October, which was when college basketball teams are allowed to begin official practice. The workouts, conditioning, weight lifting, and other things we were participating in were considered training, and not practice since we never worked on actual team philosophies or plays. During the preseason period it's against NCAA rules to do anything practice related. You are only allowed a certain number of hours in the gym throughout the week and you can't participate in practice-like activities.

Once official practice began we worked on our offensive plays, defenses, and the coach's philosophy. During those times I realized being a high school student athlete and being a college student athlete were very different. Being a college student athlete is absolutely exhausting. During October my schedule looked something like the following. Wake up at 6 a.m. to be in the weight room from 6:30 a.m.—8 a.m. Since I was an incoming freshman, unaware of how important making your own schedule was, I was stuck with an 8:00 a.m. class every day. After that I had two or three classes before a break around lunch time. Sometimes I ate during my break or I had mandatory individual workouts with my coaches. Individuals were a workout by yourself or with a couple other teammates, specific for the position you played. After individuals I usually had two more classes. After my last class of the day, I either had a break or had to rush to the locker room to get ready for team practice.

On those days that I was lucky enough to have a break, you can bet I would head to my room to squeeze in a nap. After practice was over around 8 or 9 p.m., depending how coach felt, I'd go eat dinner, shower and by 10 p.m., I'd finally return to my room. If I didn't pass out, I had to find the energy to do homework and study. I'd have to try to get as much rest as possible just to get up the next day and do it all over again.

We had weight training four times a week and on the one day we didn't, we used that time slot for the first practice of the two-a-day sessions. That schedule was very typical for college basketball players regardless of the school. Some people think being a college student athlete is easy, but they truly have no idea. To compound things, once the season started this schedule would include traveling to away games and trying to keep up with one's studies while being absent from classes.

I made sure I managed my time well enough to complete whatever work was assigned to me. I wanted to continue to be the model student athlete. After all, I wasn't just doing it for me, I was doing it for my mother and those that looked up to me. I always made sure I was as dedicated in the classroom as I was on the court. During my time at Morgan I was on both the academic and athletic first team. I graduated Morgan with accolades on and off the court and a cumulative GPA of 3.5.

My first season as a Lady Bear was right around the corner. All that was left were midterm exams and projects and "Midnight Madness". After that, what I referred to as "Operation Turn the Program Around" was a go. Midnight Madness is an event that takes place before the first games of the men's and women's basketball teams. It runs from 9 p.m. to midnight, with the purpose of introducing both teams. Midnight Madness gives fans a preview of what to expect. Fans are introduced to the new coaches and players, and there are multiple contests for the fans and between the teams. These competitions include dunking and a three point shooting contest. The evening finishes with team scrimmages. It's a great event that builds school spirit and lets everyone know that the season is here!

Floyd Kerr, our athletic director, told everyone that things were going to change for the better when it came to Morgan State basketball. After hiring Beas, Kerr also hired Todd Bozeman. Coach Bozeman was a great coach, with a lot of experience. Before coming to Morgan, he coached one of the best point guards in NBA history, Jason Kidd at UC Berkley. Coach Bozeman was also from the DMV area so it seemed like a perfect fit for the men's program. The men's team also had a lot of new and dynamic players. After the event both teams and fans were equally excited for the season. The men's team had been losing just as often as the girls, but following Midnight Madness, everyone in the gym felt that things would soon change!

We began having practice once a day and did weights fewer times a week following Midnight Madness. Since the games would begin in less than two weeks, the coaching staff wanted to take some of the pressure off of our bodies. Before we knew it, it was time to tip off the season. All the workouts, practices, sore days, layups, jump shots, sprints, suicides, free throws, squats, dumb bell presses, and crunches had led up to this moment and it was worth it.

Although I wore number 11 at Madison, my favorite jersey number was number 1 and I wore it whenever I had the opportunity. I wore number 1 in every tournament with No Limit and every game after the JRC program. Initially, I didn't actually select number 1. It was always just given to me. Sometimes I'd get it because alphabetically my name came up first and other times I'd get it because the jersey numbers matched the size of the uniform. Since I was usually the smallest person on my team, I would get the smallest shirt and consequently be number 1.

When I got to Madison, Dumont told me number one was an illegal number in our league, so I couldn't wear it. When I can't get number one, I try to get number 3, after my favorite player Allen Iverson, or 11, signifying double 1's, and the month of my birth. Fortunately for me, number 1 was available at Morgan.

The day had finally come of the 2006—2007 Lady Bear's season tip-off. We were opening our season away against New Jersey Tech in Newark. There I was, about to wear that fresh number one Morgan State Lady Bear jersey for the first time, and I was going to be doing so right in the backyard of my hometown. Since Newark wasn't too far from Brooklyn, my mother and grandmother came to see me play. Throughout my career I've played many games, and my mother and grandmother have been to no more than thirty games. I wish they could've seen me play more often, but whenever they do make it out to a game, I try my best to make them proud. I was starting point guard, wearing my favorite jersey number, and playing in front of the two most important people in my life. I had some fresh Allen Iverson-like braids in my hair and I instantly thought, "This has the makings of a great debut." I am always nervous before every game I play. My nervousness isn't necessarily a reflection of fear. It's more a mixture of wanting to perform at my best and being anxious to do what I love.

The coaching staff gave us the game plan. We finished warming up and it was game time. They announced the starting line ups and since this was sort of a homecoming for me, my coaches put my name last. "The starting point guard for the Lady Bears, standing at 5 foot 7 (media guide height) coming from Brooklynnnnn NY, Number 1, Corin Adams." Once I heard that, I lit up. I had the biggest smile on my face and I said to myself, "Let's go baby. It's show time." I ran over and shook the other coaches' hands and then waved to my mom and grand mom. We went back to the bench for a couple words from Beas and then we got ready for the tip.

My overenthusiasm reflected in my initial play as I couldn't hit a thing! I shot 3-14 from the field, but managed to knock down 5 of 6 of my free throws. In 31 minutes, despite an off shooting night, I managed to drop a double-double in my first collegiate basketball game. I had 10 points and 12 rebounds to go along with 4 steals, 3 assists, and 6 turnovers. Most importantly, we won the game! We led by 6 at half time, and ended up winning the game by 8. It was a close game throughout the first half. After the halfway mark of the first half I threw a beautiful, flashy no look pass after crossing over one of the girls from Jersey Tech. It sped past a couple defenders, went through Big Brit's hands crazy fast, went out of bounds and bounced off the wall extremely hard and loud. After that play, there was a media timeout. In college basketball games media timeouts occur in 4 minute intervals of every half. Whenever there is a dead ball after the four minute interval passes, the media timeout takes place.

Beas sweated just as much as we did while he paced the side lines and was one of the most passionate coaches I have ever played for. Many would say he was a little too reckless and out of control. Between yelling at us, working the refs, pantomiming what he wanted us to do, throwing his jacket off and back on, or just pacing up and down the sideline, Beas always worked up a sweat. The minute the game started he became our sixth man and played right with us. Beas was one of the only coaches I knew who gave every player on the team, the green light. All he wanted us to do was score and play defense. He didn't care what you did to score, or how you did it, he just wanted you to put the ball in the hole. If, of course, you did something crazy that didn't result in a bucket he'd take your green light away.

Aside from being animated on the sideline, Beas was also heavy handed. Once I threw that ball to Big Brit and it went through her hands, he ran right up to me and let me have it! Beas screamed, "Tiny, what did I tell you? They are not ready for those passes and they're never going to catch them. Stop throwing my f*ing ball away. Either make an easier slower pass or shoot it yourself!" He is always in the heat of the battle, so the whole gym heard him. I wasn't scared of him and I understood where he was coming from. What I was scared of, though, was that my mother and grandmother were going to jump him at half time. While screaming at me in regards to my pass, he grabbed me and shook me a little bit. After he shook me, we locked eyes and he finished his statement. He then palmed my face and whispered, "Now let's win this," and gave me a little pat on my cheek. Being heavy handed, that little pat felt and looked like a hard slap. From the outside looking in, my mother and grandmother thought he was putting his hands on me. As we walked back to the bench for the rest of the media timeout, all I could hear was Mom and Grandma calling my name. "Corin, Corin, I know he ain't just slap you. Are you okay? Don't make us get up." I just came out the huddle and gave them a hand gesture like, "Chill y'all. It's not that serious."

After that timeout, I played better. We won and I had a double-double in my debut. After the game we went to the locker room and it was just magical. The smiles on the faces of the upperclassmen, the coaches, and even the trainers were amazing. This win signified that we were on our way to turning things around and I personally couldn't wait to continue making it happen.

That next day after receiving so much love from the athletic department and people at our school, the Morgan State Athletics site's main article read: "Lady Bears Defeat NJIT, 63-55; Record First Season-Opening Win in 23 Years." After seeing that, I said to myself, "Wow, no wonder everyone is going crazy around here. We made history last night!"

We participated in two tournaments back to back. We lost both games in the UNC Asheville tournament and unfortunately lost in the Cornell Classic championship game. In the Cornell Classic, we beat the host team Cornell and advanced to the championship game. Even though we got smacked in the championship, beating Cornell was another historic moment in Morgan State Women's basketball history. It was the first time the program had ever beaten an Ivy League school. I led with a game high 18 points and 5 steals and made the all-tournament team. We were now 2-3 on the season. It wasn't as good as we hoped, but it was a step in the right direction. After the Cornell tournament, it seemed as though every win after made history as we were on our way to an 18-12 season. After Cornell we lost then won two straight vs Lafayette and Mount St Mary's. The Lafayette win marked the most non-conference wins in a season since 1999 and also marked the best start the program had since 1999, at 4-4. These two wins were the first back-to-back victories since February 2006, and gave Morgan its first .500 mark through the first eight games since the 1999-2000 season. After the Mt. St Mary's game, we lost two but then went on to win five games in a row beating Fordham, Delaware State, Hampton, Norfolk State and South Carolina State. The team wasn't winning five games in an entire season prior to this year, so a five game win streak was very big for the program. That win against Delaware State was one of the biggest wins of Beas' and my career together. Beas always put emphasis on two teams in our conference, Delaware State and Coppin. Those were the two best teams in our conference as well as the two teams with the most recent MEAC championship appearances and banners. We beat Del State 42-40. I was expecting to play a bunch of Diana Tarasis and Candace Parkers. After hitting the game winner, I honestly inquired, "That's Del State?" I would later regret that statement.

After beating them that first time, we didn't beat them again until my senior year. Every time we played, their Coach Davis, being the defensive coach that he was, made it a living hell for me on offense. In my four years at Morgan, Del State never really proved to be an offensive team. Their game was defense. Unless you were a top notch, powerhouse team, the box score was always going to read under 60. Coach Davis believed that defense wins games, and every team he coached illustrated that belief. He trapped me, double teamed me, box 1-ed me and did anything in his power to make sure I had as little an impact on the game as possible. A box 1 is a certain kind of defense that focuses mainly on a team's star player. The object is to limit the amount of times they touch the ball and/or score. A box 1 is arranged with one player playing the star player face to face, while the other four members on defense form a box/square in the paint.

Coach Davis was, ironically, one of Beas' best friends. So between his male ego and competitive nature, he used to say, "Look Tiny, I'm not going to let you beat us by yourself ever again. If you somehow manage to win, believe me you're going to work for it." After that I had nothing but respect for him.

He and Beas are currently working together at Morgan. I would have loved to play for the both of them. I'm sure it would have been an enjoyable experience and would've led to even more wins. After that Del State game, we began to turn heads in the conference. Other teams were wondering what was going on at Morgan. For years, everyone wrote us off as an easy win on their schedule, but this year they were going to have to earn that W.

# Chapter 12
# "BANG!"

*Self-confidence elevates performance!*
*#Tinyism*

Our win streak sadly came to an end. We lost one, won one, and then went on a three game losing streak. After getting our act back together, Hampton helped us start up another three game win streak (Hampton, Norfolk St, and South Carolina St). The win against Hampton was our first series sweep of the season and the program's very first sweep ever over Hampton. The win against South Carolina St. was our third series sweep over a team in conference and moved us to third place in the conference. In the preseason poll we were selected to be in last place, so climbing to that third spot was another great accomplishment. After that win streak came to an end we went on another three game winning streak. We beat UMES, Howard, and Eastern Shore. The UMES game was my first collegiate game winning buzzer beater. Our school website read "Morgan State's Tiny Adams dribbled the ball across the timeline with 18 seconds remaining in the contest and the game tied up at 60. Adams began to make her move toward the basket with nine seconds and pulled up just inside the three-point arc at the top of the key with three seconds left and knocked down a jumper as the buzzer sounded to give the visiting Lady Bears a 62-60 victory at Maryland-Eastern Shore, thus spoiling the Homecoming festivities for the UMES faithful."

That was one of the most memorable moments from my career at Morgan. The gym was packed. It was a close game, and the rookie Tiny Adams turned out to be the hero. Immediately after the buzzer sounded, the head coach of UMES, Coach Fred Batchelor ran right up to me, shook my hand and said, "Great shot, Tiny," while he shook his head in disbelief. I had the utmost respect for Coach Batchelor. From that game on I'd always chop it up with him, make a couple jokes and just show love, and he did the same in return. Heading into the locker room after that game was magical. Everyone was excited and all Beas kept saying to me was, "BANG! BANG! BANG!"

One time we were having a conversation in his office and he told me that I was doing a good job so far, but he wanted me to be more aggressive. He asked me what was holding me back from being the Rookie of The Year in the conference or even the Player of The Year. Beas challenged me day in and day out. He didn't believe in being average and taught the same. He said, "Tiny, this is what you gotta do." As he stood up out of his chair, he continued, "You gotta come down and just shoot the son of a b***. After you hit the first one, BANG! Then come down and hit another one, BANG! Once you hit two you're hot, so you shoot that thing again. BANG! Man I wouldn't care if you shot it every time. Just BANG! BANG! BANG! BANG!" As he got louder and more animated he did shooting motions with his hands over and over. You couldn't question his love for the game. From that day on, whenever he thought it was time for me to take over, he'd just keep shouting "BANG! BANG! BANG! BANG!" I'd look at him and laugh so hard.

We were now approaching our last game of the regular season, playing our crosstown rivals, Coppin State, in a highly anticipated match up. Their coach, Brown was another one of Beasley's best friends, so there were bragging rights at stake between them as well as bragging rights for both schools. Morgan vs. Coppin was one of the most anticipated events in Baltimore. It took the word "rivalry" to a new level. The teams hated each other, and the fans hated each other. Coppin was about 15 minutes away from Morgan, on the other side of Baltimore, so everyone in the city marked those games on their calendars and when game day came, a sold out crowd was automatic.

Beas prided himself on doing the unthinkable, and in never being predictable. When we first arrived at Morgan he made it known that he wanted to be the one to beat Coppin and end their streak of dominance. Coppin had run the conference the past three seasons with a streak in conference and tournament victories. The first time we played them at home, it started out close but I played like a rookie. I fouled out and my team wasn't able to pull off the win.

Before each game Beas would give us a speech, the game plan, and a little motivation. When it came to his motivation for Coppin all he would say is, "I want to beat Coppin's sweet a**. If anyone can do it, we can do it." After that he'd scream, we'd all get hyped up, start clapping, and he'd say it again, "I want that sweet a**, y'all!" Despite all the positive motivation, we lost to Coppin again. I played my a** off. It was the last game of the season, the crowd was sold out, and I wanted to get Coppin's sweet a** for my man Beas.

Following the game, the press read, "Morgan State's Corin Adams recorded a game and career-high 22 points, team-high seven rebounds and added a game-high five steals, but on this day, it wasn't enough." We got as close as six points after I completed an "And 1" to make it 59-53. In those last three minutes of the game, Coppin turned it on and expanded the lead to 14. We didn't manage to score after my three point play. Earlier in the game there was another "BANG BANG" episode when I hit a buzzer beater three-pointer just before halftime. Beas showered me with "BANGS" when we got to the locker room, but we ultimately lost that game.

Even in defeat, the game gave us a lot of confidence as we headed to North Carolina to compete in the MEAC's Tournament against Hampton. We were entering the tournament as the number four seed, our highest seed since the 1996-97 squad finished third. In the NCAA, each conference has its own tournament to qualify for "The Big Dance". The Big Dance is every college hooper's dream. This is the NCAA's national tournament that ultimately leads to the Final Four and the national championship title for that season. The winner of each conference tournament earns a guaranteed spot into the tournament for a chance to compete to become the national champion. The three years prior, Del. St. and Coppin St. were the winners of the MEAC conference tournament. The MEAC tournament was a single elimination tournament that spans over the course of five days.

We beat Hampton again and, of course, that win was also another historic moment for the 06-07 Lady Bears. "The last time Morgan State won a game in the MEAC Tournament, the Lady Bears defeated Maryland-Eastern Shore, 64-40 in a 2000 quarterfinal contest. Since then, the Lady Bears had not won a tournament game, going six years without a victory. Morgan State will get a chance to end a 14-game losing skid against its crosstown rival as they take on the top seeded Lady Eagles of Coppin State."

Coppin was the two-time defending tournament champions, and after competing with them in such a close game just days before, everyone wanted some of Coppin's sweet a**! We had only one day to prepare and get ready. Fortunately we got 24 hours to rest our legs and didn't have to play back to back. This was a blessing in disguise because the game actually ended up going into overtime and we definitely needed our legs.

The Morgan men's team may not have made as much progress as we did, but they were definitely on the right path. The day in between our games we went to support our men's team. In conference tournaments your overall record doesn't really matter and despite the fact that they had lost some tough battles during the season, they were always competitive. The men's team was the fifth seed and they were playing the underdog role just like we were. They managed to upset South Carolina St. by two and advanced to the Final Four of the tournament. Who would have thought that both Morgan teams would be competing in the Final Four? On Friday and Saturday both Morgan teams would be setting out to shock the world. Since it was the weekend and the first time in a long while that both teams made the Final Four, many of our supporters drove down to North Carolina to show their Morgan spirit.

Tip-off of our game was set for 12 noon and for the third time that year it was the battle of East and West Baltimore. This time it took place in North Carolina in front of fans of both teams and the MEAC conference itself. Our seniors knew that this could very well be the last time they suited up and got to play with one another.

This was their last MEAC tournament, last time playing Coppin, and the end of their best season at Morgan. I wanted to help them get their first and last win vs Coppin St. and to be sure my girls went out with a bang. After all they had been through in the past seasons, they deserved it.

Upon entering the RBC arena, I felt those same anxious feelings I felt the first game my Lady Bears and I played together in Jersey. This was one of the biggest games of my career, a chance to advance to the MEAC championship and possibly earn a berth in the NCAA tournament. From tip-off to the last whistle we fought with Coppin, and we fought hard. We battled tough and hung in there. Up until about the 6 minute mark of the first half, the game was close and we even found ourselves tied at 23 before Coppin went on a 15-8 run before the half. Beas told us at halftime that he was proud how we started the game. He said there wasn't really much to say. If we wanted to win, we'd have to step it up. He felt it in his gut that today was the day and we had to prove him right. At halftime I only had 7 points. Beas came to me and said he knew I was sort of falling back for the seniors, but just like in all our other big wins, the team needed me to get it done. Beas was right, as I was being a little more passive because I wanted the seniors to shine. I took his message to heart and proceeded to go back into the arena to warm up and get ready for the second half with a slightly different personal game plan.

After the first media timeout we were only down three, with a score of 47-44. I missed every shot I took. I was trying my best to help my team continue to keep up with Coppin, but I couldn't hit a thing and Coppin went on a 13-2 run. The score was 60-49 and we saw our chances of advancing slipping away if we didn't step up and make a run. On the next play I got the ball and went to the rack. I missed again, but I got fouled. The foul was the first dead ball after the 8 minute mark, so we went to the media timeout. During that timeout every senior spoke and conveyed the message that it was now, or never. I shook my head and told them I got this.

After the timeout I stepped on the court with more confidence than before. I was determined and focused to find a way to win this game. I walked to the free throw line and knocked them both down. 60-51. We then got a stop, Aaries got the rebound, and threw an outlet pass to me. I got the ball, ran a play for myself and hit a short jump shot to cut the deficit to 60-53. Coppin got the ball and Lala fouled Coppin's post player, Whitney Cunningham. Cunningham was a former player of Coach Graham's from Baltimore. She was one of the top rebounders and post players in the league. Playing against each other throughout the years, Lala and Whitney didn't really care for each other. So there was a little extra "oomph" in Lala's foul. That foul put Coppin in the one and one, but Whitney missed. Our next two points came from Big Brit. She got an offensive rebound and as she put it back up, she was fouled. Big Brit knocked down the two free throws to make it 60-55. Coppin then scored on a layup to make the score 62-55. On our next possession Whit and I both missed easy jump shots. Big Brit battled down low with Cunningham to get the offensive rebound. After Big Brit got the rebound over Cunningham, she kicked it out to Whit who missed, giving Big Brit an opportunity to get another offensive rebound. Brit got the offensive rebound again, tried to put it back up, but it rimmed out. Cunningham proceeded to get the ball, turned around deliberately with her elbows up, and swung the ball around to create space. She clocked Big Brit in the face and cleared her out of the way. Brit fell to the floor instantly, the refs blew the whistle and the crowd went wild. My teammates and I immediately ran over to Big Brit to make sure she was alright. As she was on the sideline getting fixed up by the trainers, the replay screen at the RBC showed the blow Big Brit took in slow motion over and over. Every time they showed it, they would randomly go to someone in the crowd to see their reaction. First they went to someone in the crowd who was watching in disbelief and then they went to a couple of Coppin fans who found it funny. Once we saw those Coppin fans laugh, we got even more furious. Lala was the angriest of us all. She was ready to get Cunningham back for what she did. Cunningham had a smirk on her face that gave us the idea that she had done it on purpose. She may have thought that she had won the battle between her and Big Brit, but what she didn't know was that she had ultimately lost the bigger battle for her team.

Upon returning to the court, we had fire in our eyes and were inspired to put together one of the best comebacks in MEAC tournament history. We were still down seven points with four minutes to go. On the next possession, Lala got an "And 1" and completed the 3 point play to make it 62-58. An And 1 is when you score a basket in addition to being fouled. After the ref makes the call, you are awarded one free throw shot. We got a stop and I finally got one of my scoops to drop. 62-60. Coppin scored the next possession to make it 64-60. But immediately after, Whit put her jets on, drove and made a layup to cut the lead to 64-62.

Beas went crazy on the sideline and called a time out to set up one of his famous defenses. It was a two point game with a minute and a half left. Beas had on a nice light colored suit, with a light colored shirt to complement it, but between running up and down the sideline, fighting with the refs and just being his usual self, he had sweat stains pouring right through. He had his suit jacket off and as he called the timeout, the cameras zoomed in on him. After about three seconds, the camera crew put a "sweat-o-meter" up on the big screen and replayed him trying to get the ref's attention. Everyone in the gym laughed, including Beas himself.

As we sat down in the huddle, he didn't even talk at first. Beas began dancing. He said, "You gotta love this! I don't care what they say, sweat-o-meter, sweat-o-heater. We gonna get us that sweet a** today. I want to run 'hot' and tie this thing up." "Hot" was a surprise defense we often ran to force the other team to make a quick turnover. We would set up in a two-three defense and on his word the first two players of the zone, Whit and I, would rush the person with the ball. As we rushed them, the two outside players would rush the passing lanes to try and get a steal. As all of this is going on Big Brit stayed in the middle just in case they didn't turn the ball over so she could protect the basket.

Once they got the ball to the point guard, Beas went crazy on the sideline again. "HOT! HOT! HOT! HOT!" As we rushed the point guard, Whit got a finger on it. After she tipped the ball, she grabbed it and as she tried to dribble it and secure the possession, she turned it over out of bounds. There were now only fifty-four seconds left in the game. Coppin had the ball and we had to get one more stop. We went to a man-to-man defense and Whit made up for her turnover. Once again with her long arms she blocked the shot of one of the guards. Shana quickly secured the rebound and dribbled ahead. Whit ran past everyone, got a pass from Shana and made the layup. It was a tie game with twenty-six seconds to go.

It was Coppin's ball and all we had to do was get a stop and we'd be going to overtime. Coppin had one of the best shooters in the nation, Rashida Suber. She was also the reigning player of the year. Everyone in the gym knew who they were going to, it was just a matter of us defending her. They ran a play for Suber, which she caught, shot, and missed. With 4 seconds left we couldn't hold onto the ball and Coppin came up with it again. Timeout. They of course ran another play for Suber and she missed again. It was overtime!

It was very rare for Suber to miss three in a row. She was upset at herself, so as expected she came out firing in overtime. On their first possession she hit a three to make it 67-64. Over the next couple of minutes no one was able to hit a shot. Fatigue was beginning to set in. At around the three minute mark, off a miss by Coppin, Whit scored a layup to pull us to within one. Coppin actually was cold the entire overtime as that shot by Suber was the only basket they scored. After Whit put us within one and Coppin missed on the next possession, Sheezy got the rebound and threw an outlet to me.

At that point I caught my second wind. I got the ball and did a couple flashy moves to get past two Coppin defenders. Once I got past them, the rest of their players were in transition defense. The crowd began to get into it and ooh-ed and aah-ed. After my second move, Beas began going wild on the sideline. I dribbled up the right sideline to cross half court, and all I heard him saying was, "BANG! BANG! BANG!" I hadn't even gotten into shooting range yet, but I had to make a play. Once I got across half court and passed the three point line, there were only two defenders left. Cunningham was in the paint and there was one guard left to beat. I did a quick in and out, followed by a pull-back crossover between the legs. After I pulled back between my legs, I pulled up for a jump shot on the wing between the free throw line and three point line. The minute it left my hand, I knew it was going in. I held my follow through extra-long, turned around and smiled at Coach Beas. I was in the moment. Beas knew it was going in also, he could see it. The closer the ball got to the rim, the louder he shouted, "BANG! BANG! BANG!" After I hit that shot the crowd went crazy and so did our bench. The score was now 68-67 in our favor, with two minutes left. Coppin stayed cold and seemed to be playing a little scared. Two plays later, they fouled Sheezy and she went to the free throw line. She missed one and made one. It was now 69-67 in our favor, with forty-nine seconds left. Coppin didn't call time out. They brought the ball up and ran a play for Suber. She shot a three and missed but they got the rebound. They called a thirty second timeout with thirty-four seconds left. The emotion in the Morgan State huddle was electric. We had the fans behind us screaming, "Hold on!" while coaches were screaming with their serious faces that, "It wasn't over." Our teammates on the bench were cheering like we had already won, while even our trainer had a word or two of encouragement for us.

The timeout was over and to our surprise they drew up a play for Cunningham under the basket. She missed a wide open layup, got the rebound and missed the put back. Their two guard got the rebound and missed the put back layup before Big Brit stepped in and secured the rebound with 2 seconds left. She held on to the ball for dear life and as the buzzer sounded we all went crazy. The bench stormed the court, the seniors ran circles around the court, the cheerleaders danced crazily while I just walked towards my team watching in amazement. Once it hit me, I found Beas and of course all teary eyed and sweaty he said, "We got that sweet a**!" After our celebration we shook hands and the look on the Coppin players' faces was priceless. That was one of the top moments I had at Morgan. To hit the game-changing bucket and help get that win for my seniors and the program was a remarkable feeling. We were going to the chip!

The way we fought and achieved that win, you would've thought that was the championship game. Between the storyline, drama, and change of events it felt bigger than it was. We still had one more game, and it was against our other rival, Del. St. What were the odds of beating both Coppin and Del St. to make our Cinderella story complete? After playing the way we did against Coppin it turned out we didn't have enough gas left in the tank to complete the sweep. We were exhausted and it showed in our play as we ended up losing in the championship game to Del. St. 55-42. Del. St. went to the big dance and Coppin went to the WNIT because they were still the regular season champs. The WNIT is the secondary post season tournament for teams who don't make it to The Big Dance.

My freshman season ended at Morgan and I couldn't have been more proud of my team and what we had accomplished. We set goals, achieved them, made history, and shocked the world. Freshman year was my favorite season at Morgan. There will never be another team like the 2006-2007 Lady Bears.

My final stats were 13.4 points, 4.8 rebounds, 2.9 assists, and 2.3 steals averaged per game. I earned honors as Team MVP/ Rookie of the Year, MEAC All-Rookie Team, MEAC All-Tournament Team, UNC-Asheville Tournament Team, and the Cornell Classic Tournament Team. Not bad for my freshman season, but I still knew that the best was yet to come!

# Chapter 13
# A Family Away From Home

*Family is verified by unconditional love and support, not just relation or name.*

*#Tinyism*

"It's often harder to stay on top than it is to get there." This was one of the many lessons I learned from both Coach Clarke and Beas at Morgan. After my freshman season, my Lady Bears and I would no longer be able to sneak up on teams like we did that previous season. After everything we accomplished, teams were going to be prepared for us. They weren't going to be sleeping on us like before. All teams were now wide awake.

At the end of each season, there is an evaluation period during which the coaches let you know what their expectations were, how you did, and what you should try to improve on. My freshman season evaluation with Beas turned into one of our many basketball conversations. We sat in his office and reflected upon the season that had just ended. We reminisced, laughed, and spoke about what could've been had we done a couple of things a little differently. Ultimately, we both were happy for each other and for our team. After a historic season, Morgan was now among the top ranks in the conference. Beas received the recognition he deserved by being named Coach of The Year in the MEAC. Beas didn't give me the typical evaluation. He simply told me that I'd have to step it up next season in all aspects of my game. After chopping it up with Beas, I got a more in-depth evaluation from Coach Clarke. Based on my performance, Coach Clarke told me I should work on my free throws, three pointers, avoiding charges, turnovers, and concentrating on a pull up game.

Coach Clarke was very instrumental in my successes both on and off the court. She was a former collegiate point guard at Fayetteville State in North Carolina, where she helped lead her team to a championship. Entering my freshman year, Coach Clarke was only twenty-five years old. I found it easy to relate to her because she had recently gone through everything I was getting ready to experience. Beas and Coach Graham were former football players, so though they may have known the game of basketball, they didn't actually experience it. Coach Clarke was my real-life guide through college, basketball, and how to manage the two. Whenever she spoke, I listened. Coach Clarke actually seemed to notice my potential before I did. She always challenged me to be better. I was ambitious and took initiative to do things on my own, but she showed me the right way to succeed. What good is working hard if you're working on all the wrong things? If you aren't doing things the right way, you're wasting your time. One of the many Coach Clarke lessons that has stuck with me was to write down my goals and focus on them until they were achieved.

In the beginning she was the one that would actually create my goals for me. Before games she'd write them down or text them to me. She'd write, "15 points, 4 steals, 2 turnovers and an allowance of one missed free throw." I'm a very goal-oriented person, and once I have a goal set, I'm going to do everything in my power to achieve it. In time I started making my own goals, both mentally and on paper. I began to make things harder for myself, raising my personal bar. I made goals that were more challenging, to ensure that I was pushing myself to the limit.

After my freshman season, I made goals before the start of every season. I'd share them with her and she'd make adjustments before we'd lock them in for the year. If I would slack off, Coach Clarke would be right in my ear saying, "You're not trying to achieve that goal, huh?" If I went a game without getting a steal, she'd look at me and just say "You're not trying to lead the conference in steals anymore, huh?" She did the little things to remind me that I had to always be on top of my game, if I wanted to achieve the things I set out to achieve. Off the court, Coach Clarke made me think more logically. She got me to simplify everything mentally. Before I knew it, I was becoming more strategic with everything I did. I'm happy she took me under her wing the way she did. Thanks to her, I think I turned out okay!

I finished my semester with a GPA of 3.2 and passed every class with A's and B's. After earning my stripes in the MEAC conference as a freshman, it was pretty evident that I was going to be a force to be reckoned with during the next three seasons.

Once the season ended we had a couple of weeks off from workouts until it was time to get back in the gym. "Basketball never stops." Both the pre-season and post-season workouts were pretty similar. We didn't train as often in the post season, but we still got some work in. During that first week off, I was able to experience what it felt like to be a regular student with a regular schedule. I even got involved with extra-curricular activities outside of basketball. I attended school events, checked out the movie theatre shows in the student center, attended a couple parties and joined a mentoring program.

The mentoring program was created and run by a former Morgan State football player, Chris Cash. Cash graduated before I got to Morgan and was also a physical educator. Between the program and studying the same subject he'd just earned his degree in, we saw a lot of each other. He became one of my mentors as well. Cash always gave me good advice about how to be successful as a student-athlete and provided some recommendations for me. Cash's program was called "Morgan Mentors, Winston Winners". The program was based out of Winston Middle School. Winston Middle School was 5 minutes from Morgan and was the school Cash worked at. The mentor program combined Morgan mentors with Winston students based on similarities, like sports and other interests. I was a part of the program during all four years at Morgan. Whenever I had free time, I'd dedicate it to my mentees.

That first year, Cash actually became the coach of the girls' basketball team at Winston, so I took a couple of his players under my wing on the court. In addition to the ones I mentored, I also tried my best to support and help the team as a whole. As for my mentees, I'd go to their games, visit them at school, pick them up to come to my games, or go hang out with them at one of the Morgan-Winston events that Cash had planned. Cash had events every couple months that allowed all of the mentees and mentors to bond, including bowling parties and small dinners at Winston.

My first mentee was Labrea Pack. Labrea was small like me, but very aggressive. She was extremely focused and always willing to fight for what she wanted. She attends Benedict College now and I couldn't be more proud of her. My second mentee was End'dya

Barnes. End'dya was more of a hooper than Labrea and was the star of the team. End'dya played the point guard position like I do. She always played hard, but had a bit of an attitude. Cash and I spent her entire middle school career working on this with her. Despite her attitude on the court, End'dya was a good student. End'dya will be trying to follow in my footsteps next semester at Morgan. She didn't get a basketball scholarship, but we're trying to get her on the team as a walk on. Although I always supported the Winston students and the program, those were my only two official mentees. Labrea was an 8th grader and End'dya was a 6th grader at the time I got involved with the program. Though Labrea graduated that next year I still kept in touch with her. End'dya and I were a little more connected because she still had two years left at Winston. While I was at Morgan, Cash brought them to our games and practices. I'd play them two on one, buy them things they needed for school like uniforms or sneakers, and just try to look out for them as much as I could. Although I don't have much myself, I enjoy giving back to those with less. Giving back, especially to children, is one of the few things that brings me more joy than basketball,

Because we had had such an historic season, my Lady Bears and I made our campus, alumni, and neighborhood proud. Everywhere I went, there would be people showing me love, especially on campus. From the janitors, to the teachers, to the administrative staff, to the students and even the school's president, Tiny was well-known and well-liked. It was humbling for me and I always made sure I showed love back as much as I could. When I had signed that letter of intent after high school and first arrived on campus, I didn't really expect any of this to happen.

I took a full week off from being a student-athlete, and then it was time to get back in the gym. Being a gym rat, I can't stay away from the gym for a long period of time. Plus, being a regular student was kind of boring. Throughout the season, most of our conference games were double headers so both the men's and women's teams were always in the same places. Being around the guy's team so often, I ended up forming relationships with most of the players. There were four players that I became especially cool with; Reggie Holmes, Demetrius Branch, Emanuel Hightower, and Vic Auja. All the way through my career at Morgan these were my "big bros". Reg was also an incoming freshman from Baltimore. He was my male equivalent at Morgan. We came in together and changed the culture at Morgan together. Our careers seemed to mirror one another's. Any accolade I earned, Reg would earn the same or something nearly as exceptional. We became the faces of each program. We had the same roles on our teams as well as similar personalities. We were the leaders, worked hard, carried our teams, and then once we handled business, acted a little silly and made everyone laugh.

Many nights, you could walk by Hill Field House after midnight and catch us in the gym getting shots up. By my sophomore year at Morgan, I actually had the keys that unlocked the gym and the rims. At any given moment I could wake up and go to the gym to shoot around. My coaches got annoyed with me contacting them so many different times and decided it was best that I had my own key. I was responsible and as a coach you didn't want to discourage your players from getting better. Having access to the gym anytime I wanted was very convenient, and Reg and I definitely took advantage. All those random hours, late nights, early mornings, nights after tough losses, all paid off, as Reg and I ended up as the all-time scoring leaders in Morgan's history. Reg surpassed the great Marvin "The Human Eraser" Webster to become the all-time scoring leader on the men's side with 2051 points, and I surpassed them both with 2058 points. Reg is currently playing professionally in Europe. He had a stint in the D league and also played in Bulgaria, Morocco, Poland, and Turkey.

Emanuel Hightower, aka Buck, was one of my biggest supporters at Morgan. If I asked Buck to do something for me, he'd try his best to get it done. Buck even used to wash my hair and blow dry it for me when I had braids. Our friends made fun of him though, so I stopped letting him do it. Buck was also a very talented guy, and was both very artistic and athletic. One minute he could be doing some kind of graphic design project and the next he'd be in the gym catching an alley oop. Buck was from Maryland and he walked on the team. He didn't get much playing time, but he always worked hard and pushed his teammates at practice. Buck lives in Arizona now, where he's working on his clothing line, 4given Love, as well as several other projects.

Vic Auja was a pure shooter from Canada. He was the oldest of our little crew. Vic was one of the smoothest dudes I ever met. He was handsome, a gentlemen, dressed nice, had all the latest gear and that great jump shot. Vic was like a big brother to us all. He held us down, taught us many things, and was just a blessing to be around. He brought life to everyone around him with his energy. Unfortunately, he passed away recently due to an unexpected cancer that took over his body. It's been a couple years now and it still doesn't seem real. "RIP Big Bro, we miss you like crazy down here. Keep watching over us!"

Demetrius "Deezy" Branch was a small, crafty guard. The first time I saw him, I thought he was the cutest thing on campus and had a crush on him for about two weeks. Once we got cooler and closer though it was best we remained friends. Deezy was popular at Morgan and had all the girls he wanted so I probably didn't stand a chance anyway. He was a great shooter and he just could flat out hoop. He didn't really get along with Coach Bozeman's system, but he did well whenever he had a chance to play. Deezy was from Kansas City, but he had an up-North swag like he was from New York. His swag was what drew me to him and by my junior year we were inseparable, until he became a workaholic and stopped attending Morgan. He remained in Baltimore and shared an apartment with Buck. He and I did it all together; freestyle rapped, worked out, shopped, went out to eat, partied, and he'd come to my games. Deezy has been there for me an infinite number of ways that makes me consider him my full-fledged blood brother. The trust and loyalty between us is never ending. We've even spoke about my brother Raling and he tells me not to worry, because it's his loss.

That first year of college proved to be a sure sign that I had made a great decision in attending Morgan. My team was successful, I was prospering individually on the court, excelling in the classroom, and I had gained a family away from home. I had a father figure in Coach Beas, older siblings in my bros and Coach Clarke, and younger siblings in my mentees from the program. People often ask me if I regret attending Morgan over Syracuse. I was right where I needed to be. Morgan helped shape me into the person I am today.

# Chapter 14
## The Emergence of Tiny

*Staying consistent is EVERYTHING...and hard*
*work breeds consistency!*
*#Tinyism*

I spent the summer of 2007 the way I spend all of my summers, playing in NYC basketball tournaments. Morgan State didn't require their players to stay over the summer, like many schools. For one it wasn't in the budget, and I honestly don't think Beas thought it was necessary. After a summer of playing with the big homies it was time to head back to Morgan.

As I entered my sophomore year things were slightly different. I was now dorming in Argonne with seven of my teammates. My roommate was, of course, Phyli. We had lost quite a few players from the 06-07 team. The seniors graduated and Brandi and Ciara decided to transfer to other schools. We had six incoming freshman, plus a healthy Mahala, who would be a freshman on court and a sophomore in the class. Two of the freshman were walk-ons. We had three seniors and three juniors. There was one junior transfer named Tamara Rogers. Tammy had played for

Coach Graham's AAU team and against Beas' AAU team. She was also a Baltimore native and was a 5'2 explosive guard with speed, the ability to jump, and was a terror on defense. Coach Graham was very excited about bringing her onto the team. He knew that with us in the backcourt together, it would be a nightmare for the rest of the MEAC. He used to jokingly say things to me like, "You gonna let Tammy come in here and take over your team." I would often overhear chatter about whose team we would be. Some people figured that since she was older that this was going to be her team right off the bat. Tammy's mother had also played for Morgan, so some thought this would give her an upper hand, especially since she just came off of a successful couple of seasons in junior college.

When you're the main focus of a team, you encounter a lot of attention. Some of that attention breeds jealousy. I felt like Tammy believed she had to compete with me. I never really paid it any mind but I'd hear people hating on me about the fact that I had the green light to do whatever I wanted. At the end of the day numbers don't lie. My response to the hate was always, "You shouldn't get mad, you should just get buckets!" That was exactly what I continued to do.

We also had a tougher schedule and teams would be prepared for us now. Every team we played focused their defense on me. I saw a lot of double teams, box and 1s, traps, and presses. I also became a focal point in the media. Before, during, and after games I'd be expected to do radio and newspaper interviews or see unsolicited stories in the local newspaper's sports section. I'd see my picture followed by witty titles that involved my nickname, along with descriptions of my performance from that past game. I'd feel honored and though I may have earned it, it still was pretty shocking to me.

We had a better team on paper than my freshman year, but we didn't seem to possess the same heart. Freshman year we always played hard, were scrappy, and just went all out. Following that season we seemed to lack the same will to win.

Coach Batchelor of UMES still had a salty taste in his mouth after I had hit that game winner the year before. He challenged us to play our first game of the season in their gym as he was seeking revenge in a do-over. We accepted the challenge and following the game, the summary read as follows: "Morgan State sophomore guard Corin Adams started off in much the same way she ended last season, as the team's leading scorer and rebounder. The 5-foot-6 Brooklyn, N.Y., native scored a career-high 23 points, including three treys, grabbed a team-high six rebounds and added three steals to lead visiting Morgan State to a 77-71 non-conference victory over Mid-Eastern Athletic Conference foe, the University of Maryland Eastern Shore (UMES). The win, which didn't count toward the league standings, was the third straight over UMES and marked the Lady Bears first back-to-back season opening wins, since the '83-'84 season."

As sweet as that felt, the glory was short-lived as we proceeded to lose our next two. I was anxious to get back on the winning side of things. Before certain games I get this indescribable feeling that I know that I'm going to have one of those games, meaning either a high scoring night or just an overall great game. In the warm up line before the game vs North Carolina Central, I barely missed. Most hoopers will tell you if you don't miss in the warm-up line, you're either going to miss every shot or not miss any at all.

The next morning the sports story read, "Coming off of back-to-back heartbreaking four-point losses last weekend at the

Longwood Classic, the Lady Bears were eager to return home for their home-opener against North Carolina Central (NCCU) and get back in the win column. Morgan State fans were not disappointed, as they witnessed sophomore guard Corin Adams record the school's first triple-double. Adams scored 11 points, dished out 10 assists and tied the school mark for steals with 11. Morgan State Coach Beasley, while proud of Adams' accomplishment, said he was disappointed in Adams' lack of second half scoring. 'Those are numbers that are good for her personally, but I'm disappointed that she had 11 points at the end of the first half and ended the game with 11 points,' said Beasley. 'She's not where I want her to be—a scoring machine. To not score any points in the second half is disappointing.'"

This was the story of my life sophomore year. No matter what I accomplished, how many assists I had, or even if we won, Beas wasn't satisfied unless it was accompanied by a 25+ point night. He wanted me to be the Player of the Week in the conference as often as possible, so not scoring a ton of points was unacceptable. In the MEAC, the other statistical columns didn't get the accolades that points did. To Beas the other aspects of my game were good, but all he wanted to see was "BANG!" He wanted me to have that killer instinct every time I stepped on the court.

In the early part of the campaign, we were scheduled to play St. John's University in Queens, NY. I was looking forward to that game all season as I was going to get another opportunity to play in front of my friends and family. Just thinking about the thrill of performing well in front of them and helping my team pull the upset excited me.

There we were. A couple of days before New Year's, I was back in my hometown, and it was game day. My adrenaline was rushing and I was in the zone. Right before tip-off I looked around the gym, saw my friends and family, and got extremely nervous. As soon as the ref threw that ball up in the air, my nightmare began. I kept thinking to myself, "Let's go, you can't let them down." I missed my first three shots and I was 3-4 from the free throw line. It wasn't long before St. John's began to break the game wide open. Not only was I missing, but I was also forcing up bad shots.

I began to focus on how badly I was playing and that I was embarrassing myself in front of my friends and family. It showed on my face and in my play. I'm a very emotional player. Early in my career if I felt I wasn't playing well, you could read it on my face and in my body language. Coach Clarke helped me get out of that habit, but after the first media timeout, I definitely had the pout face going. Everyone saw it including Beas, so he sat me down for a while.

During my career at Morgan, unless I was in foul trouble or we were winning by a ton, I played the whole game. When Beas took me out I became even more frustrated. Eventually he put me back in and I missed my next four shots. The game was one of the best offensive showings for St. John's that season as they set season-highs with 97 points, 37 field goals made, 14 3-point field goals made, a 56.1 shooting percentage and 23 assists. I finished the game 5-26 with 13 points, 4 rebounds, and was upset at myself for the way I played. I was embarrassed, to say the least. Whenever my team loses a game I blame myself and think about all the things I did wrong.

Following the game I didn't want to see anybody. Of course, I went to speak with my family and friends, but I kept the conversation and interactions brief. I'm a sore loser and everyone close to me knew it. I literally cried the whole way back to

Baltimore. While talking to Lane and Charisma, I tried to keep it together, but I kept replaying the game in my head. I even questioned my ability to compete with the bigger schools. St. John's was in the Big East, which was one of the best conferences in basketball at that time, so that win would've been huge for our team.

Our next game was three days later and we lost again. I had another terrible night. This was the first game of the New Year and it was starting off badly. For the next couple of weeks, I lived in the gym. We were in winter break at this time. Classes weren't starting for another three weeks, so I had a lot of time on my hands. Our next game was against Coppin, so I had to get it together fast! Fortunately we beat Coppin and ended their regular season streak of fourteen straight wins. I finished that game with 18 points, 7 rebounds and 6 assists. Beas loved the fact that we were the ones to end their conference streak and regular season streak. He felt as if we had their number and I'm sure they felt that way too.

During that game I finally had the killer instinct that Beas wanted me to have. Game after game I emerged as the scoring machine he was looking for. I scored twenty against NCA&T, twenty-seven against Norfolk St, and twenty-five against Bethune. I always had the ability to create for myself and others, but now it was a matter of being consistent, adjusting to defenses, and knowing when to shoot and when to pass.

Through February we put together a seven game win streak. During that streak (a team record), I averaged 17.7 points a game. The streak ended when we lost to Coppin and Del. St. before starting preparation for the MEAC tourney. We entered the tournament as the sixth seed and defeated 11th seeded Norfolk St. This improved our record to 19-10 on the season, thus setting the school record for victories on the Division I level, surpassing the previous year's mark of eighteen wins. It was also the second consecutive year that Morgan won its first MEAC tournament game since 1996-2000. Unfortunately in the next round Del. beat us by 20+ and eliminated us for the second year in a row.

Although our season didn't end quite like we wanted it to, I actually exceeded my expectations. I averaged 16.6 points, 5.1 rebounds, 4.3 assists, and 4 steals a game. I earned Team MVP, Morgan State University's Female Athlete of the Year, MEAC Conference First Team, and MEAC Defensive Player of the Year, made both the Longwood All-Tournament Team and the VCU All-Tournament Team, achieved the first triple double in school history, was 3rd in the Nation (NCAA) in steals, and led the MEAC Conference in assists and steals. With all of those accomplishments, my sophomore season proved to be a great stepping stone for what was ahead of me.

# Chapter 15
# Becoming Legendary

*Whenever opportunity presents itself, take advantage!*
*#Tinyism*

Entering my junior season, I wanted to be as focused as possible. The coaching staff named Phyli and me captains, and that meant I had to become a better leader. Unfortunately, on the court I was the quiet type. I never talked trash, spoke to anyone, or did any of that animated stuff that most players do. I didn't mind being a leader, but I like to do so by example. On the court, I'd tune out everyone, focus on the game and not say a word. The coaching staff tried their best to break me out of this habit, but I didn't become a vocal player until I became a pro. Coach Clarke did her best to help me improve in this regard.

The coaching staff helped me by giving me more responsibility and holding me accountable. One of the major responsibilities I was given was being an SAAC representative for our team along with my teammate, Aaries. SAAC was the Student Athletic Advisory Committee. SAAC was made up of student-athletes who provided insight on the current experiences at their schools. Every athletic team at Morgan chose two representatives. We'd meet to talk about events we were planning, fundraising, community service, and to ensure support at the different sporting events. I also volunteered to host multiple events. One of my favorite events to host was the Athlete Auction. It was a fundraising event where we auctioned off athletes from the different teams. The bidder would pay to share a date with the athlete, with food and drinks provided. I kind of felt like a pimp, but the Athlete Auction was fun. Once I got that mic in my hands, I came alive and so did the event. We raised a lot of money and it was a good time for everyone present.

My personal goals that season were to break into the top five all-time in three key statistics; points, assists, and steals. Focusing on the existing records before the season started enabled me to calculate what I needed to do per game to make it into the top five in each statistical category. People viewed me as one of the best female basketball players to play at Morgan, so I wanted my resume to reflect that. If I was in the top five by the end of my junior year, I could strive to become number one in each of those categories by the end of my senior season. If I was able to double my current numbers at the end of my sophomore year, I would place in the top ten in every offensive statistic. I often thought, "Your jersey number is number one, so why not be number one?" At the end of the day, I didn't want to be good, I wanted to be great!

We won our first game of my third season for the third year in a row, and also won our first tournament. That year, we won the UNC-Asheville tournament. We beat William and Mary in the first game and Fairfield in the championship. I received all-tournament team honors, and was named the tournament MVP. We then beat

North Carolina Central and headed to our next tournament at Marshall, The Fifth Third Classic. We lost the first game by two, and won the consolation game by six. Despite being the third place team, I made the all-tournament team and also scored my 1000th point.

Through our first ten games we had only lost that one game in the Classic. I found myself moving up in all of the all-time leading positions. After starting 9-1, we became a bit inconsistent. We went .500 all the way up until the MEAC tournament. Every game, I was getting closer to my goals of becoming Morgan's all-time leader in points, steals, and assists. I also ended up improving in every category except rebounds and steals. I averaged 18.2 points, 4.4 rebounds, 4.3 assists, and 3.5 steals, while my field goal, free throw, and three point percentages also increased. Once again, I earned Team MVP, MEAC Conference First Team, UNC-Asheville All-Tournament Team, UNC-Asheville Tournament MVP, Marshall/ Fifth Third Classic All-Tournament Team, WBCA Player of the Month Honorable Mention (for December), and I was top five in the nation in steals (fourth). I finished first all time in assists, second all time in points, and third all time in steals. Being in these positions at the end of my junior year paved the way for me to truly be viewed as the best female player at Morgan. Being in the top three in all statistical categories meant that I could well end up in first in these categories and make my mark in the history books.

During my junior year I had one of, if not the best, games of my Morgan career. In the 2008-2009 season, the MEAC began to get a lot more exposure and attention. That season they began to play a few games on ESPNU. Up until that point, I had never played in a nationally televised game. On February 23, 2009, I was in a zone like no other! We were on the road at Hampton. Between coming off a loss versus Howard, and having my friends and family around the nation tuned in, I had to make sure I killed. I scored a career high thirty-two points (eighteen in the first half), shot eleven for nineteen, and also dished out seven assists, which helped me move into number one all-time in assists. That Hampton game is one of my most memorable moments as a Lady Bear. I still watch film from that game to this day. Whenever I'm feeling down or need to shake off a slump, I pop that tape in. Between the announcers showing me so much love and seeing exactly what I'm capable of, it always does the trick and gets me back on track.

I dominated the MEAC conference that year and felt that I should've been named Player of The Year that season. I was second in the Conference in points, first in assists, and second in steals. The person who finished ahead of me in points was only ahead by 1.2 points and was behind me by .3 steals. I felt like I got snubbed, and that feeling gave me the motivation to finish off my career with a vengeance. From that day forward, my newest goal became to be named player of the year my senior season!

I was still doing great academically. I made the Dean's list every semester since freshman year. Through my last semester of my junior year I only had one C on my transcript. Everything else was A's and B's. Unfortunately, I had to drop anatomy during one of my semesters and that left me short a few credits. I had to make up that class, plus thirty more credits, and complete my student teaching to fulfill all my requirements for graduation. In college, there are advisors assigned to keep you on track. With my hectic schedule, I rarely had the opportunity to talk to mine. I spoke to my advisor, Dr. Thomas, only when it was time to create my schedule. Dr. Thomas was a cool guy and we had a good relationship. He also taught a couple of the Phys. Ed. classes at

Morgan. He kept up with what I was doing on the court and I kept up with the work he assigned off the court. He liked the fact that I made it a priority to handle my business the same on and off the court, but I don't think he was aware of my plans to graduate in only four years. Dr. Thomas failed to advise me of some very vital information about my final two semesters that could have very well ruined my dreams of playing professionally.

During the last two semesters of school, all education majors have to student teach and take a certification test. In the fall semester you teach twice a week and in the spring semester you teach every day of the week. After my junior year, I had about seven or eight more classes to take. Before speaking to Dr. Thomas about student teaching, I just figured I could split it down the middle and take four classes each semester; a fairly light schedule for me. After learning about student teaching, however, things got scary for me. Dr. Thomas burst my bubble of having a light senior year. After talking to him, things went from an easy road to graduation, to a seemingly impossible one.

If I was student teaching eight to four every day, there would be no time to attend classes during the day, and with team practices at night, there wouldn't be much time for night classes either. I didn't want to be here another semester because that would delay me from playing professional basketball. I had thought to take as many classes as possible on campus during the summer, but Morgan didn't offer the classes I needed during then. I decided to meet with the head of the physical education department to see just what could be done. I also had to make up the anatomy class I had dropped, plus take the other seven or eight classes. After stressing for a couple days, we came up with a plan.

In retrospect, I don't know how I did it, but once I put my

mind to something I get it done! First I had to take the anatomy class off-campus at a nearby community college because it wasn't offered in the summer at Morgan. Taking the class off-campus meant I'd have to pay for it out of pocket, because my scholarship was only good at Morgan. I also had to come up with room and board as it wasn't in the women's basketball budget to allow players to stay in the summer. I had to talk to the people in charge hoping that they would help me out which seemed like an impossible mission. The head of the hospitality department didn't really know who I was or seem to care about my situation. All he knew was that I was asking for free room and board for the summer. It took a lot of back and forth, as well as calling in a couple favors for people to vouch for me. In the end I was granted housing for the summer, but no meal plan. The plan for the summer was to get anatomy and one other class out of the way. The other class I needed was kinesiology, which wasn't offered during either the summer or the fall semester at Morgan. My only option was to try and get a kinesiology teacher to grant me independent study access in the summer. I've learned that most teachers would be unwilling to do an independent study in the summer unless there was a big group of kids. Luckily for me, my strength and conditioning coach, Coach K, was one of the kinesiology teachers. Despite some begging, he was initially turning me down because the strength and conditioning coaches focus on working with the football team during the summer. We ultimately worked it out, where I'd act as his assistant and he'd teach me in a hands-on way while conducting workouts. He'd explain things to me, give me readings to do, and test me based on what I was taught.

I found some unlimited leagues in Maryland, but nothing like what I was used to in NY. Between my hectic schedule and doubting the competition, I didn't even bother. The men's basketball team made their student athletes stay during the summer sessions to catch up on classes and to work out. They had a very cool coaching staff and I got cool with all of them. One in particular was Coach Sam Brand. Sam was one of the best shooters in Morgan history. No matter when or where he shot the ball, you just automatically assumed it was going in. He had graduated from Morgan a couple years before. Sam was responsible for the player development of the men's team. I had worked out with him and Reg a few times before. I'd watch him conduct a workout and since he knew how much I loved the game, he'd ask me if I wanted to jump in. I didn't always join in, because although I was a great player, I lacked basic fundamentals and the discipline to perform most drills. I felt as though I'd mess up their workouts or worse, embarrass myself. No one had ever taken the time to teach me the fundamentals of the game. All the coaches I had throughout my career just let me be myself, so I was ignorant to the basics. My skill and talent had come from watching my favorite players, teaching myself, and playing with the boys.

Once I settled in for the summer and had my schedule planned out, I asked Sam if he'd mind if I worked out with them. Of course he said that he'd love to have me. I warned him right off the bat that he'd have to be patient with me. He said "Tiny, when I'm done with y'all, both you and Reg are going to be the Players of the Year. Your game is going to improve like crazy." I was excited and ready to work. Being named player of the year was my ultimate goal, so I couldn't wait. Before long, I really thought I was a Morgan State Bear as opposed to a Lady Bear. I spent my whole summer in the gym with Sam and the guys. I was in the weight room with them every day, open gym, and individuals. Sometimes at night it would just be me, Sam, and Reg working on any and everything. It was hard to break a lot of my bad habits, but eventually I learned the right way to do things.

After learning fundamentals like coming off screens, turning into shots off my inside foot, creating space, and the proper way to do a pull up jumper, the game became so much easier for me. I became a better shooter and a smarter basketball player. I understood timing, eliminating extra movements before shots, and was even out there doing euro-steps. I still use the very same drills and pointers Sam taught me that summer. Without him I wouldn't be half of the player I am today. He might not think so, but I owe Sam a lot!

# Chapter 16
## Senior Year

*Decision making is one of the most important parts*
*of being successful!*
*#Tinyism*

The summer went by extremely fast due to my busy schedule. I got a good night's sleep every night because of the simple fact that I always passed out. My fatigue led to a scary moment one night. I had just gotten in from a long day. My plan was to shower and go right to sleep. I got the bathroom nice and steamy and as I entered the shower, I fainted. I re-gained consciousness and I called my bro, Deezy. We immediately went to the emergency room. The doctor's in the ER said the cause was exhaustion and/or dehydration. They gave me some prescriptions and I ended up staying with Deezy that night to be safe.

That summer I bought a car, so whenever I had free time, I'd take short road trips to see friends or family. I took trips to Georgetown in DC to see Kenya and to work out with her and her team. I'd also go see Charisma at Temple or go chill with my family members in Bowie, MD. I passed my anatomy class with a C and I got an A in my independent study kinesiology class with Coach K. Anatomy was only the second C on my transcript, but it is one of the toughest classes to take so I was okay with that. I actually worked harder for that C than any A on my transcript. Learning the ins and outs of the human body was very challenging. I should have studied a lot more than I did, but nonetheless I passed and put myself one step closer to graduation.

I also made time for one other person close to me, Kareem Hayes. "Reemo" was the only guy up until this day that I opened up to and let into my life after Jeff. There were other guys throughout my Morgan career that tried to elevate our relationship to more than friends, but they didn't make the cut. I wasn't doing it on purpose, but they just couldn't make it past that two week period without turning me off. If they weren't ambitious, sports-minded, decent at basketball, able to hold a conversation, or mentioned sex too often, I simply friend-zoned them. I always think about the long run when it comes to my boos, so if I didn't think they were compatible, I wasn't going to waste my time. The DMV area was also ranked #1 when it came to transmitting HIV/AIDS, so I wasn't with it. Reemo worked at Morgan when I first met him. Right now he's currently pursuing his Bachelor's degree in Sports Administration there.

I met him right after my junior season. Once the basketball season at Morgan is over, intramurals take place. At one point intramurals were more popular than our Lady Bears' games. The crowds were either larger or relatively the same. Most of the time, the seniors of the men's football and basketball teams would play, along with the regular students that hooped at Morgan. My junior year I tried to play, but the athletic department didn't let me due to fear of injury. Since I couldn't play, I ended up coaching the team I was supposed to play on. My team was very talented and lost in a very close game in the finals. One of our games was held in the main gym (the field house) and after our team won everyone headed to the auxiliary gym to watch the other games. Reemo was at my game and when we all went to the gym, I saw him with one of my homeboys from the football team, Kayo Bracey. He and Kayo played on the same semi-pro football team together. Kayo was either playing or going to support his old football teammates. The football team usually had their own team in the league. I saw Reemo leaving with him in the gym, and I thought, "Damn who's that? He's cute but I've never seen him before."

On the way to the auxiliary gym we walked through the student center to socialize, where I saw Kayo and Reemo at the steps. Kayo and I had this thing we'd do every time we saw one another. It wasn't a hand shake, but whoever saw the other person first would try to fake dunk on them and scream, "Ahhh!" like we were Shaq. I saw Kayo and Reemo talking to some friends, so I snuck up and dunked on him. We shook hands, talked a little, and then he introduced me to Reemo. Reemo asked if I was about to coach again. I said no and joked that I was going to scout to prepare for our next couple games. We laughed and he said he wished he could play for me and wished me luck the rest of the season.

At that time, BlackBerry phones were very popular. Immediately after our short conversation, my BBM went off. BBM is a messaging service for all BlackBerry users. When I received the message, Reemo pulled out his BlackBerry and said, "Ah, you know you gotta give me your BBM now!" From that point on, I looked forward to talking to him every day. I was under the impression that he attended Morgan, and I was excited to get to know him better. After a couple weeks of great conversations and hanging out, I was feeling him a lot; he was exactly what I looked for in a potential boo. He was handsome, athletic, loved basketball, had a car, and all the girls wanted him. Prior to the bomb he dropped on me, I had met his son, Kamren. Seeing him with Kamren made me adore him even more. At the time I wasn't sure about where things would lead, so I wasn't really worried about baby momma drama or being a potential stepmother. I was just going with the flow at that moment.

After the month passed, he told me he was feeling me a lot also, but there was something he needed to tell. Whenever someone says they have something to tell me, I automatically expect the worst. After thinking of a million and one things it could have been, he told me that there were things I didn't know about him and he wanted to be man enough to tell me. Reemo told me he actually had two kids, was twenty-eight years old, and that he didn't attend Morgan, but actually worked there. Prior to this outpouring of information, we talked about everything, or so I had thought. At that time I was a twenty-year-old college student without a care in the world except school and basketball. That information was dropped on me like an atomic bomb. I honestly thought we were the same age, or he was a couple years older than me at the most, certainly not eight years older and not with two kids.

That's all I thought about day and night. I wasn't mature enough to deal with these things. The situation put pressure on me and if I wanted things to continue I'd have to change how I behaved. After he told me, I began to act a little differently. He noticed this and said he would respect whatever decision I made. He didn't want to lose me, because he liked the bond we had and it would be hard to just let me go.

We tried to continue as just friends because I wasn't really comfortable with the whole sugar daddy/stepmom thing, but I was miserable and I didn't want to be just friends. We weren't in a relationship, but we both knew what was between us. We were number ones to each other, always there for one another, and rarely putting anyone before the other. Throughout my last two years at Morgan, Reemo was there for me physically and emotionally. No matter what, he'll always be dear to me, it's just a matter of seeing if we can be that couple we always wanted to be.

After the summer, I had two weeks to chill until the fall semester started back up. I returned to Morgan knowing I had to take the maximum number of classes possible. Usually the maximum number of credits you're allowed to take per semester is twenty. That semester I had to get a waiver that would allow me to take twenty-three! Just imagine my schedule during that semester. I had preseason workouts, eight classes, student teaching twice a week, practice, weight lifting, individuals, and games. A typical day for me was waking up at 6 a.m. for workouts or to be on my way to student teaching for a couple hours. After that I had classes, individual workouts, practice, and sometimes a night class. I'd try to squeeze time in to eat, sleep, study and do homework. Every decision I made was vital because my graduation depended on it. If I didn't pass each of those classes, I'd have to take them over the next year and I couldn't afford that. In order to reach my goals and turn enough heads to go pro, I had to have an outstanding season.

Prior to kicking off my senior season, I received some pre-season honors. The coaches and sports information staff of the MEAC voted me to the pre-season first team, and I was crowned the MEAC's pre-season player of the year. I was honored to receive that accolade. It meant that my talents and hard work didn't go unnoticed. Between my hectic schedule and the preseason honors, I sort of felt like the pressure was on. I had a lot to prove, so time management and focus was very important. Although I had a lot of classes, they were fairly easy to me. They were mostly education and physical education classes. I had racquetball, swimming, first aid, and CPR, which really just required participation. I also had teaching classes that outlined things like child psychology and lesson planning. The classes were pretty easy but they still required my focus. At the same time it was also a lot of knowledge to take in and remember.

After checking in with Dr. Thomas, I learned I had to also take a speech proficiency test, writing proficiency test, and pass a senior compilation exam. The proficiency tests were a piece of cake, but the senior comp was a recap of all the things I learned since freshman year. I may have gotten A's and B's in all of those classes, but that didn't mean that I remembered all the information. I didn't save all of my notes so I knew that comp test was going to be challenging. I spoke with some of my fellow classmates, old teachers, and alumni students to help me get an idea of what the test was going to include. Once I touched bases with them, I did my best to prepare. Ultimately I passed, but I felt like the test was a bit unfair. They had a couple review classes to tell us what would be on the test, but there were several things being reviewed that we hadn't actually learned.

Midway through the semester it was time to tip-off the season and this time we lost our first game to UNC Greensboro in their gym. I entered the game exhausted and stressed from all that was going on. Basketball has always been my outlet to relieve stress and frustration, so I had been looking forward to this game since preseason. Game day is when I let out everything negative in me. I store all negativity mentally and take it out against my opponents. To kick the season off, I erupted for thirty-one points and tied their school's gym record for most points scored there in a game. Though we lost by seventeen, I still felt good about the game. Teams usually played box one on me or doubled-teamed me. Since Reg and I were both seeing those same defenses, Sam taught us ways to beat them by ourselves and our teammates. He taught us how to read the defense and use space to our advantage.

A week after that game, I had another homecoming game vs. a Big East school in Seton Hall. This was another game I looked forward to because I'd have all of my family and friends in attendance. Seton Hall was hosting a tournament to kick their season off. Like most schools who host tournaments, they picked us to play against in the first game because they felt we'd be the easier team to beat to advance to the championship game. My mother and grandmother were in attendance, but I had all of my big homies from St. John's Rec in attendance too, including my big sis, Stass. The next day the story read, "Corin Adams stepped to the charity stripe with 7.7 seconds remaining in the game and calmly knocked down two free throws to clinch Morgan's 58-55 non-conference victory over host Seton Hall in the opener of the Anaconda Sports 'The Rock' Seton Hall Basketball Classic on Friday evening at Walsh Gymnasium. The victory, which spoiled the Pirates' home opener and gave them their first loss of the season, was Morgan's first over Seton Hall in three meetings and its second over a BIG EAST opponent. Adams' free throws gave her a game-high 17 points."

The championship game was against VCU. We had been 0-2 against them in my previous games played, so we really wanted to win this one. Unfortunately though, we lost in double OT. I made the Seton Hall All-Tournament team, but I would've preferred to take the trophy back to Morgan.

Fourteen of our first fifteen games were on the road, so we did a lot of traveling, which was sort of draining. In addition to being tired I also had to make sure I handled business with my teachers and my student teaching mentor. We often left on Friday to travel to games so I'd miss class and student teaching. I worked it out with my teachers prior to leaving and also made sure any day I missed, I made up immediately.

We had a tough non-conference season, winning only three of eleven. Each game was close, but we just couldn't get over the hump. Going into the conference schedule we were on a five game losing streak, including an OT loss to Brown University in the Brown Classic. By the time conference games started we were on winter break and I was a little depressed. Basketball was supposed to cheer me up, but since we were losing I wasn't in my happy place.

When we came back from our last tournament at St. Peter's, where we lost both games, I went right to the gym. We got back at about 2 a.m. and I just dropped my stuff and went right to the gym. I set my music up and I was in there for hours. It was my senior year, so I knew it would be my last time playing these teams. From that point on, I had to approach every game like it was my last, because in a sense it was.

Conference play started at the beginning of January against Coppin, as usual. Coppin had built a new arena to host their games. A new gym was long overdue, and luckily for us we were going to be the first team they played there. Usually our games were double headers but the men's schedule had them playing Coppin at a later date. We made a pact with the men's team that we would win both games and make a bold statement that their new gym was our new gym! Since it was our rival school it was only fitting that we added some motivation to the game.

The new gym was amazing. It had a replay screen, state of the art bleachers, and was a place that every hooper would love to play. We broke our five game losing streak and beat them by eleven. I scored a career high five-three pointers and ended with twenty-five points along with five rebounds, and five assists. It was just what I needed to give me my mojo back. We won eight of the next nine games and I was again playing like the MEAC player of the year. Our only loss during that nine game stretch came against Hampton, who would go on to win the championship that year. We played them on ESPNU, lost 74-37 and I only scored nine points, which proved to be a season low. As Coach Clarke and Coach Beas always told me, the team goes as I go!

After Hampton we played South Carolina St. away. The next game came with a story that read, "Corin Adams quickly rebounded from her season-low nine-point performance Monday night at Hampton and scored 23 of her game high and career-tying 32 points in the first half to lead four Morgan State players in double figures in scoring. Adams finished the game shooting 11-of-19 from the field, including 4-of-7 from three-point range. Adams, who connected on her first three attempts from three-point range, finished the first half going 4-for-5 from beyond the arc. Adams also added a team-high five assists and a team-high three steals for the game, giving her 339 for her career, 17 shy of becoming the school's all-time leader." Even though we fell short of upsetting NCAT, I became the school's all-time leader in points, steals and assists. I tallied four steals in that game to make it official. We fought hard, but didn't have enough in us to win.

I was now the all-time leader in every statistic I had set out to lead. I had ten games to separate myself from the others and make my records nearly unreachable. I added another goal to my list. I wanted to be the first person in Morgan's history to score 2000 points and be the all-time scoring leader in points for both male and female teams. I knew it would be a hard task to achieve, but I needed the motivation. In just seven games I achieved one of my mid-season goals when I scored twenty-one points in a win vs Norfolk State. That game gave me 1994 points, four more than the great Marvin Webster had. With the second goal six points away, and with only three games remaining in my career I wanted to make sure I went out with a bang. I did just that: "Corin Adams, who entered the game as Morgan's all-time leading scorer, male or female, with 1,994 points, surpassing Marvin Webster (1,990), added 18 points to give her 2,012 for her career. Adams also tallied a game-high seven assists, as well as a game-high eight steals in the win vs NCAT. Adams scored on a layup at the 7:39 mark of the first half, giving her the 2,000th point of her career. 'I knew the 2,000 points wouldn't matter if we had lost. I couldn't sleep last night and I was really ready to beat them my last time out,' added Adams. 'I think we are peaking at the right time before the tournament, but we still have Coppin State. This win can put us in sole possession of second-place and hopefully give us an NIT bid.'"

So here it was, my last regular season game as a Morgan State Lady Bear. It was fitting that it was a home game. We were going to play Coppin in the last rival game of the year and it was my senior night. For most basketball players senior night can be a bit emotional. Presentations are made and the school's PA announcer sheds light on all of the achievements and highlights of your career. Everyone's eyes are on you and as the announcer speaks you can't help but reminisce. Throughout that week, the seniors kept making bets about who was going to cry first, and things of that nature. My teammates never saw me show signs of weakness, so they really wanted to see me show some kind of emotion. In addition to being senior night, it was also the day of one of my big tests in Anatomy II. I figured if I stayed focused on the game and my test there would be no way I'd get emotional, because my mind would be elsewhere.

My whole family was there: my mom, grandmother, uncles, aunts, and most importantly my grandfather. In addition, I had my Morgan bros, close friends and Reemo in the stands. This was the first time my grandfather was going to see me play and what better stage than in my gym for senior night? Just as we referred to Coppin's gym as "our gym," Reg and I also called Morgan's gym "our gym." We would tell people they might as well change the name from Hill Field House to "Tiny's and Trigger's Field House".

We had five seniors on the team and of course the announcer saved me for last. After everyone got their introductions, my emotions started to go crazy. Seeing them get their awards and be recognized for all their achievements was a beautiful thing. They hadn't achieved what I had, but had accomplished their own personal goals and were indeed a part of the success we had over the past few years. We did exactly what we set out to do, which was to turn Morgan into a winning program.

The announcer began to just simply say my name. I tried my hardest to fight the tears and remain strong, but I just couldn't do it. As soon as he said, "Tinyyyyyyyy Adamssssss," all the memories came rushing back, and each with plenty of tears to accompany them. They finished announcing my accomplishments, the crowd gave me a standing ovation, my teammates cheered, and my family stood there taking it all in. Right up through pictures and warm-ups, I just couldn't stop crying. Every pic taken that night had me and my cry baby face in it. Thinking about it now, my relentless crying was actually kind of funny. As the game started, I came out hot from three point range and as I continued to score, I still had tears in my eyes. We won the game and I finished with twenty points. Unfortunately the senior night festivities made the game run a little later than planned, so I wasn't able to take my test for anatomy. My family was there so we hung out after the game, but missing that test really worried me. The game was close so I couldn't leave before it ended like I was going to try to. We were up by a lot at one point, but let them come back so there was no way I could leave. Luckily the teacher agreed to let me make it up and I passed.

I was awarded player of the year and MEAC first team prior to the beginning of the MEAC Tournament. I didn't travel with the team ahead of time because I couldn't afford to miss days in school. I missed the banquet where they gave out the awards but they honored me before our first game against Bethune-Cookman. Bethune had beat us earlier that year and I figured the perfect time to get them back would be in the tournament when it really mattered. We played terribly in the first half and ending up falling short. "Morgan State's Corin Adams ended her collegiate career scoring 23 of her game-high 26 points in the second half. Adams, who is the school's all-time scoring leader with 2,058 points, also added a game-high six steals, five rebounds, an assist, and a block against the Lady Wildcats. The Lady Bears (17-13) scored the first four points to start the second half, but still couldn't really get into the flow of the game. Morgan trailed 49-31 with 8:58 to play after a layup by Bugg. That's when Adams, the MEAC Player of the Year, began to take control. She hit a three-pointer and then scored on a layup to get the Lady Bears going. Brittany Dodson scored on a layup and Adams knocked down two free throws, before following with a three-pointer from the right corner to cap off a 12-0 run and bring the Lady Bears within 49-43 with 5:34 to play. Unfortunately, that would be as close as the Lady Bears would get, as Bethune-Cookman responded with a 9-3 run to increase their lead to 12 points at 58-49 with 1:34 left in the contest."

And just like that my career at Morgan was over. I wanted to try and make another run to the championship game and maybe even the NCAA tournament. Our bracket was very winnable, but we didn't handle business the way we should've. I concluded my senior season averaging 19.4 points, 3.5 assists, 3.5 steals, and 4.1 rebounds a game.

Although going further in the tournament and making the NCAA tournament would have for sure boosted my stock, I actually achieved more than enough to turn some heads. My senior year accolades were: MEAC Preseason POTY, MEAC Player of the Year, Full Court Press Top 25 Mid-major Players Honorable Mention, Seton Hall All-Tournament Team, Georgia St Tournament Team, Brown Tournament Team, 1st team All-MEAC, and 2009-10 Eastern College Athletic Conference (ECAC) Division I All-Stars- 2nd team. I became the All-time leader in steals and points, and was the first in Morgan's history to score 2000 points. I became the all-time leader in points for both male and female. I tied the Fleming Gym's (UNC Greensboro) scoring record with thirty-one points. I broke the single season scoring record and record for most games played as a Lady Bear. I also surprisingly finished 9th all-time in rebounds. My total statistics at Morgan were 2058 points, 564 rebounds, 455 assists, and 404 steals. I was featured in Sports Illustrated Faces in the Crowd on 3/22/10. Last but certainly not least, I was a 2010 WNBA prospect.

*The night I scored my 2,000th point*

# Chapter 17
# The "Dawn" of My Pro Career

*Never allow a letdown to become a breakdown.*

*#Tinyism*

The WNBA had been a lifelong dream of mine, but when my senior season was over I was comfortable with the idea of playing overseas. I could build my resume there, then try to make a run at the WNBA. My mind was on Europe, but if an opportunity for the WNBA presented itself, I was going to go for it.

After we lost to Bethune-Cookman, I had many Facebook messages, texts, missed calls, and emails to answer. Around a dozen were from basketball agents interested in signing me. Signing me meant that they would be solely responsible for representing me and my professional career. After speaking with each, I advised them I'd be in touch as soon as possible. Immediately after, I called my mom, of course. My mom is a business woman and always knew better than I did when it came to things like this. We didn't know a thing about where to start, but my mom was a contractor so this was sort of right up her alley.

Since this was the most important decision of my career my mother thought it would be best to meet in person with each of the agents. Unfortunately, I wasn't going to be able to attend any of those meetings. I still had student teaching and classes to finish up, so my mother and grandmother decided they would conduct the meetings to find an agent. They ultimately met with three different agencies. I did want to have some kind of say in the decision, so I researched some of the agents; unfortunately the ones I liked were too busy to meet. I didn't agree with how we opted to select my agent, but time was running out so we had to decide quickly. My mother said if they didn't have time to meet, how could we trust that they'll have time to do right by me and my career? After meeting with the three agents, we exchanged our thoughts. My mother and grandmother let me know who they thought would benefit me the most and why. The WNBA draft was right around the corner, as was the recruiting period for overseas. Although I wanted a little more time to think about things, there wasn't really any time to do so.

We ultimately decided to go with a first-time female agent named Dawn Jackson. We liked her ideas and plans for me, so she was our choice. My only worry was that I would be her first client, which meant she might not have many connections. My mother sold me on the fact that as her first client, I would be all that she focused on. I would also be the one to define her legacy as an agent. I learned that she had played basketball and was a well-respected lawyer. Since she'd been successful in all of her other endeavors, I tried to give her the benefit of the doubt that it wouldn't be any different for her as an agent.

We notified Dawn, she sent the contract, and we made it official. Immediately after signing, she got right to work. She told me her plans, asked me mine, and kept me in the loop as things progressed. I wanted to be informed of what was going on every step of the way. I'm pretty sure we had one of the most unique client-agent relationships, but it worked for us. Dawn's plan was to get me drafted and in a WNBA training camp. She also wanted to get me an endorsement deal. If either of those plans didn't work out, she then would focus solely on getting me overseas. Her goals mirrored mine so everything was cool. Dawn also mirrored my ambition. Although she may have been new in the game, she made sure she contacted everybody she could and pitched me to them all. She was in contact with WNBA general managers, coaches, and scouts. She also contacted the top apparel companies, as well as the up and coming apparel companies looking for sponsorship. Dawn had big dreams for the Tiny Adams brand and the way she worked to try to make it happen sold me on her. I started believing that maybe making it is possible after all.

Prior to the draft, she forwarded me emails from the LA Sparks expressing their interest. Even though they had my one of my favorite WNBA point guards, Becky Hammon, the San Antonio Stars also told her they liked my style of play and wouldn't mind bringing me in for training camp if I wasn't drafted. The dream was being brought to life by Dawn and her will to get things done.

One afternoon after student teaching, my friend Tawanna Cook from NCA&T (aka Tweet) texted me. Tweet and I came into the MEAC the same year and have always battled head to head on the court. She was named rookie of the year over me and won a couple of MEAC championships to go along with it. Over our four year career, we were viewed as two of the top point guards in the conference. We were always competing to beat one or another, but became cool with each other off the court. Tweet had the same hoop dreams I had as far as going pro.

Texting me was her way of showing me love and being happy for her fellow MEAC hooper. She said that she heard I might be the first player from the MEAC to be drafted. She wished me luck and told me to hold it down for the "set" (the set being the group of MEAC guards). Initially while reading her text I was a little confused as to what she was talking about. I read the text three times and kept asking myself, "The first to be drafted? The WNBA?" Of course, after reading the text I was excited, but I also became curious to know what she had heard. I asked what she heard and who she heard it from. Tweet told me that she had just finished talking to her assistant coach who mentioned that I was on a couple of mock WNBA draft boards and was predicted to get drafted in the last round. I had no idea what a mock draft was, and I had no idea where to find that information. She explained it and sent me the link. A mock draft is a prediction of what round players are likely to go and what teams are going to draft them. The information is based on inside scoop or opinions of people who watch and break down the sport for a living. One of the mock drafts had me going in the last round to the New York Liberty. The other one Tweet and her coach saw had me going as the very last pick to the Phoenix Mercury. Either would have been fine with me. I didn't care where I went, I just wanted to make the dream a reality. After seeing the mock draft for myself, I bought into what Dawn was telling me more and more. Before signing with her, I wasn't anywhere on those mock draft boards, so that meant she was indeed sparking people's interests.

After a while I even began to help Dawn get more clients. She had proven to be a great agent who worked hard for her client. I was copied on her every move and I respected her for what she did and how she did it. My basketball network is very large. Anybody affiliated with basketball either knows me or knows of me. A lot of my friends who were also graduating that year and looking to pursue a professional career needed agents so I connected them to Dawn. Dawn had her eyes on other clients she wanted to bring on board, so after getting in contact she used me as a reference to assure them they would be in good hands. I'd talk to them player to player and vouch for Dawn.

With all of this going on, I still had business to handle to make sure I graduated. There would be no professional career if I had to attend another semester. I left Dawn to handle my career and I began to refocus. I had to focus on my anatomy class, student teaching, and also the teacher certification test. The teacher certification test was going to be similar to my senior comp exam, but a little more detailed. The certification test was broken into two parts, Praxis 1 and Praxis 2. Praxis 1 was a general knowledge-based test similar to the SAT. Praxis 2 focused more on my area of study, Physical Ed. Praxis 2 tested everything from anatomy to proper teaching techniques.

I knew April was going to be my month. The WNBA draft, my certification test, and the end of student teaching were all in April. Unfortunately not everything worked out the way I planned. I didn't have any problems with my classes or student teaching, but the main problem was the certification test. I passed Praxis 1 very easily, but Praxis 2 was challenging for me. After doing my best to prepare, I failed Praxis 2 by two freaking points. In each state the required score for aspiring teachers is different. The state of Maryland requires one of the highest scores in the country. Maryland requires their aspiring teachers to score an 85 or more on the certification test to assure that every teacher would be more than qualified. I scored an 83, which was good but not good enough for Maryland. If I had gone to school in any other state, the score would have been accepted.

So now the task at hand was passing the certification test. There were only two more test dates prior to my May 15th graduation date. The education department decided that regardless of your GPA or academic standing, if you didn't pass the certification test they weren't going to allow you to walk or officially graduate. So the pressure was on. The second available date for the test was actually a couple days before graduation, so I wouldn't have been able to get the scores back in time to be allowed to walk. I had one more attempt to take this test and pass it! Like the senior comp exam, some of the questions on that test had never been taught at Morgan. I had taught myself from the study guides I used to prepare. This time around I purchased more study material because I just had to pass. Failing to graduate would not only hurt my future, but I'd feel like I had let a lot of people down. I was going to be the first in my family to graduate from a university. I was at the point where I was willing to do anything to make sure I passed. It was just my luck that I missed the required score again, this time by one measly point! I couldn't believe it! Pulling my scores up and seeing that 84 damn near destroyed me. I called my mom and told her about the situation. She comforted me and then did as she always did, had my back. She said that it was okay to be down about it now, but come that next morning I better do everything I can to assure that no matter what I'd be graduating. My mother said, "You've earned the right to graduate. Don't let this new BS rule about not passing an exam stop you without a fight." After talking to her, I was ready to blow Morgan State up if I didn't get to walk. That's how effective her motivation was to me. I had a cumulative GPA of a 3.5 and juggled basketball all four years. I just pulled off passing a near-impossible two semesters to fulfill all the requirements necessary to graduate. If anyone who deserved to walk across that stage, it was me!

I spoke to the education and physical education departments. They knew and loved me so I was fortunate to convince them to work with me. There were a lot of other students in the same position as me, so it was a hard task at first. I harassed them for weeks and eventually they gave in. The plan was to take that last available test, which was a week or so before graduation. Usually it takes weeks to get the scores back, but they worked it out so they would find out the score the day before graduation. I assured everybody that there was no doubt I was going to pass this time. Third time was the charm. At that point, a weight was lifted off my shoulders.

I bought even more study material and prepared to knock this test out. The way things worked for graduation eligibility was that everyone who was cleared to walk received a card. That card confirmed you were eligible to walk across that stage. When graduation day came, your name was called, you'd walk up to the stage and hand your card to your advisor. You'd then walk across the stage and shake hands with the administration of your department. There were many other students on the same mission, to make sure they got their card. Unfortunately not a lot of them were successful, so I had to keep it a secret that they had done me the favor they did. I even had to fake that I was still in the same boat and equally upset.

I also experienced another let down when I didn't get drafted by the WNBA. The draft was April 8th and the WNBA season started on May 15th—the same day as graduation. In a way not getting drafted was both a gift and a curse. If I had gotten drafted I would have had to choose between handling business at school, attending training camp, and my first game or graduation. I didn't truly care if I got drafted since I had other options, but after witnessing all the work Dawn had done, I got my hopes up. A week before the draft, Dawn spoke to three teams on a regular basis.

The NY Liberty said they knew who I was, but weren't interested. It wasn't a sign of disrespect to my game, but they had just traded for WNBA All-Star Cappie Pondexter. With Cappie on the way, they had no need for a guard. Dawn's pitch to them was the fact I grew up watching them and I was a living legend in NY.

Dawn had sparked some interest with the LA Sparks organization. Up until three days before the draft they were on the fence between me and a couple other guards, but they stopped responding to Dawn and didn't draft me.

Lastly, Dawn spoke to the San Antonio Stars. They said if I didn't get drafted they would invite me to training camp. The week of the draft Dawn had signed a couple other clients who she thought would also be drafted. She attended the draft in NY with one of her clients. Dawn was very optimistic when the day of the draft came. I could hear her energy through the phone. She had high hopes that her clients would get drafted and in return it would be a dream come true for all of us.

Unfortunately, neither of us was drafted and Dawn was very surprised. It hurt her just as much as it hurt us, but all that did was motivate her even more. She was upset, but now it was time to get on the overseas grind. As she began putting things in motion for career possibilities in Europe, I got over the let down and got back to focusing on graduating.

The day came to take the certification test again. When I

walked out of that classroom I knew I passed! I felt like I got a 100. I felt so confident, I even went to Morgan and assured everyone in the education department that I passed and there was nothing to worry about. They expressed how happy they were for me and actually gave me my graduation card. I called my mom and we celebrated on the phone. With only a week until graduation, I began to get mixed feelings. I reflected on my time at Morgan and reminisced on all I experienced there. I had this sort of love-hate relationship with Morgan. I joked with my friends that I was never coming back, but deep down I loved Morgan. Morgan made me into the person I am today and I'm thankful for all the things I experienced there.

Since it was my last couple of days in Baltimore, and I didn't know what was in store for my future, I made sure I enjoyed it. I hung out with my teammates, bros, Reemo, and my fellow "Morganites". I began to pack and one thing I realized was that I had a lot of stuff. After making some tough decisions, I decided to give half of my stuff to my mentee End'dya. I gave End'dya twenty pairs of sneakers, some clothes, hoodies, movies, and anything else I couldn't take back to New York. It killed me at first, but after thinking about it, I felt good. I even gave her some of the high school stuff that I brought with me. She and her mom then gave me something in return. They gave me a personalized trophy that said "World's Greatest Mentor". The feeling I got when they gave me the trophy trumped the one I had when I gave her half of my things. That same night End'dya sent me a picture of her room wall. She had hung up my two jerseys from high school and a poster of me from Morgan. She didn't know it at the time, but that meant everything to me.

A day or two before graduation I had everything all packed up and I was on the phone with my mom. I was telling her how excited I was and that I hoped I made her proud. We had a heart to heart conversation and a great mother-daughter moment. She told me she'd miss me while I played in Europe and that she wished I could be there to help her settle into the new house, as we had recently moved from Brooklyn to Staten Island.

My mother expressed how lonely she'd be, and mentioned she might get a dog. A friend of mine at Morgan knew someone who was breeding puppies, so I told her if she was serious I'd get her one and I could just take it back with me after graduation. She thought about it, said yes, and that next day I went to pick up the new member of our family. After picking him up and taking him to get his necessary shots, it was official. Fittingly, I named our puppy Buckets. Buckets was a three month-old pit bull puppy. He was one of seven in his litter. I could tell he was the sweet punk of the bunch. He had spots all over him like he was mixed with a Dalmatian or something. He was all white and had the cutest little face. Between him being slightly different from the rest and being so darn cute, I decided he would be the one we took home. Since the time he was a puppy, Buckets never really was a loud dog. He rarely ever barked or whined. He just always seemed to be cool and calm, like me. His demeanor was perfect because he had to stay with me in the dorm for a couple days. Also since my mom was driving my car back home after graduation, I'd have to sneak him on the bus home with me. He was little and fortunately for me, well behaved. That allowed me to leave him with friends those couple days on campus while I took care of last minute things. I've grown to love him like he was my first born child, which is what I often call him.

The day after getting Buckets, my family came into town. This was also the day I received my scores from the certification test and you wouldn't believe it—I had failed again, this time by three points. I was heartbroken. I already had my card though, so I was not going to give it back. Once I found out, I avoided all of the administration. I couldn't take the chance of them telling me I couldn't walk. My family had just arrived in town and tomorrow was graduation. They were going to have to escort me off campus if anything, because I was walking across that stage! I carried on as if I passed. I attended graduation rehearsal, went out to celebrate and had a wonderful night.

Graduation Day came and went and it was great. My family was happy and I was happy. Even though they gave me a side eye on the stage, the people in the education department were happy for me. Walking across that stage felt amazing and symbolized the close of one chapter and the opening of another. After taking pictures and taking it all in, I went out to eat with my family and said one last goodbye to Morgan. I had a great run, but now it was time to prepare to start living out my dream as a professional basketball player. At least, that's what I thought.

*Class of 2010*

# Chapter 18
# Senior Year: Tiny Setback #3

*Never burn bridges, especially if you can't swim.*
*#Tinyism*

After graduating cum laude and getting ready to leave Baltimore for good, I had plans of going home for a few days and then spending the summer in Atlanta. Dawn had gotten word of a new basketball league that would serve as a developmental league for the WNBA. The name of the league was the WUSBA. The Women's United States Basketball Association was founded by Duane Jenkins. The league was based in Atlanta and had teams all over Georgia, as well as other states in the south. The inaugural season was going to be 2010, and Dawn thought it would be a good idea if I played.

Jenkins had appointed Dawn the Director of Player Personnel at the time, so she was responsible for getting players and making sure the rosters were well equipped with talent. Since she was responsible for getting players, it was only right that her clients were among them. For Dawn this was a perfect opportunity. Not only could she get her clients jobs for the summer, but it also gave her the opportunity to meet more potential clients. Since this was Dawn's first year dealing with the women's basketball world, I helped her staff the teams. Playing summer ball in NY for prizes like trophies and sweats didn't compare to the WUSBA at all, so it was easy to convince fellow New Yorkers to play. The WUSBA would pay $300 a week, provide housing, and have top notch competition. Since Atlanta was the home squad and one of the best locations in the league, I asked Dawn to put me on that team. She did so and I gave her the names of the best hoopers from New York to also place on the team. Once our Atlanta roster was full, we jokingly began calling it the NY team. I gave her names of other hoopers from NY, girls that had just graduated from college, and girls just looking to get their foot in the professional basketball door. Training camp for the league was set to start around May 17th, and the season was supposed to run until August. I had some of my closest friends with me, like Stass and Kimbo. We were excited because we had plans to win the league, and we'd be in Atlanta all summer. Since this was going to be my warm up for the overseas season, I made arrangements not be home again until May of 2011. Since I wasn't going to be home, I told my usual summer job that I wasn't going to be able to work, and I also sold my car. Paying for insurance and trying to find somewhere to store it while I was away seemed like too much of a hassle.

Little did I know that events would turn out to be the complete opposite of what I expected. Suddenly the report date for training camp of the WUSBA was postponed and soon after, the league as a whole was postponed. The WUSBA ended up folding, and all hell broke loose. Prior to the league being postponed, I had helped Dawn sign some twenty to thirty players. Those players expected their summers to be accounted for, so they passed on jobs, school, vacations, and many other things. I felt terrible. Not only did I feel bad because I was experiencing another setback, but I also felt bad because I ruined a lot of peoples' summers. It wasn't my fault, but I got them involved so felt like I was to blame for the mishap. Some people had already made their travel arrangements to get to their respective locations. They booked flight, train, and bus tickets that couldn't be refunded. Jenkins and the WUSBA caught a lot of heat. From 2010-2012, Jenkins tried to get the league up and running time and again, but each time he tried there would be different obstacles in his way. Either he didn't have enough players, proper housing, air conditioned gyms, or enough coaches. Some people went as far as trying to sue him and some even submitted stories to the newspapers calling him a fraud.

The day after the league folded, I received an unexpected email from Dawn. The email was sent to all of her clients and was short and right to the point. Dawn stated she could no longer represent us because she didn't have money to pay her FIBA license dues. This came as a shock to me because I was under the impression that she was a certified agent. I didn't know that being WNBA and FIBA certified were not the same. I later learned that she was banking on her salary from Jenkins and the WUSBA to pay for her FIBA dues. All the hard work she did and everything she had set up for me was out the door. Here it was not even a week after graduation and it seemed like everything was going downhill for me.

I understand that it wasn't her fault, but I blamed her for the way my professional career started. Actually, I blamed her, my mom, and grandmother. Sh**, I blamed everybody! I was heartbroken. My dream was shattering right before my eyes. I thought I would have been better off had I signed with another, more experienced and secure agent. I now had no job, no agent, no idea what to do, and I even had no car.

I contacted the other agents I had turned down, but you can imagine how that went. Most of them didn't even respond, which was their way of saying "Don't come running back to us now." The timing of this was terrible, as it was right in the middle of the recruiting period for overseas teams. Dawn was the only one that had my film and other things needed when trying to draw interest from teams. I harassed her to try and get everything back. In the beginning she wasn't taking my calls or emails, so it was very frustrating. The fact that she was ignoring me, made me dislike her even more at the time. "First you leave me out to dry and now you don't want to give me my stuff back?!" She finally responded and mailed me my things. Dawn was also the only one who knew who had been interested in me. I tried to get that information, but I was unsuccessful. I had no one in my corner or any resources with which to pick up where she had left off. It took me some time to get over the hurt, but we now keep in contact via Facebook. I'm not one to hold grudges, it's just when it comes to something I'm very passionate about it takes me a little longer to get over it. Whenever we speak, Dawn tells me she's proud of me and always knew I'd become the person and player I am now. Everything happens for a reason!

Since I missed summer ball the previous year, there was no way I was going to miss it this summer, too. I had to be prepared and stay in game shape in case I did get that call. I continued working out and playing in every tournament I could. The whole issue opened my eyes to the fact that this professional basketball thing isn't guaranteed, so it was important that I focus on my plan

B, teaching. I decided to register and take the Praxis 2 again, but this time in New York. I planned to take the test at the end of July, so that gave me about two months to prepare. I didn't know what was next for me basketball-wise, so come September I wanted to at least be able to live out my second dream. Since I didn't pass the certification test any of the three times I took it in Maryland, I never officially graduated from Morgan State. I had no degree, which was a requirement when applying for a job in the education field.

I spent a lot of my time networking to try and find an agent or any kind of contact that could possibly help me get overseas. I eventually got in touch with someone I had known for a while, but didn't know was involved with the professional basketball world, Chris Mooney. He was very close to WNBA star Epiphanny Prince and her coach Apache from Exodus. He later became Epiphanny's manager. In addition to making sure her every need was met, he also coached college basketball at Farmingdale State University in Long Island. He also served as a middle man for players, agents, and coaches. He had a large basketball network and knew where the talented players were. Mooney always liked my game and how I carried myself. He was going to connect me with a well-known agent he knew that was going to take care of me, Athos Antoniou from Cyprus with top notch clients and contacts. Mooney assured me I was in good hands and based on the research I did on Athos, I believed him.

Throughout the summer Mooney and Athos contacted me about interests and possibilities but nothing came through. It was always between me and either a WNBA player or college player from a top conference. As soon as I found out who the competition was, I'd look them up and their stats were never as good as mine. It seemed like a political thing, like all that mattered was what school you went to and if you were a WNBA player or a draft prospect. There were some girls that got jobs that were averaging under five points and assists a game. They were either role players or not producing. I couldn't understand how they were beating me out of jobs. I realized it's not what you know, it's who you know!

Some time had passed and I hadn't heard from Athos or Mooney. During that period a lot of agents started reaching out to me via Facebook. On a daily basis I was getting friend requests from people with names I couldn't even pronounce. Nine times out of ten if I saw a foreign looking name, I knew it was either a coach or agent looking to see if I was available. The fact that I was signed to an agent ultimately made them shy away from me. In the beginning I didn't understand it, but it came down to the commission of finding a player. They didn't want to share their commission with an agent just because they represented a player.

I also used Facebook like it was my daily diary, updating what I was doing and how I was feeling. One day in the middle of August, I put a status up saying that I knew if the "basketball gods" just gave me one opportunity, I would deliver. Some of my Facebook friends liked it and commented with words of wisdom, including a person named Fernando Toro. Toro was the coach of the Cabo Rojo Turistas, a women's team in the professional league in Puerto Rico. The Turistas was the same team Stass had played on the year before. I had connected with Coach Toro back in May. He contacted Beas first who gave him my number. He called to ask me to come play for his team. Dawn told me to turn him down because I'd likely be on my way to play overseas when Puerto Rico's season started. The BSNF (Baloncesto Superior Nacional Femenino) league in Puerto Rico seasons are short, going from August to the beginning of November, while overseas seasons run from September to April or May, so in a way Dawn was right. If I did get an overseas deal, it wouldn't have been possible to play in Puerto Rico.

Coach Toro wrote that he had a position available if I was interested. I immediately told him I was interested. We spoke for a little bit and he told me to be ready to report to Puerto Rico in about two weeks. I still hadn't spoken to Mooney or Athos for quite some time, so I decided not to tell them anything. I only told my family and close friends after I signed the contract. After signing the contract, Coach Toro updated me on a daily basis as to how the team was doing. The season had already been running for a couple weeks or so. Coach Toro had three Americans on his team, and I knew them all. The Americans were Tweet, my friend from NCA&T, my friend Slinky (aka Nicole Michael) from Queens/Syracuse, and Vionca Murray, who was also from Syracuse. This made me much more excited. I was going to Puerto Rico with a chip on my shoulder. I wanted to make sure I performed at a high level and made every team and coach that passed me up, wish they hadn't!

# Chapter 19
# Puerto Rico

*Sometimes you're placed in situations that you can't control.*
*At that point, it's very important to focus on adjusting and whatever*
*it is you CAN control.*
*#Tinyism*

It had been a rough three months as I encountered things I didn't see coming at all. The next two weeks were spent working out, getting everything I needed for PR, and talking to my new teammates. I had always played against Tweet and Slinky, and the thought of actually being on their team often crossed my mind. They were as talented as me, so playing with them had always been something I wanted to experience. I knew that playing with them would be exciting to say the least. I played against Vionca a couple times, but we just knew of each other and had a lot of mutual friends.

I would often talk to Tweet and Slinky to see how the games went. I was ignorant of how things worked in the professional basketball world, both the good and bad. Puerto Rico opened my eyes to some of the bad things that can occur in the professional basketball business. A couple of days before I was set to arrive in

Puerto Rico, Coach Toro learned that I was friends with Tweet and Slinky and asked me not to communicate with them until I arrived. For whatever reason he didn't want me to mention to them that I was coming out there. Although it was already too late, that made me skeptical as to what was going on. We actually brainstormed to try and figure out just what Coach Toro had up his sleeve. We realized that Coach Toro was replacing Tweet with me and was also going to release Vionca. Since Cabo Rojo was in last place the season before, the BSFN allowed them to have three Americans. They weren't winning many games and Coach Toro wasn't pleased with Tweet's and Vionca's performance. In the Puerto Rican league, teams switch players all the time. They have very little patience for poor performance. At the end of the day it's about winning, so if you're not producing, they don't believe in wasting time or money.

Replacing Tweet changed my mood from excitement to guilt. I felt bad because I was taking Tweet's job, which she worked so hard for. It was a touchy situation, but at the end of it all, we remained cool. The biggest disappointment was the fact that we weren't going to be playing together after all. She ended up living out her other dreams, getting a master's degree and coaching college basketball. To this day I still wonder what it would have been like to play with her. Maybe later down the line, they'll be a MEAC alumni game and we can get the opportunity to finally be teammates.

When I first arrived in Puerto Rico, I didn't know what to expect besides nice weather, lots of the Spanish language, and arroz con pollo (rice with chicken). When I landed, the president of the team, Juan Garcia, and his wife greeted me at the airport and welcomed me to Puerto Rico. The ride from the airport to Cabo Rojo was about two hours. That whole ride was spent site seeing and thinking. One thing I noticed immediately was the amount of stray dogs and horses. I was used to seeing stray dogs in NYC, but I've never seen so many horses. There were horses on the highway literally in the same lanes as the cars.

Also, you are never far from a McDonald's! We stopped there and while I ate, Juan informed me of the rules, terms of my contract and that after he took me home, I'd have my first practice to prepare for our game in a couple days. I wanted to make sure I showcased my talent to the best of my abilities. Besides the chip on my shoulder, knowing that they could get rid of me served as motivation. Those first couple of practices were very easy. The team had five or six players that played the bulk of each game and we didn't have much of a bench. With that being said, practices weren't that competitive. We even had a sixteen year old on the team. She was shorter than me and you could tell she just started playing basketball. Some practices we didn't even have ten players to play a full court game. We'd end up doing shooting drills, working on plays and conditioning. My teammates had other priorities like school, work, and children. It was in Puerto Rico that I quickly learned if you weren't an import player, it was rare to take playing in a professional league seriously. This was sort of recreation for them, which is why the coach brought Americans in.

The games were way more competitive than practices. Throughout the season, I actually ended up playing against more and more of my friends from New York, as well as many other talented Americans. The first couple of games I wasn't performing close to my full potential. It took me the first half of the season to adjust to the pace of the professional game and my new role as a player. With Cabo Rojo I had to be more of a point guard than a do-it-all kind of player. Coach Toro wanted me to think the game more. I had to approach the game differently mentally. I had to know where everyone was supposed to be on court, the reason behind running plays and who the plays were for. Cabo Rojo was my team, but not my team, if that makes sense. Slinky was an amazing scorer, so she was our go-to player. She was the equivalent of a female Kevin Durant, a tall player with a guard skill set. We had a native left handed scorer named Aixanell. Until we got our third American, Coach Toro wanted me to run all the plays for them and if there was an opportunity, take one to create for myself.

Between adjusting to going from being the number one option to the last, and worrying if I was doing my job, my performance suffered. Whenever I have to think during a game, I don't perform as well. It's very important for me to be able to do things naturally and freely on court. Coach Toro wanted me to run the team in a different way than I was used to, and that caused me to think time and time again. If he called a play, he wanted me to run that play all the way through and execute it in the way he envisioned. In the beginning I'd call a play, deviate, and do my own thing. Sometimes it would have a positive result and other times it wouldn't. Since my teammates weren't used to playing with me, the only one that was able to adjust when I improvised was Slinky. My other teammates wouldn't expect me to do certain things, so it would often result in a turnover. Whenever I committed a turnover or didn't run a play as it was laid out, Coach would take me out. This affected me mentally because I hadn't been subbed out of a game for a mistake during my whole college career. I usually just walked back to the bench upset and thinking to myself, "What the f***?"

After being in Cabo Rojo for a couple of weeks, the team changed again. To replace Vionca, Coach Toro brought in another MEAC player named Amber Bland. Amber went to school with Tweet at NCA&T, but she was a year or two older than us. Amber was an athletic three guard with the ability to jump and shoot anywhere in the mid-range. After playing a couple games with her and Slinky, Slinky ended up leaving to play in Europe. Often time players ended up going to Puerto Rico to buy some time before heading to Europe. Between the length of the season, the budgets of the team, and the level of competition, Europe was way more appealing. Puerto Rico was a second choice for many players. Not disrespecting the BSFN league, but that's like if you had the opportunity to play in the WNBA. The WNBA would trump going overseas in a heartbeat. The coaches and administration of the leagues knew this also, so unless you had an out clause in your contract, you weren't allowed to leave until the season was over. A lot of teams forbade players to have that out clause. Slinky and Coach Toro had an understanding prior to her arrival, so he knew her leaving was going to happen sooner or later. Once it was officially known that she was leaving, Coach Toro asked me if I knew of a big girl we could bring in. I gave him a couple of names including April McBride. April was also a MEAC hooper who graduated the same year I did and played for UMES. She had gone neck and neck with me for MEAC Player of the Year our senior year. She was a fundamentally sound big that could score and rebound very well. April was a walking double-double.

Coach brought April in that next week. We went from MEAC rivals to teammates. There had always been some animosity between our schools, but nothing was really ever personal. After playing and living together, we actually realized how much we complimented one another on and off the court.

I didn't really have much time to adjust to my new role. After April arrived, I still was in a bit of a slump. That year Renee was actually playing in PR as well. We played her team a number of times and after each game she noticed I hadn't been playing to my full potential. I started to believe my time in Puerto Rico was going to come to an end soon. I was stressing, we weren't winning the games we should, and Coach Toro was taking me out of the game more and more. I was still contributing and helping my team, but it wasn't anywhere close to what I could have contributed. I'd just think, listen to music, and try to figure out ways to get better. It was hard to get gym access, but Coach Toro began to figure out ways for me to get into the gym to release some stress and get better. I eventually vented to Stass and to my closest friend, Charisma Wright.

Charisma and I have been friends since I was a freshman at Madison. Charisma was vital when it came to me finally turning my season around in Puerto Rico. Without her support and love, I'm positive I would have been sent home. Initially, I met Charisma through basketball, by playing against her. She went to Midwood, so we were rivals. Charisma was a great athlete, but soccer was her main sport. She was the city's leading scorer in soccer. When it came to basketball, she just played defense and made the open shots when she got a chance. My sophomore year at Madison, her brother George Wright was an incoming freshman. George and I were very good friends. We hung around the same group of people and I'd even go to his house after school to hang out. I'd see Charisma and say hello, to not be rude. I started seeing her more at the tournaments I was playing in with Munch. She'd either be playing or there supporting her teammates from Midwood. One time, I had a game in Manhattan, and I got to the gym a little bit early to watch Exodus and The Gazelles play. Kimbo, Kenya, and I ended up sitting next to her. Charisma has always been a "girly girl," despite being a tom-boy at heart. She has been someone I adored for the simple fact that she's beautiful, both inside and out. Prior to hanging with her at that game, I assumed she was stuck up like most pretty girls in Brooklyn. I learned she was the complete opposite. After seeing her at a couple more games and hanging out with mutual friends together, we exchanged numbers. I'd go to her house and end up hanging out with her and George.

We got to the point where we started to speak every day. A mutual friend of ours noticed our relationship and asked me to put a word in for her. She wanted me to hook her up with Charisma, as she was a little shy, so I served as the middle man for them. Down the line, Charisma felt as though that person might not have been as interested as I said she was. That wasn't the case at all though, so I tried to persuade Charisma to stay involved. After telling her how beautiful she was and that she may have been a little intimidating, she shockingly flipped the script on me. She replied via text, "Well, maybe I'm interested in the wrong one!" I was left speechless. Charisma had experimented a little with girls, but in NYC at that time about 85% of girls that played sports did, so it was normal. Some girls went through it as a phase, and some turned it into a lifestyle. It was a phase for Charisma, as she's been with an NFL player for the past eight years. When she came on to me, I was flattered, but definitely shocked. Knowing most of the girls I played with and against were experimenting with other girls didn't bother me. I just felt like that wasn't me. Their sexuality didn't faze me. Throughout high school there were times I was curious, but I decided I would keep my experimenting to chemistry class.

After that conversation, I still tried to connect her with my friend, but if you didn't know any better, you would have assumed she and I were together. We cared for one another, and since we were always around each other, a lot of people thought we were dating. On an emotional level, I treated her like a significant other, but at the end of the day we were just really, really good friends that flirted with each other once in a blue. It was just a genuine relationship where the love, respect, and support between us was mutual. We never lied to each other or kept secrets and to this day it's the exact same between us almost a decade later.

One night after a subpar performance, I wrote a depressing status on my BlackBerry Messenger (BBM) saying, "Maybe this isn't what I'm meant to do." Immediately, Charisma let me have it! She assured me that this was exactly what I was born to do. After screaming at me via text, she comforted me in a way that lifted my spirits. She brought up memorable moments that she had witnessed and reminded me of my records at Morgan. She told me to man up and handle business. Tough love. That next game, I did exactly what she said to do—handled business! We were playing the defending champs at home and I went off for 31 points and 11 assists. It was by far the best game I played in Puerto Rico. Everything just felt right that day. After that performance, everything began to go smoothly. We were winning more games, I adjusted to Coach Toro's system, and I was finally playing to my full potential. We made the playoffs, and how fitting was it for us to face the defending champions again in the first round! In a three game series we eliminated them and went on to the Final Four.

I ran the team exactly how Coach Toro wanted me to while playing and being able to create the way I wanted to. In those two months, I became a more complete, professional basketball player. I knew how to get my teammates the ball, what plays to call for them, and when and how to create for myself. Unfortunately, we lost in Game four of a five game series to Renee's team, Juncos. Every game was close, but we just couldn't pull out the necessary wins. A couple more plays in our favor, and we would've advanced to the championship. I turned my season around thanks to Charisma. I made the All-star team, averaged 15.5 points, 6 assists, and was second in the league in assists. I'm more than grateful for my experience in Puerto Rico. Without learning how to be more of a general, there's no way I would've became the player I am today.

*Playoffs in Puerto Rico against business partner/idol/friend Renee Taylor*

# Chapter 20
# Taking a "Gamble"

*Exhaust all options when trying to obtain a goal,*
*because you never know what can happen!*
*#Tinyism*

During our playoff series, Coach Toro had an Italian scout come to the games to see if he'd be interested in signing Amber, April, or I. Initially I was told that a team in Italy wanted to sign me. The coaches liked the way I played and wanted to work out their budget before contacting me with further information. Once again I began to get that feeling of excitement. I thought the plan would be to go home for a couple days, be ready to head back out of the country, and continue to fulfill my dream. My Plan B was to get the film of my 31 points and 11 assists game, and send it out to whoever I could. Coach Toro had promised that he'd get me a copy of the game, but by the time I was ready to leave I hadn't received it.

Throughout my whole time playing in Puerto Rico I spoke to Mooney only once. He had heard I was killing in Puerto Rico and said it was good that I was there to stay in shape until they found me something. I never told them I was going there, but it didn't seem like they had an issue with me being there. Even though I spoke to Mooney, I never actually heard from Athos. I even wrote Athos about the Italian team being interested in me, and he never responded. I left Puerto Rico on Halloween which seemed to be a little foreshadowing. I felt like things were going to get very dark from here on out unless I made something happen. With the thought of breaking my contract with Athos weighing on me, I asked around to see if anyone could help me find a more suitable agent. Athos had nothing but the best clients and partners, but in my case that was the exact problem. He was pitching me for the high paying, high caliber jobs and that wasn't getting me anywhere. I understood that he was well connected, but the fact of the matter was, I wasn't as respected as the rest of his clients. I was from a low ranked, mid-major school, from a conference that hadn't produced many female professional players. I needed him to get me somewhere that would allow me to get my foot in the door and prove my capabilities. When you work with the best, it's very rare for them to go beneath what they're used to.

After deciding to terminate the contract with Athos, I sent him an email thanking him for all he'd done for me up until that point. I wasn't rude, because burning bridges isn't my style. I told him I wanted to take my career in another direction. He replied with a simple "Okay and good luck," and that was that. I was officially a free agent. November was approaching and between then and January, teams were looking to bring in players for the second half of the season. Most of my friends were being represented by the same couple of agencies. One agency represented Renee and two other friends from NY who were also guards. With our similarities in mind, I tried to get on board with that agent. It seemed to have been in my best interest considering they all had jobs in Europe at the time. Their agent represented a lot of female basketball players and had clients in the WNBA and Europe. I inquired about the agent to Renee and she had nothing but good things to say. When I was coming out of college a couple people had actually referred this agent to me, but I had already signed with Dawn, so I never reached out to her.

Before heading to Puerto Rico I had met and played against her at the West 4th St tournament in NYC. Renee was on this agent's team and we played them in the playoffs to go to the championship. Every summer up until that point she had a team in the tournament, which was made up of her clients. That was the first year Munch and I put a No Limit team in that division, so we were the 'underdogs' and new kids on the block. Every year the agent's team either made it to the championship or won it. This particular year we upset them, and I put on a show and single handedly took over that game. I had just finished school and had gone through that whole situation with Dawn. Prior to the game, I learned that all of their players were professionals and with the way my career was going, I wanted to prove to myself that I could hang with them. That's exactly what I did.

When I initially contacted the agent, I started the email off by saying, "Hey, I don't know if you remember me, but..." and then I sent my stats and told my story. She wrote me back and said, "Hey Tiny, I remember you. You killed us at W4. How could I forget?" After a series of emails, we made it official and she became my agent.

Once November rolled around, my mother thought it would be a great idea to spend some time with our family in Tampa. My grandmother had just moved down there and we both were due for a little vacation. We drove down with Buckets and stayed for about three weeks. With hopes that my new agent would find me something while I was there, I packed my bags as if I was going overseas from Tampa. Since November was my birthday month, all I really wished for was a job overseas. While in Tampa I only spoke to the agent a few times. Since she had so many clients, there wasn't really a need for small talk. She was definitely an all business type of person. From time to time, I would check in to see how things were going and if anyone had shown interest, and every time I contacted her I felt as though I was bothering her. She responded, "Not yet! I'll contact you when I find something." Responses like that rubbed me the wrong way. I always felt like she may have had an attitude while writing to me.

One day prior to my birthday a friend of mine contacted me about a job in Germany. I didn't know if it was going to go through, so I didn't bother to tell my agent about it. I ultimately emailed her about the situation, but phrased it in a hypothetical way. She didn't like the idea of someone helping me to get a job and let me know that. That was sort of our second little beef. I didn't hear from her until February when she said she may have something for me in Iceland. Since it had been months since hearing of any opportunities, I had begun working for School Professionals, subbing for Physical Education teachers at different charter schools all around NYC. I needed the money and I wasn't doing anything on a daily basis, besides working out. After a couple weeks of substitute teaching, I was offered a more permanent position.

I emailed my agent and asked about my status and what she suggested I do. She told me to take the job. She tells her clients all the time, if they can make money, make it, because it's not guaranteed she would find them a job. This made sense, but it also made me lose a little confidence in her. I felt like she wasn't really confident that she'd find me a job. I decided that I didn't want to just sit around and wait for her to find me one, and that I had to be proactive! I went online and saw that there were a number of exposure camps and tryouts coming up. I believed that once these people saw my talent in person, I could get a job sooner. I registered for two WNBA tryouts and also an exposure camp that would take place the same weekend as the NCAA Final Four.

After registering and paying for everything, I received a forwarded email from my agent about an exposure camp that she was hosting. Her camp was the same time as the exposure camp I had already paid for. Initially I thought about attending both, but after reading through her email, I noticed fees for participating. I was already out $2000 from the three events I had paid for, and there was no way I was going to go into more debt. On top of that, I didn't like the fact that she considered charging me. I was her client so I felt that as my agent she should've waived my fee or provided me some sort of a discount. That made me a little upset so I didn't even tell her about my plans to attend the WNBA tryouts and other camp.

The first WNBA tryout went well. I was one of the top three guards at the camp, so I was optimistic. I networked with everyone and the staff seemed to like me. Unfortunately I was ignorant of how things worked in the WNBA, and that tryout basically turned out to be a publicity stunt and money maker. At the end of the camp they explained the rules for training camp and team's roster spots. Training camp only allowed fifteen players who competed throughout the camp for eleven roster spots. At the end of the tryout, the coach said that whoever they chose would be an alternate for training camp, which meant they'd be on call once someone got cut from training camp. In essence, you'd be an alternate for the alternates.

The second WNBA tryout turned out to be a disaster. When I landed at the airport, my rental car reservation didn't exist and as a result I was an hour late for the tryout. I knew showing up late would give me a strike in the coach's eyes, so at that point I didn't have much confidence. Once I arrived I saw some people I met at the first tryout and they told me what I missed. I did well during the drills and games I participated in, but I felt like they already had a good idea of which players they were going to pursue. This team actually had a training camp position available, but when it came down to selecting 15-20 to stay after the first cut, I didn't get picked.

I tried to remain optimistic about the camp, but I wasn't too pleased there either. The competition was decent, but there weren't many scouts in attendance. The only people I noticed were the participants, staff of the event, and friends of the people that participated. They had advertised that there would be scouts from the WNBA and Europe in attendance, which was my primary reason for attending. Camps tend to say scouts will be there because they know that'll get people to register. There are a lot of scams preying on the fact that they know how desperate players are to make their dreams come true. I've heard about certain camps hiring people to sit in their stands with polo shirts and clipboards pretending they're scouts just to scam participants out of their money. It sucks that people would do such things, but it's the reality of the basketball world.

Since the camp was during the weekend of the Final Four, my coaches from Morgan were able to come check me out. NCAA Final Four weekend is a very popular event, and many times coaches attend seminars and conferences as well as the games.

Despite the fact that the camp didn't turn out to be what I expected, I still wanted to get my money's worth. I figured I was already there, so I might as well make the best of it. The way the camp was set up, first we'd participate in different drills, and combine related activities where they recorded our scores. After the combine related activities, we were split into teams. We practiced for 30 minutes with our team, and then we played a series of scrimmage games. The combine activities tested speed, agility, vertical leap, and efficiency while shooting during different drills.

The first day we played the scrimmage games, the teams were set up according to our registration info prior to our arrival. The second day, they remade the teams based on skill and talent. One side had the better prospects and the other side had the people they felt were less talented. I fortunately made it to the better prospect side. By the second day I was annoyed with the way things we were going, especially since it didn't seem like there was anyone of importance in the stands. During the second day my team was being coached by an agent by the name of Charles Gamble. This was his first year as a certified agent. He had a couple clients in the camp, and I'm sure by participating on the staff in the event, he was looking to sign more. After one of our games, a teammate and I were having a casual conversation. She had just finished her last collegiate season and asked me for some advice about agents since she knew that I graduated the year before. I told her about my experience with the agents I dealt with, my time in Puerto Rico, why I came to the camp, and also that nine times out of ten people shy away from helping you if you're already signed to an agent. I told her my plan from here on was to not sign with an agent until he or she delivered. That way the next time someone approached me with a potential job, they wouldn't have reason to shy away from me. Charles overheard me and offered his opinion. He said some agents don't like to work without having a contract because of the simple fact that they can get screwed out of commission or look bad in front of their contacts for submitting a player someone else already submitted. Our discussion turned into a heated, but respectful debate. I told him the situations I had experienced, which made him understand my suggestion to her. Initially he took offense because he thought I was telling her she should pimp the agents and go with the highest bidder, but that wasn't what I meant at all. Once the camp concluded I made sure I networked and got all the staff members' email addresses. Before I left the gym, I sent everyone (including Charles) my information and made sure that they received it. Although I felt the camp was a waste, I still wanted to make the best of the situation. Before I left the gym, the directors also assured me they were going to send me film from the camp and also send it out to their "overseas partners".

I wasn't in the mood to really check out Indiana (where the camp was held) or any of the Final Four events, so I went straight to the airport. Once I arrived back in New York, I checked my phone and I had an email from my agent. I guess there really were a couple people in the stands at the camp, because word got back to her of how I was killing at the camp. In the email, she expressed anger towards the fact that I went to this other camp instead of hers. She took it as disrespect that I went to the other camp and also that I didn't even bother to tell her. I explained that it was already paid for and I couldn't afford to attend hers. She asked why I thought I had to pay for her camp knowing I was a client of hers. I forwarded the email that she sent to me to show her just why I thought I needed to pay. She said that it was a mistake and her clients always attended the camp for free. We agreed that it would be in our mutual best interest to terminate our contract. We hadn't seen eye to eye for some time, our communication wasn't good, and I also stated that there was a chance I was going to be attending some tryouts abroad. With no hard feelings, we terminated our partnership and wished each other the best.

I got some email addresses for coaches and agents off eurobasket.com and began networking. Initially, I garnered a lot of interest from teams and agents, but it seemed like after initially talking to them I never heard back from them again. I began working closely with two European agents. One agent was out of Poland and one was from Germany. The agent in Poland swore he had a team for me, but nothing came through. The German agent never made any promises, but he failed to seal any deals either. By mid-August I began having some doubt and figured I'd be on my way back to Puerto Rico. I felt like I deserved to play in Europe, but if nothing came, Puerto Rico was my next best option. I knew all I had to do was make a call to Coach Toro, but before I did I wanted to make sure I absolutely had to.

One day that summer someone from Romania added me on Facebook. They told me they had submitted my name to a team and there was a good chance the team would take me. Weeks later they told me that the team had gone with another guard with professional experience, but if I could pay my airfare they could arrange for me to try out for a couple teams. At that point I was willing to do whatever it took to get across them waters. I told him I would think about it and get back in touch. I spoke with my mother and we both knew that my talent would speak for itself. We figured there was no way all the teams I tried out for were going to turn me down. Before I even responded they contacted me saying that they spoke with a friend that worked at a travel agency. The friend found me a discounted ticket at $800 and all I had to do was put up half upfront and the other half when I landed. After receiving that info I thought it was a definite sign that I should go through with it. I sent them $400 dollars by Western Union and they sent me a confirmation email and number. Initially I was so excited that I didn't thoroughly check it out. Days went by and I hadn't heard from the person again.

We were getting closer to the date and I wanted to make sure I had all the details correct. I had asked around and teams in Romania were indeed conducting tryouts. I pulled up the confirmation email and realized I had been scammed. They spelled my name wrong, the dates were from two years ago, and once I checked the confirmation number for the airline it didn't exist. I had gotten scammed out of $400. I sent multiple threats and after a while they finally responded. They apologized and said they'd send my money back. Of course, they never did. They even had the nerve to congratulate me when I eventually got overseas. I've vowed that one day I'll either play in or visit Romania to find them and get my money back!

I experienced an even more devastating let down after that. I had managed to get in touch with a Ukrainian coach of a top league team. He wanted to sign me and a post player I knew of. The only problem was he wasn't really able to give in-depth details at first. The Ukrainian league had been going through some issues that stemmed from the previous couple of seasons and the coming September was when it was set to make its comeback. I honestly wasn't banking on the fact that the deal was going to go through. It finally came down to contract negotiations and making flight reservations. The coach sent us the contract and everything seemed legit. I sent it back, and I thought it was official and safe to get excited. A couple days went by, and I didn't hear from the coach. I began connecting with the other player because I believed we were on the verge of being teammates. I learned that the coach had been communicating with her, but not me. After about a week he informed me that the Ukrainian Federation decided they were only going to allow one American per team. Since the other player was a post player, he was going to choose her instead of me. In professional basketball guards are a dime a dozen. There will always be a bigger market for post players and centers. Once again it seemed as if my dream was taken right from under me. The other player ended up complaining to me about the living conditions, salary, and many other things, so maybe it was best that I didn't go.

By the end of August, Charles contacted me with a very low paying job in Europe. Money has never been my motivation for playing, so I told him he could submit me. His contacting me gave me hope that things were finally looking up. He was surprised by the fact that I was willing to go play for such a low amount. Despite the deal not going through he said he had some other deals he could submit me for. September rolled around and I still wasn't really interested in going to Puerto Rico, so I decided that I was going to wait a little longer and substitute teach.

Around noon on September 11th, 2011, Charles sent me a text in all caps. He said he had a team that wanted to sign me as soon as possible and they were paying very well. I wrote him back right away telling him to make it happen. He asked for some information he needed and said he'd contact me back tomorrow. Surprisingly he actually called me two hours later overly excited. He said, "Corin, this is the fastest deal I've ever made happen." By 2:00 p.m. he had a contract in my email and a possible flight date for me. I was still in shock, but I didn't want to get excited until I was on a plane. By 4:00, after looking over the contract with my mom and making sure everything was okay, I sent the contract back and it was official. For the 2011-2012 season I was going to be playing for Boa Viagem in Portugal. All I needed to do was get some fingerprints done and I'd be on my way.

After signing the contract I made a reference to the discussion at camp that Charles and I had had. I said, "Now if I was signed to another agent you wouldn't have even considered helping me or making this deal happen, and I wouldn't be going anywhere!" He laughed and said I was right. He was aware of my "agent phobia" and surprisingly never made me sign an agent-player contract. He put me on his list of clients and that was that. Charles gained both my respect and loyalty. I may not have signed anything, but if anyone asked I made sure I told them he was my agent.

# Chapter 21
# Portugal: Tiny Setback #4

*One bad decision can ruin everything you've worked for up until*
*that point. It's definitely better to be safe than sorry!*
*#Tinyism*

A couple weeks before I spoke to Charles about Portugal, I rekindled a friendship from back in my college days. I had recently gotten back in touch with one of my good friends from Morgan, Indira Mahasin. Throughout the years we had stayed in touch via social media, but we weren't communicating nearly as much as we did during those couple weeks. One boring night during Hurricane Irene, we reconnected and exchanged phone numbers. From that point on we spoke every day for the next six months. In the beginning most of our conversations were catching up and reminiscing. I had no idea she had been staying in Brooklyn since we graduated in 2010. I jokingly blamed her for not letting me know she was in town and unfortunately when we did arrange a date to hang out, I unexpectedly had to leave for Portugal.

Indira was someone you always wanted to be around. She was witty, ambitious, and just fun to be with. She seemed to have this unique aura of her own. Between her energy and social skills, it was hard for her to go unnoticed. She was also one of the pretty party girls at Morgan that everyone wanted to be associated with. I initially met her through basketball, as she was the manager of the men's team. Throughout our years at Morgan, I always admired her from afar. She always had a lot going on, but no matter what, she took care of business. Indira even managed to be the President of my imaginary fan club. That was one of our ongoing inside jokes throughout school, in addition to her calling me "Itty Bitty". Whenever I'd see her, she'd scream, "Itty!" and re-assure me that she was still the President of my fan club, so I had better make sure I acted right toward her.

We stayed in touch even after I signed with Boa Viagem and left for Portugal. We had a mutual respect for each other, and shared a passion to obtain our respective goals. She'd hold me down when needed, and I'd do the same. The relationship I developed with Indira helped me sustain a successful season in Portugal. I didn't struggle as much in Portugal as I did in Puerto Rico, and Indira always provided a little extra motivation when needed. Unfortunately, things weren't going as well for her. She had shared some very personal information with me; her mom was battling cancer. The moment she told me, my heart dropped. I had no idea she was going through something that serious. The way she was handling things showed how strong she really was. I was devastated when she told me, so I couldn't even imagine the pain she was feeling. Her opening up to me about this made me feel like our friendship had been solidified. From that moment on, I wanted to be the best friend I could for her.

Unfortunately, her mother's health wasn't improving and she passed away, may she rest in peace. Once her mother had passed, I decided that I should give Indira space. I figured I might be a reminder of her mom, or trigger an unwanted memory in some other way by staying in touch. I felt like in many ways I associated with her mom, and I didn't know what effect that would have on her. I decided to send her flowers, and let her know if she needed anything she could contact me. After her mother passed we didn't really communicate as often. We're still cool to this day but it's not the same at all. Whenever we do speak, it's like we never miss a beat, so I'm grateful for that. The chemistry is always there and we always enjoy ourselves.

The competition was much better in Portugal, as was my coach's style of coaching. For the first half of the season, my team had only one play. Coach Marcos believed in running a motion styled offense that would be dictated by what the defense did. Coach Marcos was a cool, laid back kind of coach. Whenever I had questions about my performance or general things about the game, he'd answer and also tell me not to worry. There would be times during games I'd do exactly what he wanted, and he'd just smile at me and wink. He never seemed to mind when I made mistakes. He just told me what I did wrong and moved on. The fact that he was hardly ever negative made it much easier for me to adjust to playing in Portugal. After a couple games I gotten used to him, my teammates, and the competition.

The Portuguese league allowed each team to have a maximum of two Americans. My fellow American and roommate in the beginning was a power forward/center named Sherida Triggs. Triggs was also represented by Charles Gamble. Triggs was a couple of years older than me with two years of European experience. My team was located on an island known as Terciera Island. Terciera Island was a beautiful, and was located in the

Azores area of Portugal. Triggs had been on the island about three weeks before I arrived. I followed her lead that first month. She was a graduate of Old Dominion University and one of the most skilled big girls I've played with to date. She was like a female Tim Duncan. She could pass, shoot the mid-range, run the floor, and create for herself on the block. It was a pleasure to play with her as she made my job easier. She also had good hands, so catching my crazy passes wasn't a problem for her at all. We had a pretty decent starting five, but we lacked a productive bench. Boa Viagem hadn't been in the top division for long, so winning wasn't expected. Prior to the season, we participated in a preseason cup tournament and despite it being our first few times playing together, we turned some heads.

Our first two regular season games were against the worst, and best, teams in the league. Those games gave us an idea of what we needed to work on, and also where we stood. We beat the worst team by twenty and lost to the best team by twenty. I didn't play as well as I wanted in the game against the best team. Alges, who later went on to win the championship, had two Americans who were graduates of Vanderbilt. After the Alges game I was of course hard on myself. Following that game I averaged 18.9 points and 4.1 assists in the next ten games. Through those first twelve games we were 9-3 and one of the hottest teams in the league.

Unfortunately, after our fifth game, Triggs left the team due to family issues and we had to play two games without her. That two week span really helped me. I was more depended upon to help the team win, so that forced me to step my game up a notch, which in turn gave me more confidence. Despite how talented Triggs was, she really only gelled well with me. There wasn't as much team chemistry with her as there was her replacement, Lady

Comfort. Lady made an instant difference when she arrived, both on our team and the island as a whole. Lady was bigger than Triggs and had the ability to get everyone involved. She was a better passer and facilitator.

The weeks before she arrived it had been raining and kind of cold on the island. As soon as Lady landed it seemed like she brought the sunshine from Florida with her and brightened up all of our days. In addition to our team, there were three men's teams on Terceira Island; two top division teams with three Americans each, and a second division team with two Americans. Prior to Lady's arrival we had all hung out once in a while, but her personality and hospitality quickly brought us all together much more often. We became more like a family after Lady arrived. Besides hanging out at the bars or clubs on the island, we'd have "family time", which consisted of good meals cooked by her in addition to either card games, NBA games, or just good laughs.

The two top division teams were Lusitania and Terceira. The second division team was Angra. On Lusitania there was Ricky Franklin, Brian "B Milly" Mills, and Marcel "Cel" Momplaisir. Cel had been playing in Portugal for about three years and was a New Yorker from Queens. He had been blessed to find love on Terceira Island, so he also lived there with his wife. Ricky was from Milwaukee and played on Lusitania the second half of the previous season. Ricky was their point guard, so whenever we could, we'd get in the gym and get shots up together. Ricky and I had a similar game, minus his ability to post up. B Milly was secretly my favorite out of the three. B Milly played sort of like Dirk Nowitzki in his prime. B Milly played positions 2-4 and had the ability to score quite smoothly. You'd never expect him to do some of the things he did, but once he did them you'd be jumping out your seat with excitement. On Terceira's team there was Nate Bowie, Durrell Nevels, and Tony Murphy. I had known Tony from playing in the MEAC. He was a couple years older than me, but I remembered him from Norfolk State. Tony was also from Jersey so he was the one I related to the most. Cel was from Queens, but he was also way older than me, so I just looked at him as a big bro. Nate and Durrell had played together at the University of Arkansas. Nate was about my height, but he was a flat out scorer. Tony played the wing and reminded me of Dwayne Wade. Durrell was an athletic forward, who made his living by out-working his opponents on the glass. On Angra, there was Terrence Mack and Drew Gibson. Mack was just a big bully. Mack went to school with Cel at Rhode Island. Looking at him you wouldn't expect him to play basketball. He looked like he was an NFL player. Mack was from Philadelphia and Drew was from California. Drew was the point guard for Angra, and he controlled the game well while knocking down big shots when needed.

Each team had a few natives that spoke English and hung out with us. During that season, I hardly got homesick. I had my island family, so the only people I really missed were my mother and Buckets. I don't come home for the holidays when I play overseas, because I like to see how other countries and cultures celebrate. I also hate traveling on planes for a long periods of time, so making that trip back to the States for a couple days just wasn't worth it to me. That year, most of us stayed on the island for Thanksgiving, Christmas, and New Year's. Lady and I decided to cook a big dinner at our place after everyone got out of practice on Thanksgiving and it really felt like we were home. We may not have had an actual turkey, but we had a damn good turkey day, as well as a Christmas and New Year.

I played two seasons for Boa Viagem, but the first one was by far the most interesting. The island was very small and dramatic. There were so many things going on that I could write another book or a script for a soap opera based on what I saw. We had everything from infidelity to bar fights. It seemed like every week there was a new story circulating the island. Some of it even turned up in the local newspapers. They say what happens on the island stays on the island, but boy did we have some crazy times there.

When Lady arrived, we went on a win streak that led us into the midseason cup tournament. Cup tournaments are played by the top teams in the league to compete for both bragging rights and a gold medal. There's usually a preseason, mid-season, and end of the season cup tournament in every league overseas. By the time January rolled around we were in the top four of the league. We still hadn't beaten Alges, and I took that personally. The second time we played them it was closer but we still lost, and it was a TV game to boot. I still hadn't played as well as I wanted to. The cup tourney was held at Alges' gym, and I told myself that if we matched up against them there was no way I was going to get outperformed again!

The day before we left for the cup tournament I received some very bad news. My bro Vic from Morgan had passed away due to a battle with cancer. I had just spoken to him about a month before he passed. At that point Vic had stopped playing and focused all his attention to passing on his basketball knowledge to the youth in Canada. When we spoke, I congratulated him on a championship his team had just won and we caught up briefly. Once I heard that he passed, I dedicated my play that weekend to him.

We played three games in three days and won the championship with all the odds against us. Every game day, I wrote on Vic's

Facebook page as if he had access to his page from heaven. Prior to the first game I told him I was going to hit a couple threes for him and score twenty-three points in honor of his jersey number. After the first game I wrote, "Ain't get the 23 points for you today. Missed my FT's smh, but I got a double-double for you big homie. 20 p 11 r 4 a - we back at it tomorrow vs. the #1 team so I'ma try get it then."

The semi-final game was the matchup I had been looking forward to against Alges. Since I was playing for Vic, I had to make sure we beat them, and I performed well. We won, but it took an unbelievable performance to get it done. There were times I did things I didn't even know I could do. After each move, all I kept saying to myself was that my 6th man, Vic, had helped me out. The game was close throughout the first half, but they began to pull away at the beginning of the second half. At the half way mark of the third quarter, I began to take over. Ironically, while scouting Alges the week before, I had convinced Coach Marcos that we should use one of their plays because it was perfect for our personnel. We hadn't used the play at all in the first half, but once I called it, it worked, and we ran it six times in a row while scoring every time. The play was a down screen for Lady on the block, and after she received her screen she'd come up to set a ball screen for me. It was kind of funny that they didn't realize we were running their play. When it comes to the pick and roll, I'm a very dangerous player. I can pull up, pass out of it, avoid the hedge, get to the basket, or even hit a teammate in the corner on the opposite side of the court away from the help defense. The first couple of times I ran the play, I pulled up for 3's. After that when they started to step out, I dished it to Lady twice as she rolled to the basket. Another time I hesitated in front of the hedger and got to the basket for an "And 1". Another time they tried to help as I drove and I kicked it out for a three pointer. Once we took the lead and had the momentum there was really nothing Alges could do with us. Following the game, I wrote on Vic's wall, "26, 8 and 5 for you, big homie!! Championship game tomorrow. Swear I felt you on those last three 3s'. Whooooop RIP."

There we were, one game away from history. Boa Viagem hadn't won anything since they had won the championship in the second league. Overseas, teams move down a league or up a league each season. To move up to the top league you have to win the championship in the second league. To move down, you usually have to be in last place in the top league. Prior to my arrival, Boa Viagem was in the top league for the past six seasons since winning the second league seven years before. After we beat Alges, we met the 2nd place team Vagos, who were equally talented. Prior to the tournament we had lost to Vagos by ten, so they also were a game I wanted to win. The game came down to the wire. It wasn't until the final two minutes that we sealed the win, by two points. Between the seven and the two minute mark of the 4th quarter, I scored eleven points straight. I was fortunate enough to help my team win its first cup championship and I was also awarded MVP. For MVP they gave me a gold plated Molten ball and for winning it all, we all received gold medals. After that game I again went to Vic's wall and wrote: 'Big homie, we did it!!! Told you I was gonna get that chip for you. 24, 11, and 6 and I got MVP! I felt you with me the end of the fourth. RIP. The rest of the season will def be for you!!" It was an amazing weekend for us. It felt good to finally beat the number one team, and to win the championship for both my team and my big bro Vic (RIP Bro).

After one of the most memorable moments of the season, I later experienced the absolute opposite. The end of the season was approaching and it was time to solidify positioning for playoffs. We worked our way up to 2nd place in the league, tied with a team called Quinta Lombos. On March 10, we were set to play Quinta for second place. On March 9th, both my mother and college teammate Brittany Dodson were set to arrive in Lisbon. They planned to come to the game and hang out for the weekend. I had been looking forward to their arrival for a month. Three days before their arrival, I did one of the most stupid things ever. Right before practice we watched film on Quinta. Before I had arrived at the gym, I remember being extremely tired and even dosed off in film a couple times. My coach said that this would be a light practice. Feeling tired and hearing we weren't going to have a tough practice, I decided not to put my ankle braces on. During the last twenty minutes of practice he decided to have us scrimmage. I found the energy to play hard and compete. Though I am tiny in stature, I try my best to get "big people stats" like blocks and rebounds. I blocked my teammate and landed wrong on her foot and twisted my ankle awkwardly. My ankle immediately went numb. Although that had never happened before, I didn't think it was more than a typical ankle sprain. For the next couple days, I rested and iced, but the swelling never went down. There was no way I was going to sit this game out and I felt as though I could still play on it. All the way up until the game we treated my ankle as much as we could. Come game time, I hopped around through much of the game before Coach finally took me out. We lost the game and I experienced my first serious injury. After hanging out with my mom and teammates, we went back to the island and I went to see a doctor. It turned out that I had bruised a bone and torn some ligaments in my ankle. I was on a mission to get healthy in time for the playoffs in four weeks.

First they had me on crutches, and then a boot. It took forever for the swelling to go down. When it finally did, I couldn't bend my ankle. Scar tissue had built up and blocked my ankle from flexing. We tried everything, but that was the end of my season. Unfortunately, it was also the end of Boa Viagem's season. My team couldn't function without their point guard. It hurt to see my team go out like that and I felt terrible. That one bad decision to not put my ankle braces on ruined everything. At the time I was on pace to be the league's leading scorer and we were in a position to lock down second place. With the way we were playing there's no doubt in my mind we could've won the championship. I still wonder what would have happened that season had I been healthy, but sad to say I'll never know.

*Portuguese Federation Cup MVP*

# Chapter 22
# Portugal…Again: Tiny Setback #5

*Sometimes we're faced with obstacles that prepare us for what's ahead. You may not understand it, but it's not your job to. Your job is to get through it!*

*#Tinyism*

Once I left Portugal, my main focus was to get treatment for my ankle. I was able to walk on it, but because of the lack of flexibility I wasn't able to play without a slight limp. The first thing I did when I got back stateside was go to an orthopedic surgeon. The surgeon suggested that I go to rehab. If nothing changed, he recommended I get arthroscopic surgery. The arthroscopic surgery would clean out all the scar tissue and I'd just have to worry about getting my ankle back to full strength. I did some weight lifting exercises, but most of my sessions consisted of trainers trying to bend my ankle as much as possible, every which way. My least favorite exercise involved a baseball. They'd put a baseball on top of my foot and bend my foot against it. I cried and screamed every time. There were other people getting treated, so I'd warn them that I would be loud. After those few weeks of rehab, I received a call about a team in Dubai that wanted me to come play. They were paying very well and wanted me to come in two weeks. I asked anxiously if the trainer thought I could be ready in two weeks. He looked at me like I was crazy. I was not only worried, but I had to pass up a great opportunity.

After another couple weeks of rehab there hadn't been a drastic change, so we set up the surgery. After the surgery I'd have to go through rehab again. Most overseas seasons start around September, so I had three months to get my ankle healthy, as well as get in shape. At that point in time I really questioned if I'd get healthy enough in time.

My surgeon suggested one of the best trainers on Staten Island, Ivan Candeleria. I went to Ivan right from the hospital and we started rehab immediately. There was no way I was going to let the scar tissue build up again. Both Ivan and the surgeon explained that scar tissue is going to develop because that's what happens when you heal. They told me the best thing to do was to be aggressive with the rehab to break it up before it could build up.

Ivan's facilities were fifteen minutes away from my house. I sometimes rode my bike there to get a work out in. Ivan worked with a lot of top notch athletes, many in the NFL. He had the experience and resources I needed to make a miraculous comeback. He knew time was against me and did his best to get me back. I didn't broadcast the fact that I had surgery because doing so would be career suicide. A couple of agents and teams had contacted me about my plans, and I carried on as if I was 100% healthy. It wasn't necessarily lying. I believed by the time it was time to leave, I would be good. I just didn't want to tell them what was going on and hurt my chances of consideration. No team wants that liability of dealing with an injured player.

A couple of agents showed interest in signing me but I didn't communicate with them because I was going to stay loyal to Charles. A lot of them were more connected than Charles, but I told them I couldn't just leave him out to dry. He had gotten me my first job and I wanted to give him the opportunity to deliver my second. I figured in the worst case I could go back to Portugal, since I had unfinished business there and they wanted me back. A couple teams contacted me with offers and I directed them to Charles. Unfortunately nothing really came close to what I was making in Portugal, so I didn't accept any offers. I spoke to Coach Marcos every couple of days to update him on my progress. Ideally he wanted to have the same team as the season before. He also felt that if I hadn't gotten hurt, we could have won another championship.

After a month, things were going in the right direction. I still hadn't received any better offers, so I resigned with Boa Viagem. My coaches and the management of the team were a little worried about my health and whether or not I was going to be able to play when September rolled around. I asked Ivan's opinion based on his experience and he believed I'd be okay.

I sent Coach Marcos videos, pictures, and statements from Ivan to assure him that there was nothing to worry about. Around August I began to shoot and do light drills. As long as I had my brace on, I was able to do about 75% of the things I'd normally do. I still had this baby limp when I ran but it wasn't as bad as before. My ankle lacked strength and flexion, but it was better than it was when I first came back. The last month of rehab we really turned it up. My other issue was getting in shape. I began to work out twice a day because I knew once I got to Portugal the season was going to be starting and we were going to be competing in the pre-season cup tournament.

It was now time to head back to Terciera Island. Only this time, I was experiencing totally different emotions than the ones I had the first time I went. This time my emotions were dominated by doubt and worry. I had never really doubted my ability to perform but I honestly questioned myself now. A lot of times when athletes get injured, they go through a battle between their physical and mental health. There's this sense of fear when it comes to getting back on the court. Right before I left for Portugal, I went to see Ivan and the surgeon to be sure everything would be okay. The surgeon said my ankle lacked about 15 degrees of flexion. Ivan agreed and said that with two or three weeks more of rehab I would be able to make that difference. Ivan gave me exercises to do on my own and stated that would be just as good as rehab.

After I arrived in Portugal we had our first practice. That was going to be my first time testing out my ankle, and if I couldn't keep up I didn't know what I was going to do. I did well and was able to do most of the same things I usually did. I was just a step slower and still not in the shape I needed to be in. After the first practice I felt confident and was going to work my ass off to get ready for the preseason tournament. Before and after every practice the trainer would massage and maneuver my ankle to break up the remaining scar tissue. I also did things like box jumps, hill runs, agility drills in the sand, pool workouts, and extra conditioning. I continued to improve and every step of the way my teammates and coaching staff supported me. That made me want to get back to the old Tiny not just for me, but for them too.

Some of my teammates were experiencing injuries of their own, and this angered management. They didn't like the idea of us beginning the season that way, but at that point there was nothing we could do. Entering the preseason tournament, my main goal was to show management that despite what it looked like, my ankle wasn't going to affect my performance. I heard them talking about letting go one of our native players because she had torn her ACL and wasn't going about her rehab the way I was. Her progress was non-existent and they didn't want to waste money paying her, so they were considering letting her go. In the first game I had a triple double! We played against one of the top teams so it was a close game. Unfortunately, we made some last minute mistakes that cost us the game. Despite the loss, I proved that I was still going to be able to perform. I felt some discomfort and fatigue, but as long as I worked hard and got back in shape that wouldn't last long.

Since my ankle wasn't performing the way it would normally, I experienced pain and complications in other areas like my knees, Achilles tendon, and the arch of my foot. I had to make sure that I not only nursed my ankle back to full health, but I also got around to making the surrounding muscles and joints stronger.

Some internal issues with the team began taking place. I began to get exhausted mentally and physically. I wasn't as hungry as I'd usually be and I tended to just do enough to get by. In practices I didn't go as hard as I should have. I tried to preserve energy because I was tired and sore. We still didn't have a bench, so during practice there wasn't anyone to challenge me. I justified my lack of effort as trying to get my teammates better. By trying to make them better I did less because I would defer to them. Eventually Coach Marcos noticed my lack of effort and desire to work hard, so he called me out about it. I knew he was right so I didn't make any excuses. I just shook my head and said, "Okay coach, I got you." His calling me out was a wakeup call. I began to reapply myself and go hard. We went on a little win streak after that and everything seemed to be going well.

Since my arrival, the team had set up two appointments for me to see the orthopedic doctor in Portugal. He told us the same thing I had heard from Ivan and my surgeon back home, but he told my team that I shouldn't be playing. By December I finally began feeling like the old Tiny. I was in shape and less sore and tired. Around mid-December they took me back to the doctor for a follow up. During that visit he gave me an ultimatum. He said since had I arrived my ankle had only improved flexion by five degrees, and I still had ten degrees to go. The options were to continue to play and see if I can get it to improve another five degrees, or forfeit the rest of the season and undergo another surgery. He had sensed my animosity towards him from the previous visits, but this visit went well, or at least I thought it did. I told him regardless of the fact that my ankle still wasn't able to fully flex, I was feeling regular. Since I felt good I wanted to take my chances playing the rest of the season and if it didn't improve I'd talk to my surgeon back home and decide what was best. I didn't trust his judgment, but he was one of the most respected surgeons in the country, so my team's management had contrary feelings.

When I left his office I was just frustrated, because there was no way I wasn't going to play unless I absolutely had to stop. After the visit we had a couple games left before the Christmas break. The two games after the visit I averaged twenty-five points and felt like I was completely back. There was only one game left before the break with a full week in between, so I made sure I got in the gym consistently to prepare. I wanted to go into the break on a good note. My plan for the break was to go to London with my teammate and also come back to work a basketball camp with Coach Marcos for children on another island in Portugal.

The day before the game I got a message from Coach Marcos

asking to meet me before practice. As soon as I read the message, I felt like something was wrong. I called my mom and she said to hope for the best. I had no idea what the meeting was about, but I just knew it couldn't be about anything good. I asked Coach Marcos what the meeting was about, but he didn't answer me. We had a great relationship, so if it was something good he would be excited to tell me. I went to the gym to meet with him and the manager of the team. They told me that they had just spoken to the doctor and he had told them that my ankle was never going to get better and that I needed surgery. This infuriated me because he had told them one thing and told me another. Coach Marcos said that even if it was true that my ankle is only at 80%, they wanted a player at 100% health. I began to get emotional and started to yell and plead my case. I told them that with my 80% ankle I was still top ten in three categories and my stats were the same from last year, so what was the problem? After that I got smart and asked, "If y'all are so worried about my ankle, why do I play 40 minutes a game?" They concluded the meeting saying they were going to release me and send me home. They gave me some paper work and I told them I'd look it over and get back to them.

With tears on my face they had the nerve to ask me to practice later that day and to play the next day. Because I loved my teammates, and the fact that I'd have to prove to other teams that I was able to play, I agreed to it. I sat back down, wiped my tears and told them that I was going to play, but under two conditions. One, I didn't want them to tell the team about me leaving until after the game. I wanted them focused on winning because that's what I had been looking forward to all week. The second condition was that if and when they publish an article about me leaving, they didn't say anything about my ankle. They had to promise to tell the press that it was due to family issues, because I didn't want them hurting my chances of moving on to another team.

I went on to practice like nothing had happened. I practiced hard and prepared for the game. As I got ready to leave, my American roommate Tamyra Davis came storming into the gym with tears in her eyes. I had no idea what was going on, but she kept asking if Coach was still here. I calmed her down and she said that our house had been robbed. Immediately, I understood why she was so upset. We got in contact with the coach and he arranged for some of the staff of the boys' team to go back to our house with us. We had to call the cops, and I wanted to see exactly what they had taken. They had taken 400 Euros from me, and T's iPod, as well as three months' pay she was planning to take home with her.

The cops came, we gave a report, and they checked us into a hotel to be safe. I sat there on the bed and tried to process the day I was having. What are the odds of getting both released and robbed in one day? This was definitely the worst day of my life. I began to look at the paperwork they gave me about my release from the team. I still didn't technically have an agent at that point, so I reached out to a couple I knew and told them my situation. All of them told me that since they were releasing me, even though I was still physically able to play, they'd have to honor my contract and pay me my full salary. The paper they gave me only stated that they were paying my travel expenses and my salary up until the month of December. Once I saw that I felt like they were trying to be snakes. I felt like they weren't as loyal to me as I was to them. If they would've properly rehabbed me in the first place I would've never been in this situation.

On top of that, they weren't as concerned about our house being robbed as we felt they should have been. All they kept saying was, "Don't worry, just rest, because we have a big game tomorrow." At that point, we weren't concerned about the game. My anger got the best of me and I ended up telling T and my other teammates that I had been cut. T and I were on Skype with them from the hotel room telling them about the robbery and I just let it out.

I later received a message from the girl that tore her ACL. She told me to meet her in front of the hotel by myself. To my surprise, she showed up by herself in tears. I didn't know what her issue was, so I consoled her and tried to get it out of her. She told me how the team had cut her off, how she had nowhere to live, her school wasn't being paid for, and how sick her mother had been recently. Feeling her pain, I told her that they had just done the same to me. I told her they had also cut me and that I was going home next week some time. She was shocked and began crying more hysterically. I asked if she just wanted to vent or if she had come for some other reason. Once I asked her that, she began to look around suspiciously. The doorman at the hotel was at the door waiting for me because it was late and he had to lock up. She looked around and saw him and turned her back to him. She then proceeded to tell me that she was the one that had robbed our house. I flipped! I pushed her and began cursing her out. I started screaming at her, "WTF? Why would you do that? We're all going through our own issues. That doesn't mean that you can steal from us. WTF is wrong with you?" She gave me the money back, but said she didn't know where T's iPod was. She gave it to the person that helped her in the robbery, and would try to get it back. I took the money and pushed her out of my way. She asked if she could come up to apologize to T, but I told her she would get her a** beaten like I should have done. I looked back and before I went upstairs, being the softy that I am, I offered her 100 euros. She didn't accept it and I said, "You sure?

Because evidently, you need it." She refused again and didn't take it. T was still up and as I proceeded to tell her what had just happened, she wanted to find our old teammate and beat her a\*\*, like I knew she would. I calmed her down and she said that she shouldn't be able to steal from us and get off that easily. I agreed and we called our families to see what would be the best thing to do. We decided that we wanted to report her to the police. We called Coach and he was reluctant to do so. He didn't want word to get around that it was her, or that it involved people from the team. He felt like since she gave it back it was all good. Once again, we felt like they didn't care as much about us as they did the team

Despite the night we had had, when it came time to play, I played my heart out. I wanted to win that game for my teammates and to be able to show management that they were making a mistake. Unfortunately the game came down to a last second shot, and I missed. Missing that shot felt like the end of the world to me. I had played so well, and so had my team. We went in the locker room and Coach Marcos told the team that I was leaving. He didn't tell them that it was because of my ankle, but they immediately had questions. Everyone in the locker room began crying including him. Seeing how emotional and loving they were tore me up inside. I couldn't believe that this was really it and I was no longer a part of the team.

After the game I went home to pack. I wrote Coach to make sure they told the press it was family issues, and asked that he give me copies of the last three games. He wanted to have one last talk because things between us weren't too good at that point. He came over and we talked. That talk turned out worse than the two prior events. Things escalated and it turned into one big screaming match. It came down to me pulling out my contract and telling him I wasn't going anywhere or signing any release until they paid me all of my money. I told him my contract stated they could only release me if I wasn't physically able to play. Since I was playing forty minutes a game that clearly wasn't the case at all. He tried to rationalize things and said the reason they were releasing me was because they cared about me and wanted me to get healthy. I shouted, "If you were so worried about my ankle why did you play me today, again, for 40 minutes? Clearly I'm still able to play. I'm not leaving until you honor my contract."

After that things got even more heated. I'm sure T was in her room shocked at how we were behaving. After all the screaming, he said that I lied to him that I would be 100% and that wasn't the case. We argued some more and I said, "Bottom line, I'm still able to play. I showed that today even though we lost by two points. So regardless of how you feel, I want my money." He stormed out and the next day asked me to meet with him and the manager again. He stated because of our relationship he didn't want to end on that kind of note. I gave in and we arranged another meeting. In the meeting he apologized, and so did I. We negotiated some things and came to an agreement.

Before signing the papers, we had a heart to heart. He said he knew what my plans were and that he just wanted me to get 100% healthy. He noticed I was playing better, but he knew the type of player I was, and I was nowhere near my full potential. I may have managed to put the same numbers up as the season before, but the competition wasn't nearly as good as last year. He believed that if I was 100% I would have been averaging double my previous stats. I told him I'd take into consideration what he said and keep him posted. We hugged and before I left we talked a little more. I even offered to help find them a replacement for me. I found them two players, but when it came down to the financial negotiations, since they still had to pay me, it didn't work out. Before I walked out he asked if this was the last time he'd see me. I said, "I don't know, why?" He proceeded to tell me that he had been planning to retire the first season I came, but I made him love the game and coaching again. He said that in the future, if possible, he wanted to either coach me again or coach beside me. I was shocked, but he said that once I finished playing if he was still coaching or affiliated with Boa Viagem he'd like it if I was his assistant coach, or maybe even the head coach if he wasn't coaching. I hugged him again and said, "Sure I wouldn't mind it." After that I walked out and went back to my apartment to pack and prepare to head back to the states.

# Chapter 23
# 2013

*Never allow yourself to lose focus of your long term goal, ever!*
*#Tinyism*

Once I arrived back in NYC, I contacted as many people as I could to find a team for the remainder of the season. I hadn't spoken to Charles since I decided to resign with Boa Viagem. From that point on, I figured our business relationship was over. Throughout the season I had been talking casually to some other agents. I had gained an interest in becoming a certified agent later down the line. I even inquired about the certification process after my first season in Portugal. I had intentions of representing myself and some of my friends, but FIBA rules stated I had to be done hooping before beginning the process. Thomas Prodromou was one of the agents interested in signing me after my first season in Portugal. He was also one of the agents that helped to make sure I handled business with Boa Viagem before I left. Since I really didn't have an idea of what to do, and trust had been formed, I asked TP if he'd be interested in helping me. Given the situation and lack of time, I didn't have to sign a contract with him. I was prepared to give him my loyalty though, just as I had with Charles. TP sparked interest from a couple teams, but somehow word had got out from Portugal. They didn't want to take a chance signing me because they heard about a recurring ankle injury. The fact that there were multiple teams asking about my ankle led me to believe Boa Viagem hadn't kept their word. Not only had they released me, but they were now impacting my career and future opportunities. Since the rumor had spread about me having an ankle injury, it was pretty much impossible to find a team for the second half of the season.

I seriously wondered if my professional career was over. For weeks I slipped into a bit of a depression. Since basketball wasn't my primary source of income anymore I began to substitute teach again to get a couple of dollars in my pocket. Working with the kids brought me some much needed joy. I also began spending time with my closest friends to brighten my mood. Working with children is rewarding, but also really draining. I'd leave my house at 6 a.m. and return at 6 p.m. Commuting from Staten Island to the city via public transportation takes between forty-five minutes and an hour and a half, depending on traffic. After a typical work day I usually just went home, walked Buckets, and by 8 p.m. I'd find myself dozing off. Most of the time, I'd be too tired to even think about hitting the gym. It was very rare for me to go more than three days without hooping, so imagine what weeks of that did to me. By the end of January I got back into the swing of things thanks to Munch and a close friend of mine, Damon Brown.

Damon and I had a lot in common. We loved the game, and loved the hustle. I tell people he's like the male version of me. Great basketball abilities, ambitious, intelligent, charming, and caring. I had met Damon at the LA Fitness five minutes away from my house in Staten Island. LA Fitness was one of the places to go if you wanted to get some good runs or workouts in. I used to go to LA Fitness faithfully and Damon would be in there outplaying everyone. He was one of the most talented dudes I've seen play ball. He was one of those people that you noticed right away and either you wanted him on your team or hated that he wasn't already. After learning he was also originally from Brooklyn, it made sense that we were so similar.

Damon's best attribute as a player was his shooting and ability to score. Add his handle and court vision in, and you have one of the toughest guards you'd ever see on court. Damon experienced some of the same issues and setbacks I had while trying to go pro. He had been sold dreams by agents, scammed out of money, and just never really got a fair shot. His only legit opportunity came when he went to China for an exposure tour. He averaged almost a triple double, but for some reason the teams out there didn't sign him. He was averaging twenty-eight points per game, ten assists per game, and seven rebounds per game, had good film and everything. We really didn't understand why nothing ever came from that tour, but that's how the business goes sometimes. Aside from China there seemed to be plenty of interest in him, but just like me, for whatever reason, things always fell through. As time went by his lack of opportunities hurt his resume and he began generating less interest.

Damon has always been one to push and support me. He was vital to me getting my game back after I got released. We'd be in the gym starting at 5:00 in the morning just grinding. Sometimes we'd have our own little "two-a-days" where we'd come back in the daytime and test the moves and drills we just did that morning.

When I went to Portugal that first season, he was genuinely happy for me. Whenever one of us got good news, we both felt like we made it.

During both seasons in Portugal, I spoke to Damon at least three times a week. He checked up on me, motivated me and was a great friend. There had even been times when I felt romantic feelings for him as a result of how supportive, genuine, and loving he was. We were working out together, talking almost every day, and he always seemed to care, so it was bound to happen. He was ideal to be my Quincy McCall, but he had been in a relationship since college, so I never told him. I didn't want to be a home wrecker, especially since I ended up getting cool with his boo. They always seemed very happy and were an adorable couple so I left it alone. There were times I thought the feelings were mutual. I didn't want our relationship to change though, so I kept things between us casual. Eventually the feelings faded and I was able to continue to be the best friend I could. I've always said though, that the moment she messed up he'd be mine!

Munch knew I was home, so he asked me to do two things. First, he wanted me to get girls down to have open gyms, and second, he wanted me to compile a team to compete in some upcoming money tournaments. Once or twice a week I'd arrange some open gyms in Brooklyn for the girls that were still in the country. As far as the money tournaments went, we competed in two. One was located in NJ and the other was located in Vegas. The New Jersey tournament took place Martin Luther King weekend and the Vegas tournament was towards the first weekend of April. Unfortunately we lost in the championship of both tournaments and received the second place prizes. After competing in the Jersey tournament, I got all the motivation I needed to revive my hoop dream.

I contacted TP and asked if he was still interested in representing me. I kept hinting at the fact that I trusted him, was over my agent phobia, and was ready to sign. By the time we came back from the Vegas tournament, I really wanted to sign with him and get the ball rolling. He said he'd do his best but he couldn't promise anything. He said he had a lot of other clients to focus on, which didn't really make me feel like much of a priority. I insisted on signing with him, but he kind of brushed me off. He promoted me on his site and began working for me, but since I didn't feel like I was going to be a priority to him, I contacted a couple of other agents. Eventually, since the basketball world is small, some other agents spoke to him about me. He contacted me, quite angry. Things got a little heated and resulted in him not wanting to help me anymore. He was under the impression that I was going to exclusively be working with him. He deleted me off of his site and took everything down he had put up to promote me. After a day or two, we spoke and realized it was just a simple miscommunication. I apologized to him. He apologized also, and we left it at that.

I started to play in leagues with Damon, and the unlimited women leagues in NYC. Game by game I was starting to get my mojo back. I was selected to participate in a national tournament that would take place in Taiwan during the summer of 2013. The coach of the team was Jared Johnson. I had met Jared before I went to Portugal the first year. He had seen me play in a Rucker Park game and wanted me to play for his league in Atlanta. Jared's league has served as something similar to a D-League for the WNBA and overseas teams. He thought I was talented and didn't understand why I wasn't signed. Since I went to Portugal I didn't make the trip to Atlanta, but we've stayed in contact ever since. I've worked with him to help a lot of people get jobs overseas.

Jared is now working for an agency in Italy and doing his best to get as many people contracts as possible. We're currently working on projects and events to host together. Jared selected me and eleven other players to participate in the William Jones Cup in Taiwan. The tournament would feature different national teams from Korea, Taiwan, Japan, and Thailand. The William Jones Cup was something I had been looking forward to for about a year. I had always wanted to represent my country in a national tournament, but due to the fact they usually only selected WNBA players, I thought I would never get the opportunity. Fortunately for me, this was it.

To participate all I had to do was pay for my flight and everything else would be taken care of once we landed in Taiwan. The flight was about $2000, but I didn't mind because it was a once in a lifetime opportunity. This was just what I needed to start my mission of redemption. The tournament was going to be televised by ESPN, and since I'd be performing in front of different countries, it would be the perfect exposure for me. That national exposure could help to land me a job for the upcoming season. Once we got closer to the date, I found it weird that tickets hadn't been purchased yet. Things seemed to become a little suspicious. The person that Jared was working with turned out to be mixed up in a marketing scheme regarding the tournament. Things didn't seem right, so instead of taking a chance and getting scammed again I decided to not go and save my money. Jared ended up not coaching either.

I had been looking forward to another high exposure event. I was asked to fill in for some friends in a three on three tournament, sponsored and affiliated with FIBA. The tournament was in NYC, but there were also others being held elsewhere. My team won, and we learned that the victory led to a great opportunity. By winning, it made us eligible to compete against the other champions in other states for an opportunity to represent Team USA in the next Olympics. The national competition took place in the TEAM USA training facility in Colorado Springs one weekend in August. That weekend felt like college all over again as athletes from all over the country competed with and against each other. We stayed in dorms and ate in buffet style cafes. Unfortunately we played with mostly guards, which was enough to win in NYC, but meant that our lack of height hurt us in the national tournament. Nonetheless it was a great opportunity and experience. I met a lot of great people and even got some TEAM USA gear.

That summer, Munch and I won every tournament we played in. It was the first time we had won championships in the unlimited division. I played in every all-star game and even got a couple of MVP awards. Since I had my game back, I recorded the games and attached them to the resume and film reel I usually sent out. I sent hundreds of emails. The recent highlights were to show that my ankle was fine and that I still had it. Some teams responded with deals, and others said they had already signed their guard for the season. At one point I received an offer from a team in Slovenia. The offer was kind of low, but I was considering it just to get my foot back in the door. A friend of mine also contacted me about a second year team in Bosnia. The team had just moved up to the top league. They wanted me to come there to help them finish top four in the league so he could lock down key players and sponsors for the following season.

I would have to take a pay cut this season, but next season he guaranteed I would be paid more and that the team would become a Euro Cup team. A Euro Cup team is a team that competes against teams in different countries. Initially I turned the deal down because the pay was way too low. I thought it was a little early to be making such a desperate decision. After a couple days of thinking about it and talking to my mom, I changed my mind. My mom reminded me that it had never been about the money for me before, so why start now? We decided that it was a great opportunity to prove myself. We figured I could just tough it out this season and things would be even better for me the next season. I contacted the coach back immediately and negotiated a little more money with some bonuses. After negotiating the best I could, I told them I was ready to sign.

The coach asked me if I knew any post players that would be open to playing under the same circumstances, to put us in a better position for the next season. I told him yes and hit the first person I could think of, Monet Johnson. Monet had gone to school with Kenya and went on to get a scholarship at Robert Morris, then played professionally in Finland and Germany. Monet had European experience, but she had missed that past season also, so I thought this would be a good move for both of us. We had been playing together for years, and if I didn't get MVP, she usually did. Mo was an undersized post player with crazy athleticism. She was only about 5'10, but with her lanky arms and ability to jump, she held it down on the block. Monet was a walking double-double. After a little convincing, Monet agreed to sign also and we were both on our way to Bosnia. It's very rare that you get the opportunity to play with a close friend professionally in another country. We were so excited about doing our thing that money really wasn't an issue for us. After winning the championships in West 4th and Rucker that summer, we set out to win one in Bosnia and that's what we ended up doing!

The summer of 2013 proved to be my best summer, socially. I did a lot of traveling with friends, including the trips to Vegas and Colorado and took time to enjoy myself. My summer was amazing simply because of the people I had around me. That summer Munch and I recruited most of the girls I looked up to, like Stass and Renee. We'd go play in a game or tournament and then get dressed up and hang out.

I developed a similar relationship with Brittany Braxton. I had met Britt randomly at one of Renee's games and we instantly clicked. Between being a fellow Sagittarius and having a mutual love for lime-a-ritas, Britt was like the light-skinned older twin I never had. It's very rare to meet people that understand you, your actions, and your heart. I can honestly say she has brought the best out of me these past couple of years. She constantly challenges me to do better and be better, whether I liked it or not. With her ambition and drive she's achieved so much in such a short period of time, and I often feel like I need to catch up. Britt is definitely one of the most real people I have in my corner and I couldn't be more appreciative of her.

*Team USA 3 on 3
tournament in Colorado
Springs 2013*

# Chapter 24
# Bosnia

*Sometimes you have to go backwards, to find your way*
*back to the front!*
*#Tinyism*

After winning the West 4th and Rucker Park unlimited tournaments, it was finally time for Mo and I to head to Bosnia. The night before we left, we had a crazy going away gathering with food, drinks, music, and friends. The gathering was at Monet's house, and from what I was told we had a great night. All I know is that I woke up on her couch, not quite sure where I was or how my night had ended. We spoke about what I did remember, and she told also stories that I didn't remember. I'm a lightweight, so by my third drink, I'm pretty much through. Considering I remembered her handing me at least four drinks, the stories she told me seemed pretty believable. I left to go home and make sure I had everything ready for our flight. I told Mo if she ever needed to be on time for something, our flight was it! One thing about Mo is that she is always late! It's so bad we have to tell her the wrong game times to make her show up on time.

After getting everything ready, and saying my final goodbyes, my mother and I headed to the airport. We usually let Buckets ride with us, but my grandmother and aunt were in town, so the car was full. I'm a creature of habit so whenever something is done out of the ordinary, I get worried. If possible, I try to do things the same way every single time. That mentality is a result of being a basketball player for so long. Throughout all my years of playing, I've done the same drills in preparation for games and practices. As an athlete the more you work on something, the more it will feel like second nature to you when it's time to perform. Repeating drills and motions trains your muscle memory. When Buckets wasn't able to come see me off I was sad, but more so worried. The first thing I said to my mom was, "Buckets always comes to the airport. It's gonna be bad luck if he doesn't come this time." At that time my mother probably thought I was just trying to convince her to let him come, but it turned out that I was right.

My coach had signed another American for our team, who was also going to be flying out of NY. Her name was Teisha King. T had just gotten out of college and this was going to be her first season playing overseas. A few minutes before I arrived at the airport, she texted me to ask if Coach had said anything about needing a visa. Apparently the airline wasn't going to let her board without a visa or return flight. Coach Lojo didn't book us a return flight because he wasn't sure when the season was going to be over. The airline didn't want us to leave without a return flight because of the ninety day immigration rule.

I learned about the ninety day rule the hard way, back when I was leaving Portugal after my first season. Basically, if you're in a country for more than ninety days, you become what's known as an illegal immigrant. In 2012, on my way back to NY, as soon as the customs agent looked over my passport, he looked at me like I was crazy. He was nice, but also very stern with me. He explained that when traveling to play for teams professionally, I need to make it my responsibility to get a work visa. He said usually they would make me pay a fine and put a dark stamp on my passport to show that I was an illegal immigrant at one point in time. Once you get that dark stamp on your passport, they don't let you back in that country and possibly even Europe again. So I definitely didn't want that to happen. I was in Portugal for about one hundred days more than the ninety day allowance, so he could've really done some damage. Fortunately he let me go with a very scary warning. My career could've really been over after that.

After telling my mom what T had texted me, she was told me, "That's her problem. You're getting on that flight with or without her." When we arrived at the check-in desk we saw T and her father off to the side. I wanted to ask her what they had said to her, but my mother told me not to even look at her. Since I knew the rules, I'd tell customs I wasn't staying longer than a month or two. I knew it wasn't the truth, but I figured things would most likely get handled once I arrived. When I got to the check in desk and gave them my passport, they told me the same thing they told T. I tried my hardest to get them to allow me on the flight, but they weren't having it. At that time it was maybe only an hour or two before our flight was departing. If something was going to be done, it had to be done soon! They told us that the only way they would allow us on the flight, was if we managed to book a return flight. That return flight would confirm the fact that we wouldn't be in Bosnia over 90 days. Our flight was around 9 p.m. and since it was a six hour time difference from Bosnia to NY, getting in touch with Coach wasn't happening. On top of that, Mo wasn't even at the airport yet! After talking to the check-in people and trying to do all we could before the gate was closed, we ended up having to buy our own return flights. We weren't really sure what date to say, we just were pressed for time, so we let them pick any date. We figured coach could just reimburse us and change the date when it was time for us to leave.

It was a Sunday and, according to Coach, we had a scrimmage game that next Wednesday. Since we had a game, we felt like there was no way we could miss that flight. T and I began to purchase our return flights, and Mo still hadn't arrived. We had 45 minutes left to get to the gate. I honestly thought we weren't going to make it, especially Mo. With twenty minutes left until the boarding time of our flight, we finally began to check our bags. Our return trip was booked for exactly ninety days from that day. As soon as we were almost to our gate, Mo came running in. After filling her in, she began to book her return trip, but it didn't go through. The credit card she used only had a $500 limit. Mo was only able to book one of the flights on that return trip. Going and coming back there was a layover in Amsterdam. Since we were pressed for time and I was sure I'd get my money back, I paid for the other half of her return ticket. Unlike me, Mo wasn't an over packer so checking her bags didn't take long at all. T and I said goodbye to our parents, and ran off to our gate. It was a close call, but we were on our way!

We arrived in Bosnia the next evening. Coach picked us up, took us to eat at McDonald's, and then it finally hit me; I had gotten a second chance at my dream. Our first team practice went well. We got to know our Bosnian teammates, did some drills, and scrimmaged a little. Mo and I were still in NYC summer basketball form, so we put on quite a show that first practice. There were sixteen girls besides Mo, T and I. As we progressed through the season, that number fluctuated up and down. One of the biggest consistencies was that we got new players every other week, and lost some as well.

My team was located in Sarajevo, which was the capital. Compared to Brooklyn, it was a small city. Despite its size, we made the best of it on and off the court. Before KK Playoff's existence the best team in Sarajevo was Zeljeznicar. They were a well-known and well-respected club in Sarajevo. One of the biggest differences in basketball between Europe and the USA is how their basketball system is set up. In Europe each team is part of a club. That club has teams at every level, either women, men, or both. There's usually a team starting from kids ten and under all the way up to the professional team. Some clubs have the same system for other sports within that club. Take Zeljeznicar, for instance. They had younger girls' teams, the women's team in our division, a men's soccer team, and even a European handball team. Based on this system, the club as a whole is more family-oriented. Kids, fans, and everyone that is part of the club has the opportunity to grow with it.

Zeljeznicar had a history of winning championships in the Bosnian and the Adriatic Leagues. The Adriatic League was made up of the top teams from all of the countries that used to make up Yugoslavia. There were teams from Bosnia, Croatia, Slovenia, Montenegro, and Serbia. Since Zeljeznicar was the team to be on for all the girls that played basketball in Sarajevo, either you didn't make the team or you were on the team but didn't get much playing time. Those conditions made it very easy for Coach Lojo to get some of their players. These were not necessarily their key players or extremely talented players, but good enough players to compete with and fill his roster. All season long players bounced from our team to Zeljeznicar or vice versa. These roster changes created some animosity and of course an in-town rivalry.

After a couple of practices it was game day! We were scrimmaging another well-respected Bosnian team, Celik. Celik was the favorite to win the Bosnian league and Mo and I were already plotting an upset. We realized we would be the underdogs all season because we were the 'new kids on the block.' It came down to me turning the ball over late in crunch time and them making their free throws after we were forced to foul. Mo played great as she had twenty points to accompany her double/double. Coach was surprised because she's not that tall, but extremely athletic. He was a little worried because Celik had some big girls from the Bosnian national team, but Mo held her own. T didn't do so well, but it was somewhat expected because this was her first professional match. I had 17 points but a lot of turnovers. Some of my turnovers came from my teammates not being ready for my passes. The other ones were just plain old stupid, unforced mistakes. Besides T, Mo, and one other older player, we had a really young, inexperienced team. Most of them weren't too talented, but they definitely played hard. As long as you play hard and play your role, I can work with you. Catching and finishing is really all my teammates need to focus on in games with me. The older player, Amra Dapo, was someone I came to count on to contribute. Amra has been referred to as the Bosnian Kobe Bryant. She was a well-seasoned vet, but still had some gas in the tank. She spent most of her career in Spain, Hungary, and Croatia playing against and with the best. She admitted that she was at the age where she just wanted to be around her family, so playing for KK Playoff was the ideal situation for her. Since a young age, she had been following her dream and playing all over the world. She was considering retiring until Coach Lojo got word she was back in town. After a couple of meetings, Amra played with Playoff when they were in the second division, and helped them get to the top division. Amra was about 6'1, but she played shooting guard. Though she was taller than Mo, Mo played the PF/C position. Amra could shoot from anywhere on the floor, post up smaller defenders, and she had great footwork, especially for a forty-three year old! She averaged sixteen points a game or better against players literally half her age! She also had a great sense of humor and personality. With her, Mo, and T, I had no problem getting assists or some good laughs in.

That Saturday we met up with a few of our teammates for drinks, hookah, and a nice time. We enjoyed ourselves and met Bosnian NBA player Mirza Teletovic. It was kind of ironic meeting him, because he played for our hometown team, the Brooklyn Nets. Despite our teammates being star struck, Mirza was very cool and down to earth. It didn't occur to us that he was like the Michael Jordan of Bosnia, until we saw how our teammates were acting.

That following week we beat the defending champions of the Montenegrin league, Buducnost. We then played in a memorial tournament at Celik for a player that had passed away the season before. The tournament games were back-to-back, so after our first win we were going to face Celik in the championship. All I could think about was how disappointed in myself I was after the last game we played against them. I knew it would be an even tougher game because there was so much more on the line! It was a championship game, they'd have their crowd behind them, and they were playing in honor of one of their own. With that in mind, I knew they would come out war-ready, and that they did. We were down as much as eighteen at one point, but my pride just wouldn't let me fold. To start the second half, I came out hot and with the help of my team, we got right back into the game. With all the marbles on the line, Coach Lojo drew up one last play for me with about ten seconds left and I scored an "And-1" game winning bucket. As I went to the free throw line to seal the game I tried hard not to think, but the main thought in my head was "REDEMPTION!" and of course making the free throw.

After I made the free throw Celik attempted a half-court shot which missed and the KK Playoff bench went crazy. Mo came over to me, we did our little 'Roc Boys' hand shake and Brooklyn salute and proceeded to shake Celik's hand. They gave us our medals and cup trophy. It felt so good to hold that trophy in the air and see the look on my Coach and teammate's faces. It was at that moment I truly believed I had made the right decision. I was only playing for $550 a month and a couple meals per day, but at the end of the day I was satisfied because I was back living my dream, and to me, that's priceless!

*Sealing the victory against Celik*

*Sarajevo, Bosnia*

# Chapter 25
# The Road to Redemption

*No matter where you are in life, you should always want*
*more out of it!*
*#Tinyism*

With my redemption season officially underway, I began to
think of other ways to propel my career forward. I was in the prime
of my career: I was twenty-five years old, the game had become so
easy to me physically and mentally, and, realistically, I had maybe
five more dominant years in me. I wanted so much more for my
career, so my primary focus was to find the proper representation.
Although I was doing well at finding my own deals, getting in
contact with those top teams was a lot harder to do by myself. With
the better teams, it's more about relationships. I needed someone
well-connected and well-respected to get me where I wanted to be.

When I arrived in Bosnia, I became a social media junkie. If I
wasn't doing something productive, I was on social media,
marketing myself. I learned who the top agencies were and what
kind of presence they had in the media. One agency would always
stand out on my feed: Two Points. Two Points is based out of

Cremona, Italy, and owned by Mario Scotti. I knew at least twenty people who were signed to Two Points. Girls I played with and against in college and professionally were signed with them. About ten people from NYC were signed with them. Even my bro Reggie from Morgan was signed to Two Points. At that point I said, "I gotta get the scoop on them! They got everybody!" I ended up contacting my friend Donica Cosby. We had played against each other in Portugal. Our career numbers were one in the same. We both had great resumes, but just never got the opportunities we felt we deserved. Donica had also experienced a lot of setbacks in her career, so I knew she'd be the perfect person to contact. Nica was a scoring machine, and after competing against each other and having mutual respect for one another, we became very cool. We both had the agent phobia, and always tried to look out for one another. Nica had just signed her contract to a team in Romania, and I'd see her raving about how perfect her agent was and how happy she finally was. As soon as I contacted her to inquire about Two Points, she was one step ahead of me. Once I hit her, she told me, "Tiny, I already put the word in for your boss, no worries!" After chopping it up, she gave me her agent's name and contact info.

To this day, if you asked what Lorenzo Gallotti meant to me, I'd simply tell you he was the male version of Tiny in Italian. Since our initial conversation, not a day has gone by that we haven't spoken. In the beginning, we spoke about me, my career, and my terrible experiences with agents and this business. I began to pick his brain about the basketball world. I began to realize he was just as caring, intelligent, and down to earth as I was. Every once in a blue, he'd throw in hints, like, "When you sign with Two Points, we can do this or that," but he never really pressured me to sign. It wasn't until after five months that I signed a contract with him and Two Points.

Despite not being signed, he was always willing to advise me. His willingness and the relationship we had formed made the partnership a no-brainer. He was also one of the few that didn't consider all my crazy ideas crazy. He sometimes even added to the madness, and helped me find ways that they could work.

I wanted to focus on my PR and marketing. Within the next two seasons, my goal was to obtain an endorsement deal. Honestly, I just wanted free gear and to be a poster child for an apparel company. I wasn't necessarily looking for money. I figured we could start the partnership out with free gear, and once I brought the company more business, I could begin to ask for compensation. I had begun to promote for an up-and-coming apparel brand called Lady Athletics. I got the email addresses of about forty apparel companies. Of the few responses I received, Lady Athletics wanted to establish some kind of partnership. They were just launching the brand, so compensation wasn't even an option. They would send me some gear, and I'd do my best to get the brand out there and try to bring them some customers. Throughout the summer, I did my part and they did theirs.

I began making a conscious effort to inspire as many people as I could, on a daily basis. Inspiring and communicating is the best way to market yourself; you begin to create bonds and relationships, making it easier for people to support you. I also looked to do more good deeds on a daily basis. Whether I just held the door for someone or gave a homeless person loose change, I wanted to be remembered for something positive. I wanted to have more of an impact on the people I came into contact with.

Several people suggested I write a book, which I thought was one of the craziest ideas ever. After talking to my mom and some friends of mine, I began to seriously consider it. I began communicating with someone who, at the time, I didn't know very well, but I knew of and respected. I noticed the similarities in our goals and actions. After speaking to this individual I decided—screw it, I'm going to be an author!

That person was the one and only Fan Favorite, La'Keisha Sutton. The way I had been seeing Two Points all over my social feed, I was seeing Fan Favorite. Prior to following and supporting her movement, I had no idea who she was. Keish was a couple years younger than me. She graduated from the University of South Carolina, and played under the legendary Dawn Staley. On a daily basis, I'd see a lot of our mutual friends shouting her out and supporting her, just as they had done for me. When Keish was at USC, she received her nickname, Fan Favorite, from her coaching staff. She ended up turning Fan Favorite into her brand, which is now one of the most well-supported movements of an athlete, worldwide. I first heard of her through Jared Johnson. We collaborated on an event during West 4th's All-Star Weekend in NY. He wanted to bring a team down from his women's developmental league in Atlanta, to see how they would compete against some of the best street ballers in NYC. Once we got things squared away, he would express his excitement to come down and have me and Keish in the backcourt together. The ATL vs New York All-Star Challenge was in July. There were a total of four teams. Jared's Atlanta team, two teams made up of All-Stars from the West 4th League, and one team from the West 4th League. After hearing so much about Keish and seeing her brand all over the place, I decided to purchase one of her shirts and do a little research on her. I was actually very excited to support her and her movement. I want everyone to shine and eat! Another one of my mottos is Everybody Eats B!

When Jared and his team arrived, I introduced myself to all of the girls. I noticed Keish in my peripheral, getting ready for the game. She was Fan Favorited out, from head to toe. I could see that she was getting into game mode.

In any West 4th Street game, there is a crowd surrounding the cage. The ones who didn't know me assumed I was from Atlanta, because I was playing with them. Being typical New Yorkers, they began to talk trash to Keish and me. It was funny, but, at the same time, motivating. As the game progressed, she and I went highlight for highlight to silence the crowd. There were a couple plays where I assisted her and she assisted me.

Since we both were putting on a show and the crowd was loving us, the trash talkers started talking more and more. Keish had gotten an "And 1" and, shortly after, one of the trash talkers in the crowd made an Atlanta reference. This time around she responded, and said, "Don't be fooled, I'm from Jersey!" I winked at him and said—"Yea, and I'm from Brooklyn." He laughed and called us traitors. By the fourth quarter, he was cheering us on and became a fan of us both. We won that game and the championship game the next day. I got MVP of the challenge. If it was up to me, I would've given it to Keish, but I didn't mind taking that nice 40" TV home to my mom!

After the game, Keish and I spoke about the game and how impressed with one another we were, and we wished each other the best. She ended up playing on Team USA, which I was supposed to play on, that went to Taiwan that same summer. I regret not going and getting another opportunity to play in the backcourt with her and making fans out of the crowd. Fortunately, the following summer we played in a couple more events and all-star games together that I arranged.

One day while I was in Bosnia, she asked me for my advice. She was one of my primary factors for writing this book. When we spoke, I told her of some of my experiences. I told her about everyone recommending I write a book, because of all I had been through, and, to my surprise, she agreed. She said, "I never really had a mentor, and from this brief friendship, I view you as my mentor. You've been through a lot and you don't let it show. Everyone has a testimony, Tiny, and you're a living one. People need to hear your story, for real."

Although she said the same things everyone else had been saying, it meant way more to me coming from her. I looked up to her and her movement. To this day, it's like everything we strive to be and strive to achieve are identical. She always tells me, "We gonna change the world T, watch."

After riding out on that three game win streak, Coach Lojo approached us with some amazing news! Instead of waiting until next year to become a Euro Cup team, he and the sponsors were confident in our abilities to compete against the tougher opponents this season. The Adriatic League was going to be starting in early October, so we had some time to build chemistry and prepare. Our first game was going to be away, against a top team from the Serbian League called Crvena Zvezda. Playing on a Euro Cup team gives you the opportunity to visit and play in many different countries, and provides more exposure for your career. Because of the budget, we drove from Sarajevo to all of our games. We even drove for our games in the Adriatic league. When I wasn't asleep in the van, there would be some pretty amazing sights to see. Playing with KK Playoff allowed me to visit six countries in an eight month time span. It was a very humbling experience, getting to see those beautiful places.

Each time we traveled to another country, we'd go to the center of each city. The centers are the downtown areas. They are made of stores, coffee shops, restaurants, and monuments. The first thing that was crazy to me about Serbia was the fact that, as soon as we passed the passport control border, we had police escorts with us at every moment. At first, Mo and I thought it was pretty cool. We felt kind of Hollywood with the sirens and police cars around us. After a while, I started to question it—"Hey, why do we need escorts? Are we going to be in danger?" Because of the past wars and the splitting of Yugoslavia, there was still some animosity between Serbians and Bosnians. On top of that, they weren't too fond of Americans, so the escorts were both protection and precaution. Despite what we were told, when we went to walk around in the center, the people of Serbia acted quite the contrary towards us. Wherever Mo, T, and I went, people would either come up to us for pictures or try to shout hello from afar.

We ended up winning the game by two points! I didn't shoot as well as I wanted to, but I played some great defense. That was T's best game to that point. She helped me force their guards into trouble, and made the game winning basket! Serbia was indeed a successful trip.

We were now riding a four game win streak. Our next opponent was the favorite to win the Slovenian League, Celje. Prior to every game, I look up the team we're playing and try to get a little information on them. I find out their best players, who I'd likely be guarding, and also watch some film, to see how they play. On this particular team, they had a WNBA draftee/Team USA 20U participant named Tavelyn James, and a Syracuse University graduate named Carmen Tyson-Thomas. They were both Two Points clients. I became friends with them after the game, but, during the game, we went at it! We lost by ten, but I exploded for thirty-four points! I tried to put my team on my back, but they had more fire power. To be considered the best, you have to compete with and beat the best. Having that kind of game against that kind of competition sparked a lot of interest from a number of coaches from top leagues.

The next game was going to be against Celik, but it counted towards the Adriatic League standings. Celik became a rival by default. Once again, we had to head to their side of town, but this time they demolished us by sixteen. That was our second consecutive double-digit loss. After that game, my team lost two players. One left due to lack of time to focus on school, and another left because she was in the Army, and it was just too draining for her to continue to do both.

We were off for a day or two and, next thing you know, we walked into practice to three new players. One player was around Amras' age; her name was Dajana Bugarin, but we called her Bugi. The other two players were young, but they were more talented than any young player we had. Both of their names were Nikolina, so we called them by their last names; Dzebo and Babic. Both Nikolinas were a part of the Bosnian National Team, so Zeljeznicar wasn't too happy about them coming to play for us. They left because they weren't getting along with the coach. Despite seeing the whole situation as our coach stealing their players, these three instantly made us a better team, and that's all that mattered.

The first game we would play was away, in Montenegro against Buducnost. That was one of the biggest crowds I ever played in front of, and also the most rowdy. In addition to that, I hit a three-quarter court shot to send the game into OT. Towards the end of the second half, the crowd started taking things to new levels.

When we started to take over the game, they began throwing fruits, peanuts, paper, and other items. The game took an extra hour and a half, because of the overtimes and the fact that we had to keep stopping to clean up the court. This wasn't the same Buducnost team we beat a couple weeks before. Just as we had added extra players, so had they. Minus getting hit with an apple, that was one of the best games I played in my entire career. I wish that three-quarter court shot was for the game and not for OT, because we ended up losing 103-96 in double OT.

We went on a bit of a win streak, primarily because the Bosnian League began. The Bosnian League was very weak. I was so grateful for the Adriatic League, because if we only played in the Bosnian League, I would've been highly disappointed. Besides Celik, there weren't any talented teams in the league. We were scoring ninety to one hundred points every game. I was averaging about twenty minutes a game; once we started blowing teams out, Coach would play my teammates, who never really got a chance to play in the Adriatic League. The Adriatic League games were every other Thursday, and the Bosnian League games were every weekend. In the beginning of the Bosnian League games, we played Celik and beat them by one point, to tie the season long series. Then, we played another Serbian team in the Adriatic League—Radivoj Korac. I didn't play so well against Celik, but I made a couple good plays down the stretch. After I hit that shot to go to OT in Montenegro, I became the buzzer beating queen. Whether it was shot clock buzzers or end of the quarter buzzers, I made some of the craziest last second shots that season. After a subpar performance, I always do my best to have a bounce back game to make up for it. In the game against the later Adriatic League champs, Korac, I bounced back amazingly. I hit a half court buzzer beater before halftime, scored twenty-four points, and helped my team win by twelve. After that game, we won the next three in the Bosnian League, to remain undefeated.

The scores of those games were: 106-72, 115-66, and 128-51. After those wins in the Bosnian League, we went on to lose the next two in the Adriatic League. The first was by two points, in a rematch with Crvena Zvezda. If I ever needed to hit another buzzer beater, it was in that game. We were down most of the game, but in crunch time I scored eight straight, to tie the game. Prior to my last minute heroics, Mo took over and started the comeback. They had the ball, with about twenty seconds left. We played great defense and forced them to miss. As I tried to crash the boards to get the rebound, their center grabbed it over me and quickly laid it back up. With about three seconds left, my teammate inbounded the ball to me, and I tried for my classic buzzer beater. As I shot it, one of the girls on the other team jumped under me and affected my momentum. The shot fell short, and that was the end of the game. I scored twenty-four points and dropped six assists, but it just wasn't enough. On the bright side, I was leading the Adriatic League in scoring.

Our next game was against Celje, right before Christmas break. I desperately wanted to win that game, as we needed to win to be sure we would make the playoffs for the Adriatic League. In the first quarter, it was a pretty even game. Unfortunately, I got into foul trouble early in the second quarter, and Coach sat me down. I was upset, because I didn't want to be out that long, but my team was holding it down in my absence. I began to coach and cheer them on as hard as I could from the side. I don't know why, but Coach Lojo decided to play zone on defense. We rarely ever worked on zone prior to that game, and it definitely showed. The moment we went zone, Tavelyn James caught fire. She hit seven threes off of the same exact play. By the time he put me back in the game, I wasn't even in my same groove. Tav gave us forty points, and Celje went on to win by sixteen.

Prior to that, Coach had always listened to my suggestions and trusted me. That loss was the turning point of our relationship, and maybe even of my Bosnian experience as a whole. The day before that game, I had asked him about possibly raising my salary. That little $550 a month wasn't doing it for me. I had heard that we had gotten new sponsors, and more money was being given to the team. I let him in on the fact that a lot of teams had been contacting me to come play for them, but out of respect and loyalty to him, I didn't entertain them. I wasn't threatening him, but I tried to let him know that I was worth the increase. I just wanted a bit more, so I wouldn't have to be as cheap as I had been those first few months. He told me he would see what he could do, but he didn't think it would be possible.

Following the loss, we had a couple days off for the holidays. During those off days, Mo, T, and I would hang out, go out to eat, and even go to watch Zeljeznicar play in the Bosnian League. Zeljeznicar wasn't as good as the teams they had in the past. They really only had one good player, and she was a Bosnian-American. She played college ball in America and a couple seasons overseas, but her nationality was Bosnian. We eventually got cool with her too, and hung out a couple times. One day after hanging out, word got back to Mo and I that Zeljeznicar wanted us to leave KK Playoff and play for them. Coach Lojo had stolen their best players, so now their plan was to steal his.

Being the loyal person I am, I had already made my mind up that I wasn't going to think about playing for them, but Mo and I are two completely different people. Mo had bills and responsibilities that I didn't, so we went to meet with them, to at least see what they were offering. The whole situation was kind of weird for me. The way they contacted us was very sneaky, and I just didn't want to be in the middle of that Playoff and Zeljeznicar war. We met with their coach and the club's GM. During the meeting, they gave us the background information on their club, their history of championships, and their future plans to bring in another American before playoffs. They also mentioned that they could triple whatever Playoff was paying us. Mo was pretty much sold. As for me, I wasn't with it. Everything sounded great, but my conscience just wouldn't let me consider it. On top of that, I knew that, when it came down to it, they couldn't beat us—so I definitely wasn't interested. Once we left their offices, Mo went on and on about how she was gone. She wanted the money and all she kept saying was, "This is a business, baby. Coach been doing the same thing to them." I just laughed, shook my head, and said, "Do your thing, son, just know we gonna bust y'all a**!"

# Chapter 26
# The Beginning of 2014

*You can plan all you want, something is going to go wrong!*
*It's up to you to also make sure something goes right!*
*#Tinyism*

On Christmas Eve, I decided to take a trip down to the center. I figured I could get something to eat and kill some time. There was a Christmas market and mini-carnival set up. There were rides, tents with live entertainment inside, and a lot of vendors. Besides noticing all the people with their families shopping and enjoying the carnival, I also noticed the less fortunate families on the opposite end. Most of them were outside the market, begging for marks (Bosnian money). Usually when I walk by the less fortunate, I give whatever loose change I have and go about my day. This particular time, after I gave them my change, I wanted to do more. I decided that, since I had no one to buy a Christmas gift for and didn't have any plans, I would come back to the center and buy a less fortunate family toys and dinner for the night. I knew it wouldn't be much, but I just wanted them to have some kind of Christmas.

I asked Mo to come to the center with me. I wanted to document the good deed, so I'd be able to relive the moment visually. When we got to the center, the first thing I did was get a couple of chicken sandwiches from this spot we go to on a regular basis. In addition to tasting amazing, the sandwiches were huge. I figured they would be perfect for a family who didn't know where their next meal was coming from. I began scouting out just who I was going to bless. One thing about the homeless people in Bosnia, if they sense you aren't from their city, they are going to harass you more than anyone else for money. They feel it's more likely for a foreigner to give them money than the people from their own town. As soon as we stopped walking, two kids ran up to us and asked for money. Although they didn't speak English, I asked them where their family was, and they proceeded to show us. When we got near their family, their eyes lit up! The fact that the kids had two Americans walking back with them meant nothing but good. When we came into contact with the whole family, I gave them the chicken sandwiches. The mother thanked me over and over. After she hugged me and finally let me go, I told the two kids to walk with me. We went to the market, and I told them to pick any toy they wanted. The market had toy baskets for sale. Each basket came with about five toys, candy, and a coloring book. I bought both of them a basket, and proceeded to give them the change. As Mo was recording all of this on my phone, another little boy came over with the saddest face ever. Mo saw how sad he looked, and she ended up buying him a toy basket too. We didn't have much to give, but seeing the appreciation from those people made me feel like we gave them the world.

The days prior to New Year's Eve were filled with a lot of wine and writing. I began to really get into a groove, and I was producing chapters almost every three days. I sent them out to my friends, family, and publishers, and I received a lot of positive reviews. I couldn't believe it at first. I thought my friends were just trying to be nice and supportive. When publishers began to tell me I was on to something, it motivated me to continue writing! The toughest part was reliving all of the heartbreaking moments I've been through. Once I made my book outline and figured out exactly what I wanted to write about, the memories began coming back vividly! There were times I had to stop writing because I was getting too emotional. It was hard sometimes, but I wouldn't change a thing that has happened to me (except maybe meeting my biological father). Those experiences made me who I am today.

Before I knew it, it was New Year's Eve—and since I was with Monet "Life of the Party" Johnson, there was no way I wasn't enjoying my New Year's Eve. Even T decided to come out with us and partake in the festivities. T was way more religious and reserved than Mo and I, so we were definitely surprised when she held her cup under one of the wine bottles. Once we saw T was down to party, we knew it was going to be a good night.

While heading to the center, everyone approached us for pictures, suggested that we party with them, and showed a lot of love. We went to five or six spots that night, and everywhere we went, people treated us like celebrities. They were buying us drinks and taking pictures. We even managed to get into a couple of VIP areas. We found our images all over Facebook and Bosnian websites. We were even pictured in a Bosnian newspaper! We brought in 2014 with a lot of love, fun, drinks, and good people.

Mo ended up leaving the team, but instead of going to Zeljeznicar, she ended up going back home to Brooklyn. A few years prior, Mo had applied to work with the Corrections

Department of NYC. She took the test a couple years before, and they were just now calling her back to participate in the preliminary interviews and academy. This was something that she couldn't pass up, because this is what she planned to fall back on once she finished hooping. I was genuinely happy for her! She had family she needed to provide for, and this was something she really wanted to do. Coach Lojo wasn't happy. He was more worried about the rest of our season and continuing to win. He asked Mo time and again if she could reschedule, postpone, or even come back after the interviewing process for playoffs. Unfortunately, none of that was possible.

Coach Lojo wasn't happy, and neither were our sponsors. They were the ones that would've had to pay for her flight back home. Since it was last minute, they wanted find a cheap flight for her. While they looked, time was running out for Mo. Her interview date was quickly approaching, and she had things she needed to take care of. Mo eventually asked Coach Lojo if she would be reimbursed if she bought the ticket herself. He said yes, because that's what our contract stated. Mo's credit card still didn't have enough on it to purchase a ticket. I ended up putting her flight on my credit card. We spoke to Coach, and it was arranged that, when the time came, I would be the one to get reimbursed.

After Mo's departure, we won our first two games. We had one game in the Bosnian League, and then we played Celik again in the Adriatic League. Although I loved playing with Mo, winning without her meant more to me than winning with her. Our first couple of months in the Adriatic League I struggled sharing the stardom. I had played on a couple teams where other teammates shined, but never more than me. While we were playing in Bosnia, I got the newspaper articles and website write ups, but Mo did too.

In the Adriatic League, she was getting all the love!

In Europe, they have a stat not really paid attention to in the USA called your efficiency rate. The efficiency rate is calculated with a formula based on all of your stats. Everything from your field goal percentage to your turnovers are computed into a plus and minus system. It's harder for guards to have high efficiency rates, because we usually have more faults in the game than bigs. On most nights, Mo would average a double/double and since 85% of her shots were layups, her field goal percentage was always high. The efficiency ratings are what decides who the players of the week are. In the first month of the Adriatic League, she got multiple players of the week, as well as a player of the month. I would feel a little envious, because I wasn't getting any love. I was happy for Mo and proud of her, but, at the same time, I wanted my pat on the back too. Most of her double/doubles were 50% mine, since I was the one assisting her. Not getting any recognition motivated me, though. That was another reason that being the leading scorer of the Adriatic League was so important to me.

Prior to the Celik game, something unexpected occurred. Two days before the game, Coach Lojo called me. He said that there was a team in Bulgaria that needed a point guard. They wanted me to come in and replace their current point guard, with hopes that we would go far in the playoffs. He said the agent could work it out to where I could get double the pay and come back to Bosnia for playoffs. At first, I was a little shocked that he would suggest something like that. He told me that I deserved it, and that we probably wouldn't make the playoffs in the Adriatic League. Since the Adriatic League would be coming to an end soon, he suggested I go and come back for the Bosnian League playoffs.

I contacted Lorenzo and my mom, to see what their thoughts

were. My mom said to go if I believed it would be a good career move. Lorenzo told me that the Bulgarian league was more competitive than the Bosnian League, and if I managed to help save their season, it would look good on my resume. He warned me that even though the league was better, the team was a little unprofessional and disorganized.

I told Coach Lojo that I would accept the offer, but I didn't want to leave until after we beat Celik! I had been looking forward to the game all week. On top of that, it was going to be on the anniversary of my favorite aunt's death. I also told Coach Lojo that I didn't want to tell the team about my departure until after the game. They still weren't over the fact that Mo had just left. I didn't want to stress them out more and hurt our chances of winning!

Since it was the anniversary of my aunt's passing, I wanted to do something to honor her. My Aunt Liz was the liveliest person in our family. She reminded me of Mo. She was also the life of the party, and so much fun to be around. Between the ages of ten and thirteen, I spent a lot of time with her at my grandmother's house. Unfortunately, during my senior year of college, she passed away due to AIDS. She was older than my mom, but you would think she was the youngest of my mother's siblings. Aunt Liz's birthday was also ten days before mine, so we would always celebrate our birthdays together. I decided that I would write her name on my shoes, and wear mismatched shoes during the game. That season, I was hooping in the Lebron 10s. I had two pairs of them, in the brightest colors ever. I had one pair that was neon orange and neon green. The other pair was green, blue, purple, and yellow.

As expected, the Celik game was very intense. They took advantage of us on the boards since we didn't have Mo, but we managed to stay in the game all the way to the end. With about thirty seconds to go, I came up with a big steal with the game tied. They fouled me, and I knocked down two clutch free throws. The next possession, they drew up a play and missed. We ended up winning 64-60, and I couldn't have been happier. I was able to honor my aunt with a win, and I was going to be leaving Bosnia on a good note.

After the win and celebration, Coach Lojo told the team that I was going to be heading to Bulgaria the next day. The looks on their faces were so sad. They all told me I better come back for playoffs, and I assured them that I would. I told them that I even left some of my things in the apartment with T, so there was no way I wasn't coming back. After the game, Coach and I spoke about the Bulgaria situation again. He mentioned that there were some things occurring within the city of Sarajevo and the government. They had recently fired the treasurer of the city. In Bosnia, the treasurer signed off on all financial checks and transfers. Since they fired him, there was no one in the office to sign off on anything. All payments were on hold until they elected someone else. At the time, he was already a month late with my payment, so he gave me what he owed from the last month, and said he would transfer the reimbursement for Mo and next month's salary as soon as he got it. At the time I believed him, but, just like most of the teams in Europe, once you leave a team and country without your money, chances are you will never receive it. He dropped me off at the bus, and wished me luck. We said our see you laters, and then it hit me—I was on my way to yet another team, experience, and journey.

I did a little research on my new team. We had a great center from the University of North Carolina who was also drafted to the WNBA. Her name was Walteia Rolle. We had a pre-season cup championship under our belt, and good positioning to make the playoffs. I even checked the girl out that I was replacing. Her name was Bjonee Reaves. She graduated from the University of Cincinnati. Her overall numbers were good and she was top ten in a couple statistics throughout the whole league. I had a hard time trying to figure out just why they wanted to let her go. The only thing that seemed fishy to me was that in the last couple of games, she didn't play much.

Coach Lojo and Vesko (the agent who arranged the deal) told me I would be traveling for ten hours after I got to Serbia and that once I arrived, I was going to go straight to practice. The next day I would have my first game with the team. To me that sounded so crazy, but dope at the same time. Thursday I played in Bosnia, and by Sunday I was playing in Bulgaria. I was convinced that this was exactly what I needed, to continue to propel my career in the right direction.

The plan was to take the bus to Serbia from Bosnia, and then the train to Sofia, the main city of Bulgaria. From there, my new coaches were going to pick me up, and we were going to drive from Sofia to Haskovo—my new city for the remainder of the season. To my surprise, the trip ended up being double the amount of time Coach Lojo said it would be. Initially I was a little upset that I would be on a train for 24 hours, but I figured it would be okay, because I would have time to write more. I ended up sleeping the whole time. Once I finally arrived, my new coaching staff picked me up from the train station in Sofia, and we drove for another two hours to Haskovo. As we drove, I broke the ice and asked them what would be expected of me. After looking at B's stats, I wanted to know ahead of time how I would need to perform. I didn't want them looking for my replacement, so, before I even hit the court, I wanted to have an idea. I realized that the woman driving was my head coach. This was going to be my first time having a female head coach. She laughed, and in this funny, high pitched voice she said, "I want you to score and score and score!" I laughed and said, "Cool, that won't be a problem at all." Once we arrived and I got settled, they told me what time practice was. When I arrived at the gym, I was in for yet another surprise—B was still there. It was pretty awkward, looking in the face of the girl you were supposedly coming to replace. I guess my other teammates weren't aware of my arrival either, because they looked pretty surprised to see yet another little black girl in that locker room. No matter where I am or where I am playing, I try my hardest to make a great first impression. Despite the awkwardness in the air, and my train-lag from traveling, I made sure I put on a show in that practice. I also made it my duty to put on even more of a show in my first game the following day.

Even though I was under the impression that I was going to be replacing B, it turned out that the coaching staff wanted us to play together. It was an honor to be on the same team with her and Walteia. They had come from the Big East and the ACC conferences, two of the best conferences in the NCAA. I was just little ol' Tiny from Morgan State and the MEAC. I've played with all types of players worldwide, and I'm one of those players who, no matter who you put me on court with, I'll find a way to co-exist and make them better.

When it came time for tip-off, it was me, B, one of our young Bulgarian players from the national team, and our starting forward Lidia—who was older than Amra! Lidia was forty-three years old, but still had it in her to compete. Lidia had gone to college in the USA. She had also played all over Europe and for the national team.

Since we only had one practice, I didn't know many plays.

Coach Elena told me all she wanted me to worry about was pick and roll. So, after Wal won the tip, the first thing we did was pick and roll at the top of the key. Off of Wal's screen, I hesitated, drove to the basket, and got an "And 1". The crowd and team went crazy! Prior to the game no one knew who I was, but after the game they all knew and began to love Tiny. We won that game 85-62. I finished the game with sixteen points and seven assists, most of which came from B. Because of the awkwardness, I tried to cater to her whenever I could throughout the game. B and I worked very well together. We both understood the game, and, having the luxury of one another in the backcourt, we just had fun out there playing off one another.

My first two weeks in Bulgaria went pretty well. We won both of our games, and I was getting acclimated to my new city. I even earned myself a sponsor that paid for my meals daily at different restaurants. After performing well in the first couple of games, the people of Haskovo took a liking to me. B and I lived in the same apartment building, so she'd often show me the ropes and how to get around town. Since it was evident that neither of us were going anywhere, those awkward moments were gone. Sad to say though, they were replaced by some very unfortunate ones. Since I had only been in Haskovo, and on the team for a short amount of time, I wasn't aware of everything that had been going on, nor did I know what we were in for.

Prior to my arrival, Wal and another girl came to the team a couple games before me. The other girl was from Belarus, and her name was Tatsiana. The two weeks I had been in Haskovo, I saw Tatsi maybe twice. We were never introduced, so I didn't know who she was. That next week, I saw her in the locker room and gathered she was on our team. Apparently she had been recovering from some kind of knee injury, so she wasn't around. I don't know if it was because of the circumstances, or her feeling the need to prove herself, but Tatsi wasn't a team player. In my opinion, she wasn't really that good. After warming up for my third game, the coaching staff spoke among themselves as if something was wrong. The situation was that only three import players were allowed to play each game. Tatsi sat out my first two games, so they made a decision to let B sit.

At the time, I didn't know of the rule, that Tatsi wasn't Bulgarian, or what that import rule meant in regards to the rest of the season. Without B in the back court with me, things became difficult for me and the team as a whole on offense and defense. We lost that game and things began to get dramatic. I tweaked my ankle at the end of that game, so I didn't practice for two days. By the third day I was good, but they just kept telling me to rest and not rush back. Something seemed suspicious about them not wanting me to practice, and that was when B filled me in about the import rule. Even though they kept telling me not to practice and to rest, I worked out on my own time. I also worked out on the side while they practiced, so the coaches could see me.

The day before the next game, they finally let me practice. Before that practice, I needed them to see that I was perfectly fine and able to play the next day. Just as I suspected, Coach Elena already had her mind made up. When it came time to scrimmage, she put me with the second team, which confirmed that they weren't going to let me play the next day. With that in mind, I murdered my teammates! I missed one time that whole practice. I was in a crazy, Jordan-like mode. It was so bad that Coach Elena made them run suicides time and time again, because she didn't feel like anyone was really playing defense on me. Contrary to what she thought, it wasn't as easy as it looked, but every time I scored three times in a row, she made them get on the line. It didn't matter who was guarding me, I found a way to score. Everyone on that starting five felt my wrath that day, especially Tatsi. After leaving practice, convinced that I had proven my point, to my surprise, they still didn't let me play. I wasn't upset because, honestly, my ankle was still hurting a tad.

To assure myself that I would play the next game, I went extra hard in practice. I even went to the gym daily to shoot by myself, conveniently at the same time the coaches were around. In my mind, I had a spot to earn, and I was going to do everything in my power to secure it. After a great week of hard work and killing everybody once again, I knew I would be playing. Game day came, and I was pumped as usual. I warmed up a little, shot around, and then headed to the locker room to hear Coach Elena give the game plan. She announced who was guarding the other team's starting lineup, and I didn't hear my name called. It was evident that I was going to be sitting once again. I was furious, and I quickly made it known.

The first game, I understood why I was sitting, but for this second game I couldn't understand it at all. All week I had busted my ass and my teammates' too. Coach Elena even referenced me and my hard work a couple times during practice when my teammates were slacking. Before the coaches left the locker room, I demanded an explanation. Coach Elena didn't speak much English, so her daughter and the manager stayed to translate. I asked her why I wasn't playing again. She calmly told me not to worry, it was management's decision. As she said that, she proceeded to walk away like that was the end of it. But it wasn't the end of it for me. I began getting more and angry. What infuriated me the most was the fact that they watched me warm up before we entered the locker room, knowing I wasn't going to be playing, and didn't say one word to me. I began to shout, "Who the f*** is management, and what is this 'decision' based on? For the past two weeks I've been busting everybody on that team's ass, including y'all beloved Walteia the 'WNBA player'. For two weeks no one has been able to stop me, or has worked as hard as me. So who the hell is management?" After I went off, they were speechless. They told me to calm down and that we would talk after the game. They left the locker room, and I got dressed. I stayed in the locker room with tears in my eyes. For a moment I thought about leaving and going home. After cooling off, I realized that wouldn't have been a good decision. I got myself together and went to the gym. When I walked back in the gym, there were two minutes left until game time. I stood by the door and contemplated sitting in the stands. When the buzzer sounded, I decided to be a team player, so I went to sit on the bench. I sat at the end of the bench and had the meanest look on my face the entire game. I didn't clap, cheer, or anything. I even wished that they would lose. Contrary to my wishes, they pulled out the win, but Coach was so fed up with Tatsiana's performance that she barely even played her.

After the game, I asked the manager of the team if management could meet me in the locker room. When I got to the locker room, it was the manager, Coach Elena, her daughter, and her husband. It was at that moment that I realized this was a family-owned team. We spoke again, and they told me that if I wanted to play, I had to respect and accept management's decisions. They said that, because of the import rule, B, Tatsi, and I would have to rotate. I got upset all over again, because, had I known this ahead of time, I wouldn't have come there. I expressed that to them, and they said they never brought me here with intentions of releasing B. They said they never told Vesko that, and they were sorry for the misunderstanding, but this was how things were going to be. Eventually I got upset and emotional again, so I ended up cursing them out again—which, in return, resulted in me not playing a third game.

# Chapter 27
# Bulgaria

*Tolerance, versatility, and adaptability can go a long way when trying to persevere!*
*#Tinyism*

Since I now knew the situation, I accepted it for what it was. I knew what the deal was now, so sitting out didn't upset me as much as before. I calmly asked them to do me the courtesy of letting me know whether I was playing or not at least a day before the game. Tatsi and I both had no-cut contracts, so there wasn't really an easy solution. Everyone within our organization knew I was the better player, and that we had a better chance to go far the more I played. Management began getting strategic with who would and would not play. For the tougher, must-win games, B and I would play. For the easier games, Tatsi would play with one of us. I wasn't sure if Tatsi played the way she did because she felt everyone was against her, but literally no one on our team was a fan of hers.

Prior to my arrival and her hurting her knee, she was averaging sixteen points in three games with the team. Once I came, everyone threw her on the back burner. It was pretty evident that the majority of the team didn't like her. In practices, she began to get nasty with players, coaches, and even with me one time. She became somewhat of a cancer, and killed our team chemistry and overall vibe. Every time it was announced that she was playing, my teammates would shake their heads or make faces. Thinking about it now, I can't even imagine the level of stress she was under. At the same time, she could have managed it a little better. I mean, I didn't manage mine in the best way, but I didn't take it out on my team!

As the season progressed, we won some big games and also gave away some big ones. One weekend in particular, we participated in the post-season cup tournament. Every matchup we had, we were the underdog. This was a new team, and the rest of the league wasn't too fond of Coach Elena and her family. They did a lot of things that upset the rest of the league. Even the refs weren't pleased with their shenanigans, and it showed via the way they officiated our games. After beating Neftochimic to get into the Final Four of the cup, everyone expected us to lose. In the Final Four, we beat Levski, a well-respected top team who had the league's player of the year, Charel Allen. Levski had the history, the fans, and on paper, the win. We ended up beating them in a very dramatic overtime win.

The next game would end in an even crazier fashion. In the championship of the cup, we faced Montana. Montana had beaten the defending champs, Dunav, on the other side of the bracket. That win gave them a lot of confidence. The championship game also ended up going to overtime, but this time we fell short. The game should have never gone to overtime, as we were up four with less than two minutes left. Unfortunately, I committed a crucial double dribble, and we fell apart as a team after that. In my eyes, that turnover cost us the game. I even told the team in the locker room that it was my fault, immediately after we lost. With the type of player I am, things like that can't happen. There's simply no excuse for it.

After reviewing the film, there is no way I can honestly blame that loss on my one turnover. We turned the ball over or didn't score on the following six possessions. Luckily, B saved us in regulation. She scored a bank three to send us to overtime. In overtime, it was pretty clear who wanted that championship more.

In the game against Levski, I scored all of my points except two in the overtime. In regulation of both games, I just couldn't seem to hit a shot. Despite not scoring, I managed to control the game and put us in positions to win. Between that turnover and not shooting well though, I truly believed I didn't show up like I was supposed to. To my surprise, neither did management. The next week was supposed to be payday. After a couple days of not hearing anything in regards to my salary, these people had the nerve to say management wasn't going to pay me, because I cost them the cup championship. As expected, I went off on these people again. There was no way I was going to allow them to penalize me for one mistake I had made.

Once I calmed down, I kindly told them I wasn't coming to any more games and practices until I got my money. They thought they were going to scare me and treat me like they did the Bulgarians on my team, but I wasn't with it. Some of my Bulgarian teammates weren't being paid, and even some of the management. They had bitten off more than they could chew, financially. They had to make sure they paid the Americans first, so those were the type of sacrifices they made. During that time, there was a sponsor up in the air about whether he wanted to give us money or not. Winning the cup would have solidified his contribution, but, either way, my salary shouldn't have been dependent on that. My contract didn't say anything about it being dependent on performance, because, if it was, I should've been getting compensated for my great performances.

The next day I did just as I said, and didn't go to practice. I told them, "Good luck with playing Tatsi, I'll be at my apartment until I get paid." After two days of seeing I wasn't bluffing, they came to my apartment with the saddest story about losing sponsors and how my turnover was crucial. I agreed with them as far as my turnover went, and said I obviously felt bad about it, but I also told them I could show them a summary of everything that went wrong after my turnover.

I decided to contact Coach Lojo in Bosnia about my last paycheck and reimbursement for Mo's ticket. To my surprise, things in Bosnia were getting pretty hectic. It had been months since people were paid by the government. As a result, they went on strike, and rioting had begun in the city of Sarajevo. Things got so crazy, they even burned down a couple of government buildings. Once I was informed of what was going on, I knew it would be a while longer before I got my money. It wasn't urgent, and Coach Lojo continued to assure me that once the money came in, I would get it. Mo wasn't as understanding. Since she had to leave in a hurry, Coach Lojo wasn't able to pay her last salary, and he was still a little bitter about the way she left. On top of that, a while after she left, she got married. In his eyes, she betrayed him and lied about the job. He felt she just wanted to go home and be with her family, and some animosity developed between them. They got into an argument, and Coach Lojo told her that he didn't care about her or her money. He said he was more focused on figuring out how to pay the players who were currently on his team. He simply told Mo that, given the situation, they were the priority. It was understandable to me, because if I was still out there and he paid Mo before he paid me, I would've been highly upset.

After hearing about the way things were going in Bosnia, I didn't contact Coach Lojo for a while. Mo continued writing him, and took to calling him out on Facebook. She called him a liar, thief, and much more. He eventually responded and went right back at her. To me, it was very unprofessional on both of their parts, so I stayed out of it.

Towards the end of the season in Bulgaria, management decided that we should try to obtain a certain seed for playoffs, to better our chances of going all the way. I'd never been a part of a team that purposely lost games, so this was very frustrating. There was one game where they left B, Walteia, Lidia, and another starter home, with intentions of losing the game. The coaching staff even stayed home. They had the nerve to tell me that, as a punishment for my turnover in the cup championship, I had to play. The punishment was me not being able to rest like everyone else. I planned on playing anyway, so I didn't care. I wanted to get my stats up, so playing didn't bother me at all. What bothered me was that we lost to the last place team in the league. I was extremely embarrassed, and couldn't believe what they did. The coaching staff had the nerve to get upset at us because we didn't win, when before the game all they kept saying was that this game didn't matter, we didn't have to win, just play. At that point, I lost what little respect I had for them, and all I could think about was how many more days I had to put up with this crap.

I began to write more, as well as plan for my summer. Since the book was more than half-way done, I wanted to begin marketing it and my brand, and I decided that I wanted to launch a website. Between the book and the website, I thought it would be cool to do a TA9 photo shoot. One day while doing laundry, I was folding my Haskovo jersey. I had a pair of KD 6s on. For those who don't know, Kevin Durant's logo is his initials in lowercase letters. Looking back and forth at my jersey and the sneakers, a thought popped into my head for a logo design I could use. I drew the letters T and A and number 9 over and over, and finally created something I kind of liked. I reached out to a couple of friends to help me create a logo. They wanted to charge me, and, of course, since I was so cheap, I tried to do it myself. One day, I was talking to my bro Buck about his clothing line. I told him I was working on a logo and he inquired, "Why you ain't ask me? You know that's what I do." It had completely slipped my mind that he was a graphic designer. I took a picture of the drawings and sent it to him. He tweaked it a little bit, and, next thing you know, I had my TA9 logo.

Once I got the logo, all of my crazy ideas started to flow. I decided for the photo shoot that I wanted to have shirts and hoodies with my logo on it, to promote the book. I also decided that I wanted to show love to everyone I knew that had their own clothing line, including my bro Buck. After I ordered the very first TA9 hoodies and t-shirts, I ordered different shirts from a couple of my friends. To help get them support, I told them I would wear their apparel in some of the shots during my photo shoot.

After I narrowed down the different kinds of shots and where I wanted to take them, I contacted the best photographer I knew, Tara Polen, aka the Sixth Woman. I met Tara from playing at the West 4th Street tournament. For the past couple of summers, she would come to West 4th and take action shots during the games. She always produced quality work, and that's exactly what I wanted for my photo shoot. After talking to her about my ideas and working everything out, she said she'd do my photo shoot for a discounted price.

Halfway through finishing the site, I decided that I wanted to create a trailer to promote the book and to do a short documentary series. I contacted a friend of mine, Senyo Topenway, aka 2 Step. We had known each other since middle school, and he was an aspiring videographer. Once I spoke with him and told him my ideas, I began preparing a list of where and what I wanted to shoot in documentary. I wanted to provide visuals of all of the places vital to my career and what I've been through. We eventually filmed at Morgan, Madison, my grandma's house and backyard, and other areas that contributed to the success of my career. I wanted to make this a big summer for myself and the TA9 brand. In addition to producing visuals and marketing for the book, I wanted to also have my very own basketball camp. I figured with everything I planned to have going on, giving back to the young women in my community would be the icing on the cake.

The time had finally come to compete in the playoffs. Although we did all that strategic losing, we still didn't end up getting the seed they wanted. In the first round of playoffs, we faced Montana, and this was the game I wanted! The series was the best of three, and they had home court advantage. Since I didn't perform as well as I wanted to the last time we played them, I wanted to be sure I made up for that turnover. Prior to that playoff game, my coaching staff had written letters to the commissioner of the referees. They stated that the refs were always against us, and said that they hoped the officiating would be better for the playoffs. They even made us customized warm-up shirts that said "Fair Game" in Bulgarian. With all the shenanigans they pulled, that first game of the playoffs had so much energy and mixed emotions that the gym was hysterical! Despite how hard we played, we lost by two points, 83-81. I finished the game with sixteen points and three assists, which clearly wasn't enough.

Since that first round of the playoffs was best of three, this next game was do or die for us! If we lost, that was it. There was a lot riding on this game, aside from going home. The game was the third of April. Since it was the beginning of the month, if we lost, we wouldn't have been able to get any salary for the month of April. There was also a sponsorship from the mayor of the city riding on this win, which would pay for the April salary.

The second game of the series was a home game, and I honestly loved playing in front of our fans in Haskovo, since we rarely lost at home. We ending up blowing Montana out, 103-55! As a team, we rarely missed any shots! In the first quarter, I didn't miss a single shot! I went 5-5! My team fed off of my energy and followed my lead. I finished the game with thirty points, twelve rebounds and seven steals.

We went back to Montana's court for another situational win or go home game. We ended up beating Montana 86-68, and advancing to the Final Four round. In the Final Four round we were matched up against the defending champs, Dunav. Haskovo had beat them in the pre-season cup, but they were definitely a better team since then.

Before the game, I recognized the coach's name on the game day flyer. I asked about him, and my teammates said he was the national team's head coach, but that wasn't how I knew him. While getting dressed, it came to me. Back when I was my own agent, I had spoken briefly with him about possibly coming here to play. I couldn't remember how the conversation went, but it didn't go where I wanted it to evidently, because I never came to play for him. With that in mind, I wanted to show him the type of player he had missed out on. Although we lost by nine, I finished the game with nineteen points, eight rebounds, and five assists. I had made such a great first impression that he came over to me after the game, and personally told me how great I played.

This series was best of seven, and, before each game, the coach would joke around with me. He would say things like, "Take it easy on us, Tiny. We're a little tired." I would respond in a similar fashion, then proceed to warm up. Unfortunately, Dunav swept us, but in Bulgaria they also have a Bronze Medal round. The Bronze Medal round is played between the two losing teams of the Final Four. We ended up sweeping Neftochimic. Days before the Bronze round started, Wal left the team. She had been drafted by the Minnesota Lynx WNBA team, so she had to leave Haskovo to report to training camp.

It may not have been Gold or Silver, but I was extremely motivated to compete for the Bronze Medal, with or without Wal. Of course, I would have loved to have her on the court. Who wouldn't want to go to battle with a 6'4 beast on their team? We won by twenty points in the first game of the Bronze Medal round. In my last game of the 2013-2014 season, I finished with twenty-seven points, twelve rebounds, six steals, four assists, a 77-74 win, and a Bronze Medal. During my time in Bosnia and Bulgaria, I earned a Gold Medal in Bosnia when we won the pre-season cup at Celik, a Silver Medal when we lost in the cup championship, and the Bronze Medal from the Bulgarian National League. I think it's safe to say my redemption season went well!

Things in Bosnia got even worse, so it didn't make sense for me to even try to go back for the playoffs. T had also left before the season was over, so that she could attend her college graduation.

Although she left school the year before, she had finished her bachelor's degree online while she was in Bosnia. Without T, Mo, or myself, they weren't able to win the Bosnian League. Sad to say, they ended up losing to Celik in the championship series of the playoffs. After a while, Coach Lojo stopped responding to me, so I never got my money or belongings from Bosnia. I guess he was over me. Like every mistake and obstacle in my life though, I take it as a lesson learned!

*Tsarevec, Bulgaria*

*Taking it to the hole against the mighty Dunav*

# Chapter 28
# TA9

*Invest in yourself, your passions, and your goals.*
*#Tinyism*

After we won the Bronze medal, my teammates and I went to a club in Haskovo, rented a table in VIP, and had a blast. Once I recovered from that night, I still had a few days until my flight back to New York. I spent that time putting the final touches on my TA9 summer campaign. The promotion and marketing of my book and brand was going to start immediately after I set foot in NY. The very first thing on my to-do list was to get my hair done! I had to make sure I looked good during all these video and photo shoots I had lined up. For the past couple of summers I had been going to my girl Des to keep my dreadlocks fresh. Des was the one who started my locks, so when I got my hair done I went to her shop in Brooklyn. To my surprise, my guy Senyo came to see me while I was in the shop with Des. He didn't live too far, so he swung by to kick it for a little. As expected, he had his camera and we began shooting a day early. He asked me about my season, how it felt to be home, and what was next for me. After Des finished my hair, we spoke about the trip we were taking to Maryland the next day. At that point I had been home for 5 hours, and there I was already planning a trip out of town the next day. Senyo and my mom thought I was crazy, but I didn't want to waste any more time.

Prior to coming home, I had ordered my wardrobe and had it delivered to my house weeks before my arrival. In preparation for the shoots I ordered three shirts and a hoody with my TA9 logo on it. I ordered a white tee, black tee, royal blue tee, and a grey hoody. The white tee, black tee, and hoody just simply had the logo on the front. I decided to make the royal tee a "Morgan edition" tee. I put my logo on the front, but I also put a cartoon bear on the back of the shirt since that was Morgan's mascot. Aside from the TA9 apparel, I also ordered three shirts from Buck's clothing line 4givenLove, a shirt from Keish's apparel brand Fan Favorite, a customized shirt from one of my friends out in Florida who was working with a clothing company called Grind Life Cvrtel, and a tee from a friend of mine named Priscilla, who was starting her own non-profit organization called P Stars.

During the website, documentary, and photo shoots I thought it would be dope to also shed light on other people who were also doing their thing. Through my projects I wanted to support and give exposure to anyone I could. In addition to the other clothing lines and Senyo, I was able to feature basketball trainers, college athletes, DJs, producers, coaches, photographers, and up and coming hoopers in my project. At the end of the day I just wanted to support the people who needed it. I knew when it came time for the release of my projects, I'd need support as well. In the end I figured if and when someone took the time to support me, they'd be supporting them too.

We were only going to be in Maryland for the day, so we couldn't afford to waste any time. We left for Morgan around 10 a.m. and got there at 1 p.m. When we arrived on campus, my first stop was the Hill Field House. I contacted current Morgan player Tracey Carrington so she could meet me there. I wanted to film a quick workout with her, as well as some profile shots of us dribbling and bonding. Tracey was Morgan's current star of the women's basketball team. I thought it would be pretty cool to feature her in my documentary. She was a Baltimore native and whether I liked it or not, she was creeping up on some of my records. She's already managed to break one of my records, and with her senior season underway she may break a couple more. While concluding her junior year, she broke my single season scoring record with 628 points in 30 games. After her freshman year I got a lot of messages from Morgan about how much she reminded everyone of me. By her sophomore year, I reached out to her and began to take her under my wing. Two years after I graduated (her freshman year), the women's basketball team went back to its losing culture. Unfortunately, Tracey didn't have as much help as I did during her first three years on the team. I helped her keep her head up, and motivated her to be better than me. I did my best to serve as her mentor. Based on the interview I conducted with her after we worked out, I felt like I had done a good job. Tracey is a great individual, with serious ambition, and I truly wish her the best. As long as she doesn't break any more of my records, she's okay with me!

After Tracey and I did our workout, we went to the coach's offices to check on Beas. I wanted to interview all the people who had been instrumental to my success, as well as visit places of importance. I was going to ask them all the same questions and reminisce. I would also speak about why that place was important to me. To conclude each location, I would do different types of profile shots. The profile shots would be me dribbling or shooting. In addition to interviewing Beas, I also interviewed Tracey, and a well-known DJ that I grew up with in Brooklyn. DJ Flow was DJ of the year in Baltimore in 2014. He was a great DJ and gave back to the Baltimore community. We used to hoop together back in Brooklyn for FYA. The full itinerary for the Maryland trip included Morgan, my Uncle's house in Bowie, and the Melo Center of Baltimore to catch up with Coach Sam Brand, the one responsible for my stellar senior year at Morgan.

After interviewing Beas, we did Tracey's interview while on the move. We walked through campus while interviewing her to sort of give a tour of Morgan's campus at the same time. Although I speak to Tracey on a regular basis, I had never really known her full story. Once I learned her story and recognized just how driven she was, it made me want to help her succeed even more. After interviewing Tracey, I went down to the football field to reflect. I spoke about my time at Morgan, what it meant to leave a legacy, and my feelings towards being back. I met up with DJ in the student center to catch up and conduct his interview. DJ wasn't always a DJ, but ironically that was always his nickname. His real name was Dwight. When DJ first started, he knew nothing about DJ-ing. All he knew was that when it came to partying, the DJ always got paid. With money as his motivation, it was pretty natural for his Brooklyn-instilled ambition to take over. He even serves as the official DJ now for certain popular young hip-hop artists like Sevyn Streeter and Shy Glizzy.

Once we wrapped up our session at Morgan, we headed over to the Melo Center. I hadn't seen Sam in a couple of years, so I was looking forward to catching up with him and featuring him in the documentary. When I arrived at the Melo Center there he was, doing what he did best: teaching the game. Sam had left Morgan's coaching staff a couple years prior and was now coaching at his alma mater, Poly HS. He was also coaching Carmelo Anthony's AAU team. As I entered the gym, Sam was showing a player the proper footwork needed to perform a move he had just tried. Watching him brought back so many memories of the long hours we had spent in the gym. Once he was done training and working out his guys, we were able to catch up. He had recently become a father, so we spoke about that experience and his transition from a college assistant coach to a high school head coach.

We then went to my Uncle Anth's house in Bowie. Unfortunately, my cousins Brandon and Tristan Youngblood were still away at school, so I couldn't include them in the interview. They both attended North Carolina A&T to pursue engineering degrees, and had finals. While I attended Morgan my uncle and his lovely wife Parthenia Youngblood were almost always in attendance for my home games. Having them in the stands always felt like a privilege to me. Playing in front of a crowd of fans is a little different than playing in front of family. My Uncle and Par were very well off financially. Their house seemed like a mansion to me. After living in that apartment in Brooklyn for most of my life, their current house always blew me away.

Before interviewing them, we shot a tour of their house. The house had three floors and was very spacious. The basement had a theatre, pool table, bar, work out room and even a sauna. The main floor had a computer room, two dining areas, a kitchen, living room, laundry room, and led to their very spacious patio and backyard. On the top floor there were five bedrooms with bathrooms in each of them. The way they lived motivated me to someday be able to live like that. When I was at Morgan and just sometimes needed to get away, I would come stay in their guest room for the weekend. The only thing they were missing that I would've liked was a basketball court.

During their interview we reminisced about when I was younger and about how much I'd grown as a player and person. My Aunt Par even pulled out some old VHS tapes of me dancing and acting silly at one of our family holiday parties. By the time we were done, I was exhausted. There was no way we were going to make it back to New York safely, so I got something to eat and took a nap. After getting my rest, we headed back to NY and got back the following morning.

That next Monday we went to visit Coach Dumont at Madison HS. Senyo had attended Madison with me, so it was a bit of a homecoming for both of us. We got some good footage for both of our documentaries as Senyo had decided to do one as well. He has been through a lot in his lifetime, both physically and mentally. When we were in junior high school he got hit by a car and things haven't been the same for him since. All of his athletic dreams were shattered, as well as some of his bones. For the past couple of years he has had numerous surgeries that were vital to his ability to walk again. Going through the struggles many young black men in the 'hood encounter encourages him to inspire and educate others using the story of his life.

That was the first time I had seen Dumont in years. We kept in touch, but being able to talk to him face to face was way better! After Madison we went to interview Munch at St. John's Rec. Surprisingly, when we arrived we found an Adidas basketball development group was there. They were trying to figure out just how they could improve their basketball shoes by giving out different pairs of sneakers and observing as people played in them. After each game they would ask the opinions of the hoopers and ask for comparisons to other brands like Nike, Reebok and Under Armour.

After interviewing Munch, I set up a workout with an up and coming trainer, Justin Bright. Justin and I grew up playing in St. John's Rec. After pursuing professional basketball and seeing that his chances were getting slim, he redirected his energy into helping others get better. To help get him more clients, I figured I could record a workout with him and include it in my documentary. After introducing him to the camera, we worked out for a couple hours. Once we got started, the Adidas reps began focusing on me, instead of the other people in the gym. This was an amazing opportunity to network, so I began to have casual conversations with the Adidas reps. After listening to them tell me how great I looked performing Justin's drills, the conversation escalated a little bit. I began talking about TA9, my professional career, and the things I planned on doing in the community. Munch, Justin and I then gathered them into the conference room and conducted a forum. They were there to get some answers regarding basketball in NYC, and how to improve the demand for the Adidas brand in our community. Who better to help them out than us? After answering their questions, and providing them with inside information based on our experiences in the NYC basketball circuit, I proposed a partnership with them. As of now we've only managed a couple free pair of sneakers, but as this relationship grows we feel the collaboration could bring more.

The next thing on my list was the photo shoot with Tara Polen. I immediately saw that she had a passion for what she did. She took her job very seriously, and it showed in her work. Tara made it clear to me that things like location, lighting, and angles all made a big difference in photos. Working with Tara quickly changed my perspective on her craft. After getting to know her and learning the ins and outs of photography, I gained even more respect for her and her work. I began taking pride in the pictures I posted on a daily basis via social media. After working with Tara, she piqued my interest even more.

On the first day of the shoot, we shot at a Park near Canal St. and 6th Ave. and West 4th Street Park. I felt shooting at West 4th St. Park was fitting because it was both the place we first made our acquaintance and a very historic location when it came to NYC basketball. On the second day we took it to my birthplace, Brooklyn! We started out in a neighborhood called Bushwick. Bushwick was well known for its outdoor street art gallery called the Bushwick Collective. Throughout that neighborhood, there are many different graffiti paintings created by artists from all over the world. We concluded the photo shoot at the Brooklyn Bridge Park. The Brooklyn Bridge Park showcased an amazing view of the Brooklyn Bridge, which I thought would look great as a background in some of my shots. After the photo shoot, Tara and I hung out a couple times, attended some Liberty games, and got to know each other a little bit.

Senyo and I would post things to social media to create buzz. Everywhere we shot, we'd take a cool picture and upload it. I made sure I had on my TA9 gear. Every time I'd post a pic in the TA9 apparel someone would comment that they wanted some gear. After weeks of people inquiring about how to get some gear, I began to look into producing some. Munch had connected me to a friend of his who printed uniforms and shirts for most of the tournaments in NYC throughout the summer. I went with Munch to meet him. The guy's name was Marlon. As soon as I walked in with my TA9 hoody, Marlon smiled and said, "Oh, that's it? I can do that easy!" Marlon didn't only do uniforms, he also did trophies, banners, and anything else needed to run a successful basketball league. This was his side hustle, so when I inquired how much he would charge me to print the shirts, he said all I had to cover were the materials. Marlon told me that he didn't want to take away from my profits. He said as an entrepreneur he knew how hard starting a business could be. Talking with Marlon about how I could pull this business off was very eye-opening.

After all these years of contacting companies to be a poster child for them and just simply get some free gear, I now would be able to wear my own stuff. I made it known that it was now possible to purchase TA9 gear, and things took off. The first order I placed with Marlon was for about fifty shirts. No way was I expecting that many people to support my brand. We were at a time when it seemed like everyone had a clothing line. The next order was for seventy-five shirts! I couldn't believe the amount of support I was receiving for TA9. People I didn't even know in different states were inquiring about purchasing gear.

Before filling that second order, Marlon had become very busy and backed up with business. Since I wasn't paying him, my shirts weren't a priority. It had been weeks since people had placed their orders, and I didn't want to keep them waiting. I used to watch Marlon make the shirts and it seemed like a piece of cake. He'd heat the machine up, press the shirt, press the logo on the shirts for three seconds, and voila! I decided to order my own heat press machine. I didn't want to have to depend on him anymore, nor did I want to keep my customers waiting. Once my machine came I was reluctant to ask Marlon for help. I was scared that he would be upset. To my surprise he was more than willing to help. Before I knew it, I was in my kitchen every other night cooking TA9 shirts up. By the time I went back for overseas, I had produced about 300 shirts and hoodies.

In addition to running a business, working on the website, and shooting a documentary, I also had a lot of other things going on. On a daily basis I helped run the Brooklyn Kings Basketball Academy. I'd also conduct personal training sessions with the youth, work out on my own, have a game, or host basketball events with Renee and Positive Influence. Positive Influence was a non-profit we partnered with to help bring women's basketball events to the city. I was averaging about four hours a sleep a night. My summer was very exhausting, but I loved every moment of it.

It was now time to launch tinyadams.com! On the website I was able to highlight everything I was currently doing. The site consisted of news, pictures, highlights, my social media feed, an online store for TA9 apparel, and two areas where I highlighted someone else doing well, on or off the court. Those two areas were Tiny's Hooper of the Week and Tiny's Spotlight. I never want it to seem like it's only about me, so I wanted to give someone else some exposure and support via my website. My site generated a lot of views and with all of the positive feedback I was getting I felt like all my hard work had paid off.

Senyo and I continued filming for the documentary. For Mother's Day, all the women in my family go to Atlantic City for the weekend. While my Grandma was in town, I had to make sure I did her interview before she headed back to Tampa. My grandparents moved to Tampa in 2011, but they kept their house in Queens. It was vital that I included 540 Beach 65th Street in the documentary, because that's where it all started! The hoop may not have been up in the back yard anymore, but for the most part everything was just like I remembered it. During our session at Grandma's house we watched the NBA Playoffs, grilled some burgers and franks, and flashed back to the good times. It had been a while since I'd had the chance to spend quality time with my Grandma. That was a great day and the best part is that we were able to document it. Between the interview and just hanging out, I think what we got on film truly illustrated just how much my grandmother meant to me.

In addition to launching the site and my brand, I wanted to give back to the community. When I got back home in May, some people from Morgan State contacted me on behalf of the Black Women in Sport Foundation. They were hosting a forum at Morgan State, and wanted to know if I'd be interested in being on the panel. Without hesitation I told them I was definitely in. Prior to this event though, the only public speaking I did was at sports camps and clinics. I never had been up on a podium so I was a bit nervous. The moment I got up there, saw my old teammates and colleagues in the audience, and saw my name and pic on the projector screen it was a piece of cake. I spoke passionately about my journey, the things I'd learned, and my assigned subject, Effective Coaching Characteristics.

Naturally, while reliving my past, I got a little choked up and teary eyed on the podium. At first I was a little embarrassed, but at the end of my speech I received a round of applause that assured me my message and emotion was appreciated. We took pictures and everyone expressed how much they enjoyed my speech. Before leaving, the board members and directors of the Black Women in Sports Foundation advised that if my schedule permitted, they'd love to have me back for future events. I never thought of myself as the motivational speaking type, but after that event I will definitely be adding that to my resume.

To conclude my amazing summer, I hosted my first annual TA9 Skills Academy! Initially I had planned to host the camp outside, but Mother Nature didn't seem to agree with that. With rain in the forecast, I had no idea just what I was going to do. I couldn't afford to postpone and I didn't want to. Fortunately for me, Munch came through and we were allowed to host the skills academy in St. John's Rec. Being able to host the skills academy in the very place I grew up playing made that day even more incredible. The day before my skills academy felt like the day before the first day of school. We all know how that feels. You lay your clothes out, wake up every couple hours, and you're just so anxious and excited to get there. Everything was the same for me, except instead of me laying my clothes out, I had to print sixty shirts for my campers and staff. My skills academy was completely free and my Coaches all volunteered. In addition to conducting drills, having competitions for prizes, and playing full court games, I had a few of my friends come speak to the forty girls that attended. My biggest interest is educating and enlightening others. I suffered due to ignorance time and time again. If I have an opportunity to help someone avoid making a mistake, I'm going to do my best to help them. The speakers talked about everything from injuries to getting in trouble with the law. Hopefully all of the campers benefited and took in something important from that day. Being able to do something like that is truly humbling and I can't wait for the second annual TA9 skills academy!

*Guest speaking at the Black Women in Sports Foundation Forum 2014*

# Chapter 29
# Sweden: Tiny Setback #6

*Always be prepared for the worst. When Plan A fails, get a grip, and then follow up with Plan B-Z.*

*#Tinyism*

After signing with Lorenzo and Two Points in February, they showed me there was no way I'd regret signing with them. Before I even finished my season in Bulgaria, teams were contacting them expressing interest in me for the next season. When Lorenzo initially told me about the first team in particular, I was surprised. I was still competing against Neftochimic in the Bronze series at the time. My season wasn't even over yet, and all I could think about was the strangeness of the situation. Prior to this there were times I've waited all the way until the end of the summer to hear from teams. Although I was excited about how things were looking, I was still in competition. I told Lorenzo that I was interested, but for now I wanted to handle business in Bulgaria. I told him to try to negotiate more money and perks, and stall as much as he could. I also didn't necessarily want to make a decision so early. Since this was the conclusion of my redemption season, I wanted to have an opportunity to weigh my options and see what kinds of offers I would get.

A week after I got back to NYC, Lorenzo told me that the team had agreed to meet all of my terms. They were even willing to fly my mother out in December, which was big! The team's name was Mark Basket. Mark Basket was a team located in Kinna, Sweden. They competed in the top women's league in the Swedish Damiligan League. After thinking about my situations from the past, I decided that even though this was the first team to contact me, it didn't make sense to decline. They were paying what I wanted, flying my mom out, and the coach even said he would help me in regards to some TA9 production in our city. Time and time again athletes tend to pass up on perfectly good opportunities for no reason. We choose to wait around thinking something better is going to come along, but in reality better things rarely ever come. I didn't want to end up regretting that I didn't take this deal, so I told Lorenzo to accept. After I looked at the details in the contract, I really didn't see any negatives involved in accepting the deal. I began to talk with the coach, Frank Alm, at least once a week. We got to know each other and each other's philosophies when it came to basketball. My first impression of Coach Frank led me to believe that we would complement each other very well. He even asked my opinion on certain things pertaining to the team. I'd give him my honest opinion, and sometimes we'd agree to disagree. The fact that he was even considering my input made me feel like we would develop a great player-coach relationship.

I really felt like things were now starting to work in my favor. I embedded the belief that this Sweden opportunity would be the turning point of my career. My plan was to lead the Swedish league in assists and steals, and place top ten in scoring. I also wanted us to compete for a championship. Off the court, I hoped to expand my brand TA9 in Sweden. I had this vision of people in the city wearing TA9 gear that matched our team colors. At home games I wanted a whole section TA9ed out and also somewhere to sell apparel in the gym. After handling business in Sweden on and off the court, I wanted to then obtain a WNBA training camp spot somehow. With this being my fifth season, I felt it was a now or never situation. Sweden was a very well respected league, so performing well could lead to a lot of great opportunities.

Before leaving for Sweden, I drove down to Tampa to see my grandparents. The drive from New York to Tampa is about eighteen hours. Fortunately for me I had the company of Renee, my little cousin Keyonna, and Buckets. With them on board, the road trip wasn't that bad. I spent most of that time bonding with Renee. We talked about things we wanted to achieve in the next five years. We spent six days in Tampa and even took an additional road trip with my grandmother and Keyonna to Renee's alma mater, Miami University. It was a perfect getaway for both of us.

Once we got back from Tampa, I had two more bits to shoot for the documentary before I departed for Sweden: Wingate Park, and an interview with my mom. Days before my departure, Senyo and I went to Wingate and got some great footage. I got to interact with some kids that were in the park, and even ended up playing a one on one. After giving a tour of the park, I reminisced about all the great times I'd had there and the impact Wingate had on my development as a player. For my mother's interview, I thought it would be cool to actually do it on the way to the airport.

The day finally came for my departure to Sweden. This time there was no crazy party prior to my departure. I simply hung out with Buckets for a little, ran some last minute errands, and recorded the trip to the airport. We conducted my mother's interview the entire ride to the airport. I adore my mom, and some of her responses and the things she said really motivated me. Hearing how she truly felt made me want to do so much more to continue to make her proud. There were no issues this time around at check in or with my ticket, and I actually had a perfect send off. Buckets' company was indeed good luck this time around.

When my flight landed in Gothenburg, Sweden, three of my new teammates were there waiting for me with a sign. Surprisingly, that was the first time someone had ever waited at the airport for me with a sign. The sign said "Welcome Tiny" with one of my recently posted Facebook pictures. The teammates waiting for me were Anna Stoltz, Emma Karamovic, and my fellow American Ashley Daniels. Ashley was from Mississippi and had arrived about half an hour before me. Ashley and I had played against each other during my second season in Portugal. We were also both signed with Lorenzo and Two Points. Over the summer, when we found out we'd be playing together, we were more than excited. Ashley was an athletic post player, who understood the game, ran the floor, and worked hard day in and day out. With her on court, I knew I'd have at least one person fighting with me during games. From previous communication, I realized that Ashley loved the game just as much as I did. There's really nothing better than playing with equally passionate teammates.

The other two teammates were from Sweden, but they were from different cities. Emma was from a neighboring city called Boras. Anna was from a city called Orebro. Emma was one of the youngest girls on the team. She played the SG/SF position and was one of the most skilled players on our team. Emma's only real issue was her basketball IQ. Since she was still young and learning about herself and the game, she sometimes made silly mistakes. Nonetheless she was a great shooter, with scoring capabilities. Anna was a little closer in age to Ashley and me, and was more experienced than Emma. She had played on the national team and for other clubs in our league. Anna played the SG position. She was a decent defender and could finish as long as you set her up well. They both were about 5'9" and Ashley was close to 6'. After we left the airport we had to drive about an hour away from Gothenburg to our city of residence, Kinna. Kinna was a small city in Sweden that reminded me of the countryside back home.

We pulled up to a little house on a hill near a soccer field and a white building. The house had two floors with two bedrooms on each floor. On the main floor there was a living room, bathroom, and kitchen in addition to the bedrooms. In the basement there was a laundry room, multiple closets, and two more rooms. For just me and Ashley to be living there, the house was very spacious. The house in Kinna was the best place I lived in overseas. The only issue I had with the house was that everyone would know exactly where we lived. After my robbery experience in Portugal I was very cautious about my living arrangements. That white building turned out to actually be our home gymnasium. So living fifteen feet away from our home gym, with a big sign above our front door saying "Mark Basket" could have caused some personal problems for Ashley and I. Fortunately during my time in Kinna, the only unexpected visitors were some newspaper reporters. From the first practice in Kinna onward I received a lot of media coverage. I'd tell my friends that I felt like Lebron James because of all of the publicity I was getting. In every article they would refer to me as the star guard. It was very surreal to me. I was used to getting attention from the media, but not to this magnitude.

Prior to our first game of the season, I learned that the immigration office in Sweden hadn't validated my work visa. Unaware of what was going on, Anna had asked if I was going to be able to play our first game. When she contacted me, I was clueless, so I just responded with, "To my knowledge, I thought I was playing, why?" She responded with a screenshot of this article, the headline of which read, "Star guard may miss premiere game." For the next couple of days all I could think about was whether I'd be able to play or not. Things were going well in practice and I was doing additional workouts on my own. The only thing left for me to do was wait and see whether or not the basketball gods would bless me. Luckily, the day before the game, Coach Frank told me I was clear to play.

Game day came, and it was sort of a weird one. For starters, it was an away game against a team called Visby. We left very early in the morning the day of the game and headed to the airport. We then took two flights and cabs to the gym. We were all clearly tired from all of the traveling, so in the first half we didn't play so well. At halftime Coach Frank let us have it. Throughout the course of the second half we managed to get it together, and pulled out the win. I finished the game with 15 points, 6 assists, 6 rebounds, and 7 steals, and received more Lebron James treatment.

Before I could even gather my water bottle and warm up shirt, a reporter came over to talk to me about the game. After speaking with me, the reporter then interviewed Coach Frank. After the game Coach Frank told us that even though we won, he wasn't necessarily happy with how we won. He was upset that we seemed like we were sleeping all through the first half, which struck me as odd. It had been his idea to do all the traveling the day of the game, so I honestly couldn't understand him expecting us not to be tired.

He concluded his speech by saying he wanted everyone awake and ready to play four to six hours before all games from that point on. Ashley and I began to question his decision making capabilities.

Although I had pretty decent numbers in my debut, I wasn't happy with my performance. I had six turnovers in that game, which is unacceptable. Our next game was a home game against the defending champions of the league, Northland. All week Ashley and I talked about how much we wanted to win and pull the upset. Sad to say, Emma, Ashley and I were the only ones who really believed we could win. All week, Coach Frank and our teammates made statements that demonstrated their lack of belief in our team. Coach Frank said things like, "We don't have to win this game. Don't worry about it." Ashley and I couldn't believe it. It honestly made us both upset. I was especially upset at Coach Frank, because, as our coach, if he didn't show confidence in our team, how were my teammates supposed to show any? That week I worked very hard to make sure I was prepared for the game. I wanted to show Coach Frank and my teammates that we can compete with anyone as long as we believed.

Even though I couldn't hit a shot, I controlled the game and helped us compete with the mighty champions. Ashley and I decided that we would do our best to show the team that we were good enough to compete. It was our first home game and we wanted to give our fans something to cheer about. At the end of the first half we were only down four points. Surprisingly the team followed our lead and we held our own. After halftime, Coach Frank decided to change what seemed to have been working in the first half. He changed our defense to this weird zone we had barely worked on, and he didn't start me in the second half. Six minutes into the second half Northland caught fire and we ended up losing by eighteen. After the game he commended our effort and admitted that this game was on him. In my eyes that was strike two against his coaching skills. His changes were unnecessary and simply didn't make any sense. I felt like we worked so hard to show that we were capable of competing for no reason at all. We did all that work just to have him take it away from us.

Things were turning out to be the complete opposite of what I thought they would be. Practices began to get more annoying and I felt like we never worked on the things we needed to get better. On top of that, Coach Frank only attended practices twice a week. We'd see him on Mondays and Fridays. When he wasn't at practice they were run by our assistant coaches Susanne and Arvid. Susanne was actually a track coach, so she did a lot of strength and conditioning stuff with us. Arvid was younger than both Susanna and Frank. Arvid was new to the staff and from another city in Sweden. Arvid's philosophies differed from Frank's, so my teammates and I would often be confused. On Mondays and Fridays with Frank we would be doing one thing, and on the other days with Arvid we would be doing another. Since practice didn't really do much for me, I began working out on my own more and more. Our next game was away against Anna's old team 08 Stockholm. Since I couldn't hit a shot against Northland, I spent that week getting a lot of shots up. Fortunately for me it paid off and I started feeling like my usual self again. We beat Stockholm 83-57. I shot 7 for 10 from the field, and scored 20 points, 11 assists, 8 rebounds, and 5 steals. That performance proved to be the best of the week in the Swedish league and earned me EuroBasket Player of The Week.

People in our town were messaging me daily with congratulations and saying how proud of me they were. It felt good to finally feel like regular Tiny again. Although some people were happy with my accomplishments and performances, I learned that there were people on my team who surprisingly felt differently. After that game Emma had informed Ashley and I that some of our teammates were talking about us behind our backs. They were jealous of the way everyone treated us and spoke about us. They said they didn't understand why newspapers were making such a big deal about us. Up until that point most of the articles addressed the fact that Mark Basket had been doing so well in comparison to other seasons. The papers often called Ashley and me the dynamic duo and credited us when it came to the team's success. After Emma told us our teammates were hating on our success, I began to stop trusting them.

After the Visby game my focus was staying consistent. Unfortunately that was a tougher task than I thought. Once again at our home gym, I couldn't hit a thing! We were playing a less talented team, but they came out hungry for a win. Despite not playing well, we managed to pull away from Solna in the last four minutes of the game. I came up with some big steals, and made a big three pointer to seal the win. We were now 3-1 and off to the best start for Mark Basket in the past few seasons. Next up was a big game against a top team. Like Northland, UMEA was very strong. There were a Euro cup team with experienced imports. Since we couldn't get it done against Northland, I was looking forward to redeeming ourselves against UMEA. Once again Coach Frank decided that we would travel the day of the game. This UMEA trip was actually way worse than the trip to Visby. This time we were cutting it close in all aspects. For starters Coach Frank forgot to pick one of our teammates up before we arrived at the airport. He didn't realize until we were ten minutes away from Gothenburg, so he had to turn around to go get her. After that, our connecting flights were only a few minutes apart. After we landed and got in the cabs, we arrived at the gym forty minutes before tipoff. As hectic as our day started, the game was even worse. We ended up losing to UMEA by fifty-three freaking points. The score was 87-34. Everything that could've gone wrong that day did. That game was by far the most embarrassing game I've ever been a part of.

I began thinking to myself that maybe Sweden wasn't "it" after all. I hated the way things were being handled here. I needed something to take my mind off the way things were going and serve as a stress reliever. I usually used basketball as my stress reliever, but at the moment Mark Basket was messing that up for me. Kinna was a small town with not much to do. You couldn't even go get a drink on a weeknight after nine. At least once a week Ashley and I would go to Boras to watch the men's team play, but that's really all we did. It was eat, sleep, walk down the hill to practice, stare at your laptop and phone all day, and then do it all over again the next day. We had planned to visit the other neighboring cities, but during October and November it rained a lot. Since we were going to play tourist, we didn't want to get lost or walk around in the rain.

In the hotel room that night after the fifty-three point loss, Ashley, Emma and I had a heart to heart conversation. In addition to venting to them, I also vented to Lorenzo. Ashley and I updated him on everything that had been going on. This loss had really done a number on me and he could sense that during our conversation. He asked if I wanted him to find me another team, but I responded no. I didn't want to be a quitter and give up on my team. Although they got on my nerves and talked about me behind my back, I still felt the need to be loyal to them. My loyalty is a gift and curse. I pride myself on being loyal and never giving up on anything, so I told him no and decided that I would figure out a way to make things better.

After UMEA, redemption was definitely necessary. Our next game was away again against Telge. We were told throughout the week by our coaches that Telge was a team very similar to us. Pushing my issues to the side, I channeled the real Tiny and put the team on my back. Every clutch play we needed late in the 4th quarter, I delivered in, whether it was a steal, assist, or bucket. We ended up winning 63-58. I finished the game with 18 points, 6 rebounds, 5 assists, and 3 steals. After the game I spoke with a reporter about how big of a win this was. We were now 5-2 and tied for 3rd place. After wrapping up my conversation with the reporter, Coach Frank came to give me a big hug and high five. He said, "That was a damn good win!" At that point I felt like things were going to get better. I was happy with my decision to stay and make it work.

In addition to venting to Lorenzo, Ashley, and Emma, I took to my blog to release a little steam. I wrote about my current feelings, thoughts on Swedish basketball, and how I wanted to find a way to consistently play like a wanted. Most of the time readers of my blog see my accomplishments and happy moments. I thought it would be a good idea to let them in on the not-so-happy moments too. Unexpectedly, a lot of people read the blog and I got a lot of feedback and encouraging words. After the Telge game I wrote another blog expressing how things took a complete 360 turn for the better. I had changed my mentality and figured out how to get back in my happy place. That next week of practices was very up-tempo and we played a lot of five on five for a change. I felt they were the best practices we had had since I arrived. Our next game was against a team in the bottom of the league, but Coach Frank informed us that we were preparing for our game the following week. That game would be for sole possession of third place. With the next two games approaching I wanted to continue playing like I did against Telge. After Telge's game I became the leader in steals and assists in the entire Swedish league. I wanted to get my stats up so I could crack top ten in scoring and hone in on my preseason goals.

Usually we had Thursdays and Saturdays off, with most of our games being on Sundays. That Friday, we watched film and coach Frank put in a couple new plays. While going through the new plays, one of my teammates tried to cheat the play and ended up colliding with me. I landed awkwardly and hurt my ankle really bad. It cracked three times and just began to throb crazily. With the game two days away I was optimistic that I would still be able to play, because it was actually the ankle with the scar tissue in it. Whenever I tweak that ankle it doesn't swell up so I wasn't too worried. Worst case scenario, I figured I would maybe rest since Sunday's game was going to be an easier game. I did want to play to get my stats up, but winning the game the following week for third place was much more important.

I nursed my ankle all the way up until game time, but it still wasn't good enough to play. Right before the game the local newspaper reporters had come by to do a big six page story on Ashley and me. I'm sure my teammates didn't like that at all, but it actually came out very nice. The story covered everything from our past, to playing against each other in Portugal. Despite being disappointed that I couldn't play, my team managed to pull the win out. They ended up winning by a few points, and I was happy and proud of them. During the game many of the younger girls stepped up in my absence. One girl in particular was named Amanda. Amanda was the best shooter on our team, and she proved it that game. Amanda hit five threes and led all scorers with twenty-three. That was her career high, so that was very big for her and boosted confidence. I went back to nursing my ankle so I could be ready to go when it came time to suit up the following week.

The next day I contacted Lorenzo so he could remind Coach Frank about booking my mother's flight. It was already November, and I wanted to make sure everything was handled in advance. Later that day Ashley told me that she and Emma had overheard our teammates saying things like, "See we don't need Tiny. We can win without her." All I could do was laugh, because I couldn't understand why they were so envious of me. It wasn't like I was selfish on the court. I was leading the league in assists for a reason. I made some of them better and they didn't even know it.

That night Lorenzo said Frank never confirmed the flight information, but he said he would call him later and keep me posted. After the news from Ashley, I seriously started to do even more for my ankle. Unfortunately we didn't have a trainer on our staff, so I was forced to do my own rehab. Since these girls were continuously talking about me, I wanted to get back to practice just so I could bust their a****. I wanted to show them exactly why I was receiving so much praise.

Once Lorenzo got in contact with Frank, Coach told him that the board decided they didn't want me on the team anymore. They felt as though I wasn't in proper shape or as fast as they wanted me to be. Lorenzo went to bat for me and Coach Frank continued with more bullsh** excuses. Coach Frank told him that some of the other reasons management wanted to release me were because I stayed up all night on Facebook, I was always sleeping on the way to games, I wasn't professional, I didn't listen to the coaches, all I cared about was running my business, and that I wasn't setting a good example for the younger girls on the team. When Lorenzo relayed all of this information to me, I couldn't believe it. On top of that they wanted me gone as soon as possible so they could bring in another guard. They also told Lorenzo that because of the clauses in the contract they had a right to release me without paying me my salary. Lorenzo didn't mind them releasing me, but once they said they weren't going to pay me, they had pretty much declared war.

I hadn't been cut from a team since the incident in Portugal. On top of that, my ankle still wasn't 100%, so I got very worried about what would happen next. Lorenzo assured me that he would take care of everything, and he did. He reminded me I was averaging close to 13 points and leading the entire league in steals and assists. The ongoing quote for this situation became, "I don't know what type of shape they're looking for, but steals and assists leader is a nice shape to me!" I went back and forth on whether to tell my mother about everything that was going on. I wanted to handle this situation like a big girl, and I also didn't want to worry her or make her think that she wouldn't be able to still visit.

My mother's birthday was October 5th, and that year she turned fifty. While trying to figure out just what to get her for her birthday I decided I would take her on a Euro Tour instead of giving her a gift. Ever since I was about ten years old, she'd always told me that when she passed away she wanted me to sprinkle her ashes off of the Eiffel Tower. For the past three years I had been planning to surprise her and take her to Paris once I got the money. Unfortunately different priorities came up, so I never got a chance to take her. Since Coach Frank was supposed to be paying for her flight to Sweden I figured a Euro Tour would be cool and inexpensive since we would be going from European country to European country. Our initial itinerary was for her to come to Sweden, then I'd take her to Paris, then to Italy to meet up with Lorenzo and visit Rome, and then we would visit Stockholm. Telling her that the team was releasing me didn't seem like a good idea, because we were really looking forward to this trip. I didn't want to make her go crazy for no reason so I waited a little while longer.

After about a week, I called my mom and told her what had happened. I needed her to calm me down and talk some sense into me. I was an emotional wreck and I just needed my mommy. Eventually she got my mind right and since I'd told her, I figured it was cool to tell Charisma. They were the two people that helped most when I was going through a tough time. Like always, they came through in the clutch!

*My signature pose*

# Chapter 30
# ...Still the Comeback Queen

*When the unexpected happens, trust yourself and your abilities!*
*#Tinyism*

Lorenzo basically had Coach Frank and Anders cornered. He told them that since I had a guaranteed contract, they had to pay me or I wasn't going anywhere, and he would get FIBA involved. Word had gotten out around town, and of course the papers were hitting me up nonstop. To remain professional, I told them I had no comment at that time. I told them that once the situation was settled, I would give them my side of the story.

Eventually we came to an agreement, and before signing anything, I met with them. I wanted closure before I left, so I asked Coach Frank and Anders about all the things they mentioned and also why it was never brought to my attention. They claimed they told Lorenzo some of it, but I didn't believe them. When it came to their jabs about staying up and being on Facebook, as well as running my business, I simply asked if any of that ever affected my performance in practices or games. They answered by saying, "No, you're a great player. You're just honestly not the type of player we thought you were." I asked what type of player they were looking for because, after all, we were winning. Their next response led me to believe that all of this was personal. Between the girls on the team hating me and talking behind my back, it all made much more sense to me. They answered my question by saying, "Yes, we are winning, but we are winning your way!" After that, I had nothing else to say to them. At the end of the day, I thought winning was the bottom line, but I guess I was sadly mistaken. After that response, I simply asked when I would get my money and wished them the best.

Ashley also met with Coach Frank. She didn't trust them, and didn't like the way they were treating me. She met with them to discuss her future. Who was to say that they wouldn't eventually do the same thing to her? Coach Frank told her he would never do anything like this to her because they liked her and wanted to actually sign her again for the next season. Ashley's meeting with them proved that they just had something against me personally. It didn't seem like this was a decision based on basketball.

In the midst of all the drama, my ankle was getting better and Lorenzo was on the hunt to find me a new team. We were pressed for time, so Lorenzo ended up arranging a two week tryout with a team in the Czech Republic. Slovanka MB was one of the first teams to show interest. While Lorenzo sorted my future out, I focused on altering my trip with my mom.

Eventually I got my money with interest from Mark Basket, on my birthday. Lorenzo and I agreed to terms with Slovanka MB and the two week tryout. Slovanka was at the bottom of their league. They had only won a single game all season, but from what I saw online, they had a decent team. They had three players averaging double figures. To me, it seemed like they just needed someone to help them get over the hump. The Czech league was also more respected and competitive than the Swedish League, so I began looking at the whole situation as a blessing in disguise. I arrived in Prague on Thanksgiving, and couldn't have been more thankful. I was a little nervous about trying out, especially with my ankle still only at 75%, but after the second practice all of that went out the door. By the third practice, I was back to my usual self, and Slovanka told Lorenzo they wanted to finalize our contract for the remainder of the season.

I began to enjoy basketball again in Prague. In my first game with Slovanka, we ended up upsetting the #6 team! I scored 12 points, 3 assists, and 4 rebounds. While I helped Slovanka get their second win, Mark Basket had only won two of their seven games without me.

That win with Slovanka meant more than anything to me after all of the bull crap I had been through the previous days leading up to the game. That win symbolized the fact that a tiny setback, almost always leads to a major comeback! Whether I like it or not, that's just the ongoing story of my life.

While in Prague, I began to slowly creep back into my happy place. Basketball was becoming fun for me again, and I was able to take my mom on what she called "The Trip of a Lifetime"! With the help of Lorenzo, I was able to alter the trip's starting point to Prague. My mom arrived a day before my last game of 2014 with Slovanka, so she was still able to see me play. My mom may have always supported me throughout my trials and tribulations, but as far as physical support at my games, she may have come to a total of thirty games, tops. With that being said, whenever she does make a game, I make sure I play my heart out. Despite a tough loss to a top four team, I dropped a double-double of 12 points and 10 assists. After the game, my mom simply said, "You know y'all wasn't supposed to lose that game, right?" Nonetheless, she still expressed how proud of me she was. Hearing the excitement in her voice as she described certain plays and how she told the other fans in the stands "that's my baby girl" softened the blow of the loss. After the game, we went to dinner and hung out with my teammates.

The next couple of days, we played tourist in Prague. We did a lot of sightseeing, eating, and drinking. After Prague, our Euro Tour officially began. Our first stop was actually the most important one. Ever since I could remember, my mom would tell me that when she passed away, she wanted me to sprinkle her ashes off of the Eiffel Tower. Prior to this trip, I had been secretly planning to take her for three years. Unfortunately, with all of my setbacks and experiences in this basketball world, I just never was able to get the funds to pull the surprise off. I figured since she always said that, it was her way of telling me she always wanted to go. When we arrived in Paris it was evening, but, nonetheless, the first thing we did after checking in the hotel was to go see the Eiffel Tower. Speaking from experience, with the lights, I actually think the Eiffel Tower looks better at nighttime. After arriving at a location that most visitors go to see the tower from afar, my mother was in awe. Seeing the look on her face was truly priceless and it also made me a little emotional. At that moment, we both cried tears of joy. My mother then expressed to me that it wasn't the fact that she always wanted to come to Paris to see the Eiffel Tower, it was the simple fact that she didn't expect to actually get a chance to see it in her lifetime. So with that in mind, she figured after her lifetime, me sprinkling her off the top would be just as fulfilling. After she told me that, my tears began to flow and this trip became that much more special.

After spending Christmas actually on the top of the Eiffel Tower, we went to meet Lorenzo in Italy. This was my first time actually meeting him, and it was a great experience. First, we had dinner with his lovely family in his hometown of Arona, Italy, and from there we drove through to Florence to sightsee and spend a couple days with him in Rome. From Rome, our next stop was Stockholm for New Year's Eve. After New Year's Eve, we took a couple days to actually relax. In every city and country we went to, we were on the move from sun up to sundown. Although I didn't get the opportunity to hit a gym during our two week Euro Tour, with the amount of walking and hiking we did, I didn't feel guilty at all. By the time we were in Stockholm, I was honestly exhausted.

On New Year's Day, I just sat back and re-evaluated my life. I thought about my past, present, and future. Despite the way some things turned out, I realized, no matter what, it will always get better...eventually. I may struggle, I may cry, I may face adversity, but, no matter what, as long as I remain strong, I WILL PREVAIL!

With that being said, I hope you guys have enjoyed and learned from my story! Thank you so much for reading, and I wish you all the best! -#TA9

*Giving back to the youth in Prague,
Czech Republic*

*Momma Tiny and I at the
Eiffel Tower*

# #Tinyisms

1. If you're passionate about something or someone, you should go for it, no matter what! #Tinyism

2. The more you play the 'game', the higher your IQ will get! #Tinyism

3. You should focus more on proving yourself right, than proving them wrong! #Tinyism

4. When dealing with new experiences, you should always be open-minded! #Tinyism

5. The more painful a mistake, the more pleasant the lesson will be. #Tinyism

6. You never really know who's watching, so make sure you're portraying the right image! #Tinyism

7. Regardless of your feelings, remain humble and grateful! #Tinyism

8. One of your top priorities should always be to protect your feelings. If you don't, then who will? #Tinyism

9. When someone is both on your mind and heart, its damn near impossible to suppress the thought of them. #Tinyism

10. Holding yourself accountable is a very vital part of achieving any goal. #Tinyism

11. Being a part of history is good, but being legendary is even better! #Tinyism

12. Self-confidence elevates performance! #Tinyism

13. Family is verified by unconditional love and support, not just relation or name. #Tinyism

14. Staying consistent is EVERYTHING...and hard work breeds consistency! #Tinyism

15. Whenever opportunity presents itself, take advantage! #Tinyism

16. Decision making is one of the most important parts of being successful! #Tinyism

17. Never allow a letdown to become a breakdown. #Tinyism

18. Never burn bridges, especially if you can't swim. #Tinyism

19. Sometimes you're placed in situations that you can't control. At that point. it's very important to focus on adjusting and whatever it is you CAN control. #Tinyism

20. Exhaust all options when trying to obtain a goal, because you never know what can happen! #Tinyism

21. One bad decision can ruin everything you've worked for up until that point. It's definitely better to be safe than sorry! #Tinyism

22. Sometimes we're faced with obstacles that prepare us for what's ahead. You may not understand it, but it's not your job to. Your job is to get through it! #Tinyism

23. Never allow yourself to lose focus of your long term goal, ever! #Tinyism

24. Sometimes you have to go backwards, to find your way back to the front! #Tinyism

25. No matter where you are in life, you should always want more out of it! #Tinyism

26. You can plan all you want, something is going to go wrong! It's up to you to also make sure something goes right! #Tinyism

27. Tolerance, versatility, and adaptability can go a long way when trying to persevere! #Tinyism

28. Invest in yourself, your passions, and your goals. #Tinyism

29. Always be prepared for the worst. When Plan A fails, get a grip, and then follow up with Plan B-Z. #Tinyism

30. When the unexpected happens, trust yourself and your abilities! #Tinyism

# Potpourri

- My all-time favorite player is Allen Iverson. I often refer to him as my father/daddy.

- My favorite female basketball players are Cynthia Cooper, Teresa Weatherspoon, Becky Hammon, and Epiphanny Prince.

- My favorite rapper is Drake. Any song or feature he puts out is amazing to me.

- I don't really like my first name. I only like it when I travel overseas and they say it with their accents.

- My middle name is Rhonda.

- I hate stretching.

- My favorite color is black (my friends think I wear it too often).

- Somehow, someway I'd like to have an Asian baby, either by adoption or birth.

- I don't know how to swim.

- My deepest fears are rejection and failure.

- I get nervous before every game.

- I love helping people if/when I can.

- I have never had a fight a day in my life. I often wonder if I even know how to.

- I don't know how to walk in heels.

- I don't know how to apply makeup.

- I am very indecisive.

- I care about what people think and say about me.

- I want everyone to like me.

- My birthday is November 26, 1988.

- I overthink EVERYTHING.

• I'm not really a spur of the moment type of person. I try to plan EVERYTHING.

• I'm petrified of being pregnant, but I do want a son.

• I hate people who aren't humble.

• To my friends and behind closed doors, I really think I'm a rapper.

• Whenever I eat a satisfying meal, my nose starts running and my throat gets scratchy.

• I curse myself out during games when I don't think I'm performing well. I'm my biggest critic.

# Glossary/Abbreviations

Box 1- a particular type of defense used in basketball, with one player playing the star player face to face, while the other four members on defense form a box/square in the paint

And 1- when a player scores a basket while being fouled. After the foul and basket, the player gets one free throw shot

Double Double- when a player scores at least ten of two different statistical categories (example: ten points and ten rebounds)

Triple Double- when a player scores at least ten of three different statistical categories (example: ten points, ten rebounds, and ten assists)

Bucket(s)- slang term for points

Free Throws- also known as foul shots. Shots by players from the free throw line

Assists- attributed to a player who passes the ball to a teammate in a way that leads to a score by field goal

Rebounds- the act of successfully gaining possession of the basketball after a missed field goal or free throw

Steals- occurs when a defensive player legally causes a turnover by his positive, aggressive action

Senior Night- a player's last home game in their senior year of competing for a team

Double Teams- two players on one person with the ball

Presses- when the defense applies pressure to the offensive ball handler

PSAT/SAT- a standardized test widely used for college admissions in the United States

ACT- college readiness assessment, a standardized test for high school achievement and college admissions in the United States

ACL- Anterior Cruciate Ligament, one of a pair of cruciate ligaments (the other being the posterior cruciate ligament) in the human knee

NCAA- National Collegiate Athletic Association

WNBA- Women's National Basketball Association

NBA- National Basketball Association

AAU- Amateur Athletic Union

GPA- Grade Point Average

HBCU- Historically Black College/University

JUCO- Junior College

PE- Physical Education

PAL- Police Athletic League

MEAC- Mid-Eastern Athletic Conference

# Career Stats

2006-2007: Morgan St. (NCAA, starting five) 13.4ppg, 4.8rpg, 2.9apg, 2.3spg

2007-2008: Morgan St. (NCAA, starting five): 31 games: 16.6ppg, 5.1rpg, 4.3apg, 4.0spg, FGP: 33.7%, 3Pts: 26.5%, FT: 70.2%

2008-2009: Morgan St. (NCAA, starting five): 30 games: 18.2ppg, 4.4rpg, 4.3apg, 3.5spg, FGP: 39.1%, 3Pts: 36.4%, FT: 75.8%

2009-2010: Morgan St. (NCAA, starting five): 30 games: 19.4ppg, 4.1rpg, 3.5apg, 3.5spg, FGP: 39.3%, 3PT: 30.9%, FT: 77.1%

2010: Cabo Rojo Turistas (Puerto Rico-BSNF, starting five): 20 games: 15.4ppg, 3.8rpg, Assists-2nd in the league(6.0apg), 2.4spg

My total statistics at Morgan were 2058 points, 564 rebounds, 455 assists, and 404 steals.

2011-2012: Boa Viagem-Angra-Acore (Portugal-Liga Feminina, starting five) 16 games: 17.5ppg 6.5rpg 3.4apg 3.1spg FGP:44% FT:82% 3PT: 26%

2012-2013: Boa Viagem-Angra Acore (Portugal-Liga Feminina, starting five) 11 games: 16.9ppg 6.1rpg 3.1apg 3.5spg FGP:44% FT:75% 3PT: 25%

2013-2014: KK Playoff (Bosnia Top League, starting five) 6 games: 11.3ppg 2.7rpg 4.2apg 2.8spg FGP:53% FT:62% 3PT:15%

KK Playoff Adriatic League (Euro Cup League, starting five) 8 games: Points-2nd in the league (19.6) 2.9rpg Assists-8th in the league (4.4) Steals-7th in the league (2.3) FGP:43% FT:86% 3PT:20%

2014: BC Haskovo 2012 (Bulgaria Top League, starting five) 18 games: Score-5th in the league(16.1ppg), 6.8rpg, Assists-2nd in the league(5.1apg), Steals-1(2.8spg), FGP: 41.2%, 3PT: 30.8%, FT: 75.8%

2014: Mark Basket Marbo Kinna (Sweden-Damligan): 6 games: 12.5ppg, 5.3rpg, 4.5apg, 4.0spg, 2FGP: 37.7%, 3FGP: 29.4%, FT: 90.9%

2014-2015: Basket Slovanka MB Tabor (Czech Republic-ZBL) 13 games 11.8ppg, 2.9apg, 2.2spg, 2FGP: 44.9% 3FGP: 21.4%, FT: 76.9%